$27.95

SOUL MATES

SOUL MATES

Religion, Sex, Love, and Marriage among
African Americans and Latinos

W. Bradford Wilcox

AND

Nicholas H. Wolfinger

OXFORD
UNIVERSITY PRESS

Oxford University Press is a department of the University of
Oxford. It furthers the University's objective of excellence in research,
scholarship, and education by publishing worldwide.
Oxford is a registered trade mark of Oxford University Press
in the UK and in certain other countries

Published in the United States of America by
Oxford University Press
198 Madison Avenue, New York, NY 10016

Cataloging-in-Publication data is on file at the Library of Congress
ISBN 978-0-19-539422-1

1 3 5 7 9 8 6 4 2
Printed in the United States of America
on acid-free paper

W. Bradford Wilcox dedicates this book to Alexander, Michael, Clara, Yonas, Simone, and, above all, Danielle

Nicholas H. Wolfinger dedicates this book to the memory of Wanda Song

CONTENTS

Preface   *ix*

1. Introduction   1
2. Steering Clear of the Street   26
3. Religion, Sex, and Childbearing   70
4. Wandering Toward the Altar   96
5. A Path to Wedded Bliss?   124
6. Conclusion   147

Appendix   *165*
Notes   *169*
Bibliography   *201*
Index   *219*

PREFACE

Soul Mates is about the intersection of two of society's most venerable and consequential institutions. Religion and family have both organized human behavior throughout recorded history. Each continues to play a central role in public life and, for many of us, private life as well. Both have also been staples of social science since the publication of seminal works by sociologists Émile Durkheim and Max Weber. Following in this tradition, we are interested in better understanding how these two institutions intersect.

Profound currents in modern family life form the context for our inquiry. Sex, love, and marriage have changed enormously over the past half-century. Perhaps most notably, Americans spend far less of their adult lives in the bonds of matrimony. Indeed, the very meaning of marriage has changed. As sociologist Andrew Cherlin has noted, marriage now represents the culmination of young adulthood, rather than one of its important early milestones. Unlike in previous generations, children are much more likely to be born prior to marriage. All of these trends are inextricably bound up with social class. Americans without four-year college degrees are less likely to marry, less likely to stay married, and more likely to have children prior to marriage. Conversely, college-educated Americans marry more, divorce less, and typically wait to have children until they are married. Finally, race and ethnicity continue to play a huge role in modern life—few Americans have been more affected by the so-called retreat from marriage than African Americans and Latinos, a major reason why this book focuses on these two groups.

This book represents the culmination of a collaboration that spans more than a decade. Our partnership has flourished in part because we bring different things to the table. Wilcox has long studied religion, while Wolfinger specializes in the family. Wilcox usually sees the forest, while Wolfinger is oriented toward the trees (including the statistical techniques necessary to do this sort of research).

Our personal lives are just as different. Wilcox is a conservative, a Catholic, and a married father with an interracial family. Wolfinger is none of these things (he is an unmarried, childless liberal, and a nonbeliever). Contrary to expectations, we have found that such an unlikely pairing is ideal for conducting research on religion and the family. As we describe at some length in this book, our polarized nation has often left us unable to see the whole truth about the social world. Many liberals would have us believe that everything that is wrong with the American family can be explained by poverty (and perhaps, in the case of nonwhite minorities, discrimination), while many conservatives inevitably point to a combination of failed values and feckless social policies. In the course of writing this book, we have come to realize that neither side has a monopoly on the truth. Inevitably the answers lie somewhere in between. So too do the solutions. As two coauthors with different worldviews, we believe we are perfectly poised to deliver a balanced, objective account.

We start by surveying the state of marriage and family in contemporary America, and talk about the competing theories that might account for how we got where we are now. Our account emphasizes the distinctive strengths and challenges of African American and Latino families. Next we talk about the benefits—and occasional liabilities—of religious participation. Subsequent chapters cover out-of-wedlock births, getting married, and the quality and stability of American marriages. We conclude with a discussion of how social policy might strengthen American families, and how religion might provide one vehicle for change.

The result of this inquiry is a finding that can variously be described as simple, powerful, and provocative: religion is a force for good in the lives of many blacks and Latinos. People who regularly attend religious services—denomination and tradition do not matter as much—are less likely to give birth out of marriage, more likely to get married, and have better relationships whether or not they are married. At the same time, we are careful to note that religion is not a panacea. Only a minority of Americans attend church regularly. Not all attendees benefit, and many nonbelievers are doing just fine in their relationships.

Collectively we have published six books. *Soul Mates*, our seventh, is by far our most ambitious undertaking to date based on the evidence we have marshaled: six national data sets, interviews with 25 clergy and 60 ordinary adults, and a year of ethnographic fieldwork, a period Wilcox spent living in Harlem and attending black and Latino churches there, in the Bronx, and Brooklyn. We also conducted focus groups in Atlanta, Dallas, Los Angeles, and New York. An endeavor of this magnitude could not have come to fruition without the assistance of many people. Chuck Stokes performed all analyses of the Add Health data and also helped out with the National Longitudinal Survey of Youth (NLSY).

Jeffrey Dew also conducted analyses of the NLSY. This book would not have been possible without their help. John Bartkowski, David Blankenhorn, Kathryn Edin, Christopher Ellison, Michael Emerson, Jennifer Glass, the late Norval Glenn, Tim Heaton, Sara McLanahan, the late Steven Nock, David Popenoe, Mark Regnerus, Christian Smith, and Jeremy Uecker provided valuable feedback or counsel on various parts of this project. Andy Roth kindly read the entire manuscript, and it is vastly improved as a result. Wolfinger is lucky to have such a great friend and colleague.

We thank Sonja Anderson, Mary Caler, David Franz, Young Kim, Tony Lin, David Morris, Sam Richardson, and Alta Williams for research assistance. Betsy Stokes provided valuable editorial assistance. We are indebted to their tireless efforts on behalf of this project.

At Oxford, special thanks are due to Cynthia Read. This book would have stillborn without her support and considerable patience.

Support for this research was provided by the Lilly Endowment, the Annie E. Casey Foundation, the John Templeton Foundation, the Bodman Foundation, the Baylor Institute for the Studies of Religion, the Louisville Institute at Louisville Presbyterian Theological Seminary, the Center for Research on Religion and Urban Civil Society at the University of Pennsylvania, the US Department of Health and Human Services (Grant 90XP0048), the William E. Simon Foundation, The Project on Lived Theology at the University of Virginia, and The Spiritual Transformation Scientific Research Program, sponsored by the Metanexus Institute on Religion and Science, with support from the John Templeton Foundation.

At the University of Virginia, Neal Grandy and Katherine Shiflett provided valuable assistance in navigating the administrative terrain of sponsored research. Cindy Brown and Bill Ernest did the same at the University of Utah. Wolfinger also thanks Sandra Earl, Sandy Stark, and Ashley Johnson for superb administrative support.

Above all, we are grateful for the counsel and forbearance of our families and friends throughout the process of researching and writing this book. Thanks especially to Mom and Dad, Amy, Andy and Liz, other Andy, Eric, the House family, Jack, Jessica, John, Korey and Sharif, Lori and Mick, Matt, Sasha, Sergie, Tim and Donna, and to Danielle, Mom, Pam, Bill, and the kids for your support over the long haul. Without your love and support, none of this would have been possible. Raymond Wolfinger, Nick's father, died as this book was going to press. He will be missed.

SOUL MATES

Chapter 1

Introduction

In 1994, David Hernandez decided to get out of the drug business in Spanish Harlem and turn his life over to Jesus Christ.[1] After his brother was killed by younger rivals seeking to expand their turf, David realized it was time for a change. "It was a tragic moment in my life, and I was searching for answers," he said. "Before, I had the view that I should make money, get ahead as fast as you can." After his brother died, he put his faith in God, joining a vibrant Bronx-based Pentecostal church called Victory Chapel that serves mostly second- and third-generation Puerto Rican Latinos. Ironically, David then joined the New York Police Department (NYPD) (he had never been arrested while dealing drugs).

David's religious awakening proved momentous not only for himself but for Marianne, his live-in girlfriend at the time. She had been in and out of relationships with men and grown distrustful of the opposite sex: "I was tired of disappointments; I was in a lot of pain." But after attending Victory Chapel, Marianne responded to an altar call, went to the front of the church, and accepted Jesus Christ into her life. She and David are now happily married, have three school-age children, and are regulars at Victory Chapel.

Michael and Latisha Brown live across the city in Brooklyn, where they attend Faith Deliverance Church, a large African

American Pentecostal church. They first met while working at a McDonalds in 1989, but they did not begin to date until the early 1990s. Soon they moved in together. At the time, Michael and Latisha were not particularly sure where their relationship was headed. Michael was finishing up a degree at Brooklyn College, and they both partied a lot—in Latisha's words, they were "club heads"—and were living well beyond their means, accruing debt on fourteen different credit cards.

By the fall of 1995, Michael began to get serious about Latisha. He told a friend he was going to propose. The following winter, Michael recalls, "We went down to Zale's Jewelers and I put down an engagement ring, and I proposed to her on February 14, 1996. We had just given our life to Christ about two weeks before, and we were married in August that year."

Latisha remembers things a little differently. She said she promised to follow Christ that winter because she wanted to marry Michael. "He [Michael] was like the best thing I had until then," she said. "So I kind of lied to say I believe in Christ and all that. I just repeated everything the preacher said." But when she and Michael began attending church and reading the Bible together, Latisha decided to make the faith her own. In April 1996, she made her own heartfelt personal profession of faith. Four months later, Latisha and Michael tied the knot. Ten years later they are happily married, work hard (she as a clerk in the Fire Department, he as a dispatcher for a taxi company), keep a tight eye on their weekly budget, and are pillars of their local church.

These two stories show how religious faith and church-going are related to marriage and family life among African Americans and Latinos in the United States. For some couples, as for the Hernandezes, the religious beliefs, moral norms, and social networks associated with their faith help foster successful marriages. In social-science terms, religion appears to exercise a causal role in shaping the relationships of churchgoing couples. For others, such as the Browns, a burgeoning interest in getting or staying married can fuel a desire to find a spiritual home where both family and "decent" living are valued and reinforced. In the language of the social sciences, these couples are self-selecting into religious communities that legitimate their commitments to family and mainstream American values. For most of the couples who form connections between their faith and family life, the link is reciprocal. Religious faith fosters a strong family orientation, and family commitments drive people to deepen their reliance on their faith and religious communities.

These stories suggest that religious faith and churchgoing are bulwarks of marriage and family life, and decent living more generally, in the Latino and black communities. In this book we find that married and unmarried minority couples who attend church together are much more likely to enjoy happy relationships—and the unmarried more likely to get married—in comparison to similar couples who do not regularly darken the door of a church. Our book shines a much-needed spotlight on thriving minority couples and on how religion often undergirds their success. These topics have been largely ignored in academic and journalistic treatments of black and Latino family life.[2]

But this book also shows that religion is not a silver bullet when it comes to addressing the challenges facing African Americans and Latinos. Infidelity, domestic violence, and divorce can all be found among the ranks of black and Latino churchgoers. Religious faith and religious participation offer no guarantees of a happy family life. Needless to say, this is true for Americans of every creed and color. What is more, religion does not influence the sexual behavior and nonmarital childbearing of African Americans and Latinos as much as it does for whites.

Nor does religious participation reduce the likelihood of divorce for black and Latino couples. Our book also suggests that minority women who attend church by themselves—that is, without their husband or partner—do not experience any benefit in the quality of their relationships.

What kinds of challenges confront ordinary Latinos and African Americans in their marriages and family lives? Many minority couples face the same tribulations as do white, middle-class couples—juggling work and family responsibilities, coping with the ups and downs of married life, and trying to successfully raise their children. But the black and Latino singles and couples examined in this book are also more likely than Anglos to struggle with making ends meet, racial or ethnic discrimination, and, for recent immigrants, the difficulties of learning a new language and customs. Equally important, Latinos and especially African Americans are more likely than whites to have been caught up in the family revolution—marked by unprecedented levels of nonmarital childbearing, divorce, single parenthood, and multiple-partner fertility—that swept across the United States over the last half-century.

AFRICAN AMERICANS, LATINOS, AND THE FAMILY REVOLUTION

Before understanding how religion is related to marriage and family life among Latinos and blacks, we must first get some sense of the size and scope of the family revolution that has so altered the contexts of courtship, childbearing, and marriage in the United States in recent years. The family revolution is characterized by four features. First, and foremost, marriage has been deinstitutionalized as the anchor of the adult life course and of family life itself: marriage is less likely to guide and govern the lives of men and women as they move into adulthood and, in particular, as they engage in childbearing, parenting, and romantic relationships.[3] Second, at the cultural level, family-centered beliefs and norms that used to prioritize the welfare of marriages, children, and families have given way to individualistic beliefs and norms that stress the importance of personal fulfillment, individual advancement, and equality at all costs.[4] Concurrently, structural factors like deindustrialization and falling wages have eroded the economic foundations of the American family.[5] Consequently, when familistic and individualistic beliefs clash, the latter are much more likely to triumph than they were fifty years ago. In a word, the moral authority of the family is much diminished in recent years.

Third, the family has less influence over social life than it once did, with many of its functions being subsumed by the market or the state. Cooking, leisure, and the provision of care are all increasingly likely to occur outside the home. Fourth, given these cultural and social shifts, it is no surprise that people are less involved in family life over the course of their adult lives: they are having fewer children, spending a smaller share of their adult lives in a marital union or with minor children in their household, and investing less in their spouses than they once did.[6] As a consequence of this family revolution, the family is less of a force in people's lives nowadays; the family is also more fragile insofar as ties between parents, and between parents and children, are more likely than they once were to be formed outside the bonds of marriage and to be sundered by divorce or the breakup of a live-in partnership.[7]

Judging by trends in marriage, cohabitation, divorce, and nonmarital childbearing, the family revolution has been particularly consequential for African Americans and, to a lesser extent,

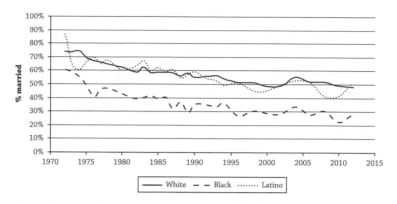

Figure 1.1 Trends in Marriage, Adults Aged 20–54, by Race/Ethnicity.
Source: General Social Survey, 1972–2012.

Latinos. As figure 1.1 makes clear, marriage rates fell from 1970 to the present, especially for African Americans. Fifty-four percent of blacks were married in the 1970s (averaged over the decade). This figure dipped to 25 percent by the second decade of the twenty-first century. For Latinos, the corresponding figures are 72 and 47 percent. Second- and third-generation Latinos living in the United States are less likely to be married than are their first-generation peers.[8] White marriage rates witnessed a similar decline to those of Latinos, falling from more than 70 to 49 percent.

From 1970 to 2011, the number of cohabiting couples rose more than fifteenfold, from about 500,000 to more than 7.5 million couples.[9] In 1995, only 2 percent of Latino householders were cohabiting; by 2012, the number was 9 percent. Among African Americans, the corresponding figures were 3 percent in 1995 and 6 percent in 2012; for whites, also 3 and 6 percent.[10]

The divorce rate is also higher now than it was in 1970, though it has declined a bit since 1981.[11] Currently, 21 percent of blacks who have ever been married are divorced, compared to 12 percent

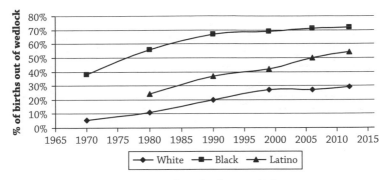

Figure 1.2 Trends in Nonmarital Births, by Race/Ethnicity.

Sources: B. E. Hamilton, J. A. Martin, and S. J. Ventura, "Births: Preliminary Data for 2006," National Vital Statistics Reports, vol. 56, no. 7 (Hyattsville, MD: National Center for Health Statistics, 2007); B. F. Hamilton, J. A. Martin, S. J. Ventura, "Births: Preliminary Data for 2012," National Vital Statistics Reports, vol. 62, no. 3 (Hyattsville, MD: National Center for Health Statistics, 2013).

of Latinos and 14 percent of whites. But here again, foreign-born Latinos are least likely to be divorced (9 percent), whereas more acculturated native-born Latinos are actually more likely to be divorced (16 percent) than are whites.[12] Moreover, foreign-born Latinos are disproportionately likely to marry their live-in partners and less likely to dissolve their cohabiting relationships.[13]

As figure 1.2 indicates, nonmarital childbearing has also risen for all Americans over the last half-century. In 1960, only 5 percent of children were born out of wedlock; in 2011, 41 percent of children were born outside marriage. Nonmarital childbearing is highest among blacks and Latinos. From 1980 to 2011, the percentage of children born outside of wedlock rose for blacks from 56 to 72 percent and for Latinos from 24 to 53 percent; by comparison, for whites it rose from 9 to 29 percent over this same period. Moreover, Latinas who were born and raised in America have higher nonmarital birth rates than Latinas who were born outside of the United States.[14]

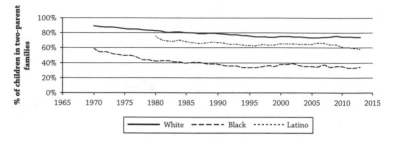

Figure 1.3 Trends in Child Residence in Two-Parent, Married Families, by Race/Ethnicity.

Sources: US Census Bureau, Current Population Survey, March Demographic Supplement, 1970–2013. Figures refer to children living with two married parents and exclude multi-racial/multi-ethnic children.

One of the most important consequences of the family revolution is that children are more likely to spend time living outside of a two-parent, married family. From 1970 to 2013, the percentage of children living without two married parents more than doubled, from 15 to 36 percent.[15] As figure 1.3 shows, 66 percent of black children, 42 percent of Latino children, and 26 percent of white children lived outside of a two-parent, married family in 2013. Given current levels of divorce, an even higher percentage of children in each of these racial and ethnic groups will ultimately spend time outside a two-parent, married family. Most of these children end up in families headed by single mothers, while others reside in families headed by single fathers, grandparents, or foster parents.[16]

The family revolution of the last half-century has dramatically altered dating, marriage, and family life for adults and children in the United States, especially among African Americans and Latinos. What are the forces driving this revolution? Many liberal social scientists contend that structural changes in the American economy have been the primary forces behind this revolution,[17] whereas most conservative commentators and scholars argue that cultural change and misguided public policies have been most important in undercutting marriage and family life in the United States.[18] We reject this dichotomy and suggest instead that a confluence of economic, policy, and cultural currents came together with sufficient force in the late 1960s and the 1970s to generate a tidal wave of family change. More generally, we agree with *New York Times* columnist Charles Blow, in that we "take enormous exception to arguments about the 'breakdown of the family,' particularly the black family, that don't acknowledge that this country for centuries has endeavored, consciously and not, to break it down."[19]

On the economic front, America began to shift from a strong manufacturing foundation (e.g., automobiles, textiles) to a service (e.g., call centers, care-giving) and information (e.g., technology, finance) economy. Many of the new information-sector jobs pay well but are not available to workers lacking a college degree—workers who make up a majority of the labor force.[20] At the same time, Americans' earning power was being undermined by competition overseas and domestic trends such as deunionization.[21]

Men's real wages stagnated in the wake of these changes.[22] Because their physical labor and skills were less valuable in the new economy, working-class and poor men were hit particularly hard. Consequently, men became less attractive as marriage partners, both in their own eyes and in the eyes of potential spouses. As sociologist William Julius Wilson has argued in *The Truly Disadvantaged*, working-class and poor men were especially unlikely to be viewed by potential partners as "marriageable."[23]

At the same time, owing to both financial need and a burgeoning egalitarian ethos, women were entering the labor force in record numbers: women's labor-force participation rose from

38 percent in 1960 to 52 percent in 1980.[24] For a few women, employment obviated marriage.[25] The combination of men's stagnating economic position and women's improving economic position meant that men's relative financial contribution to marriage and women's relative economic dependence on marriage began declining in the late 1960s and the 1970s. Even as women's labor-force participation began to rival men's, they still found themselves doing the lion's share of the housework and child care.[26] This threatened marriages by producing more domestic strife.[27] Accordingly, men and women, especially in working-class and poor communities, where women's relative gains have been strongest, became less likely to get and stay married.[28]

Changes in welfare policy and family law also contributed to the family revolution. From the mid-1960s to the mid-1970s, a raft of policy changes and court decisions—including the Supreme Court's decision in *King v. Smith* (1968), which struck down the man-in-the-house rule prohibiting women on welfare from cohabiting—made it easier for unwed couples and single parents to receive welfare and for unmarried mothers to get child support from the fathers of their children.[29] Burgeoning enrollment in means-tested programs like food stamps and Aid to Families with Dependent Children in the 1960s had the unintended effect of penalizing marriage among the poor and working class, simply because low-income adults faced the loss of their benefits if they married someone whose income pushed them over a particular program's modest income limits. As economist Eugene Steuerle has pointed out, substantial marriage penalties for low-income couples remain built into the nation's welfare policies.[30] These changes in public policy and family law undercut the economic value of marriage and lent public legitimacy to the family changes sweeping across the United States in this period, thereby helping to launch the family revolution.[31]

The 1960s and 1970s also ushered in cultural changes that eroded family-centered culture among American men and women. The counterculture and second-wave feminism together fostered an anti-institutional ethos that sought to throw off the shackles of traditional morality and to challenge the authority of institutions such as church and family.[32] Weekly religious attendance fell from 46 percent in 1960 to 39 percent in 1979,[33] and declines in religious participation were even higher among young people caught up in the spirit of the 1960s.[34] More generally, this period in American life was marked by the triumph of an ethic of "self-expression and self-gratification," as sociologist Daniel Bell has argued. "It is anti-institutional and antinomian in that the individual is taken to be the measure of satisfaction, and *his* feelings, sentiments, and judgments, not some objective standard of quality and value" is determinative of personal ethics and behavior.[35] In the face of these cultural developments, the structure associated with marriage and family life proved less compelling to ordinary Americans.

The sexual revolution made crucial contributions to the family revolution, insofar as it helped to decouple sex, childbearing, and marriage. As Nobel laureate economist George Akerlof has pointed out, the availability of the pill and then abortion in the late 1960s and 1970s helped facilitate the dramatic shifts in sexual behavior and norms that marked the era: men and women felt freer to have sex outside marriage without worrying about pregnancy. Sexual behavior and norms shifted so dramatically that the nonmarital childbearing rate skyrocketed, even though women had gained ready access to reliable birth control and abortion.[36] Akerlof argues that one reason that nonmarital childbearing rose was that men no longer felt compelled to marry women they got pregnant; in light of women's reproductive options, many men reasoned, any pregnancy was her choice and not their responsibility.[37] The sexual revolution also helped to advance the view that marriage need not be child-centered, which in turn made divorce a more viable option for unhappy spouses.[38] In the words of Akerlof and his colleagues, "Just at the time, about 1970, that the permanent cure to poverty seemed to be on the horizon and just at the time that women had obtained the tools to control the number and the timing of their children, single motherhood and the feminization of poverty began their long and steady rise."[39]

In our opinion, liberal views that privilege economic explanations and conservative views that privilege cultural or policy explanations for the family revolution of the last half-century each obscure an important truth. In the late 1960s and 1970s, a combination of economic, policy, and cultural factors arose to create a perfect storm for the American family. This family revolution has only gained strength over time.

African Americans and the Family Revolution

We have cited figures showing that the family revolution struck African Americans with particular power. Why have African Americans been especially likely to experience high levels of nonmarital childbearing, marriage delayed or foregone, and divorce? Once again, we think there are both structural and cultural factors at work.

From a structural perspective, one of the crucial issues is that the supply of "marriageable" black men with decent economic prospects has deteriorated since the 1970s. Due to a host of social factors, from racial discrimination to failing schools to residential segregation, black men have suffered from comparatively high rates of unemployment, underemployment, and imprisonment since the early 1970s. Consequently, there have been comparatively fewer black men who qualify as attractive marriage partners to black women looking to marry.[40] Over these years, black women have seen their educational and occupational status improve, especially relative to black men. Their average earnings increased markedly more than did black men's earnings.[41] Thus as their earnings have grown, black women have been less likely to see marriage as economically necessary, especially because they have been less likely to encounter black men with the means to be good providers.

Poverty in and of itself has contributed to lower rates of African American marriage. Throughout American history, blacks have been disproportionately poor. At the end of the 1960s, approximately one out of three blacks lived in poverty.[42] In 2006, 24 percent of African Americans were poor, compared to just 8 percent of whites.[43] The poor are less likely to get and stay married, because they cannot afford the expense of a wedding, they face marriage-threatening financial conflict, and they have fewer economic assets to share with one another.

As sociologists Kathryn Edin and Maria Kefalas argue in *Promises I Can Keep*, the social distance between marriage and the poor has only grown in recent years. Marriage has increasingly become a luxury good of sorts for the poor, something admired and desired but rarely attained.[44] As marriage lost much of its institutional power and cultural meaning as the only legitimate venue for sex and childbearing, it was reborn as a relational capstone of sorts that signifies that a couple is "set," both financially and emotionally, at a certain level of middle-class comfort and security.[45] Marriage has changed from an essential step on the road to the American dream to being a sign that a couple has finally attained the American dream. Thus, for poor and working-class African Americans, marriage has become both less necessary and less attractive, insofar as a middle-class, married lifestyle seems out of reach.

Not surprisingly, most studies suggest that socioeconomic factors explain part of the racial differential in marriage patterns.[46] Culture also plays a role here, as sociologist Orlando Patterson has argued, because even middle-class blacks are less likely to get and stay married than are whites from a similar class background. His central claim is that African American relationships and family life have been indelibly marked by the legacy of slavery and Jim Crow; in his words, African American couples and families "are still paying the ethnocidal price of slavery and the neo-dulotic Jim Crow system."[47] His point is that slavery—which often denied blacks the right to marry and raise a family together, prevented men from assuming their rightful roles as father and husband, often gave women sole responsibility for raising a family, and sanctioned the sexual abuse of black women and girls—has bestowed a poisonous legacy to African Americans. This is a legacy—for some, but not all—of fraught relationships between the sexes, male infidelity, single motherhood, and men who are ill-prepared to be husbands and fathers. From Patterson's perspective, slavery shaped modern black relationships and family life.[48] He attributes unusually high levels of nonmarital childbearing, single parenthood, and multiple-partner fertility among contemporary African Americans in part to "practices, values, and beliefs" that took hold during slavery and Jim Crow, when they became "routinized and normative."[49]

Nevertheless, Patterson's account fails to explain why black family life was stronger in the first half of the twentieth century than it has been since the 1960s. In our view, the legacy of slavery and Jim Crow fueled an underlying fragility in black relationships and families that made African Americans much more vulnerable to the economic, political, and cultural changes that together precipitated the family revolution of the 1960s and

1970s. That is, we suspect that structural changes (such as the decline in working-class and poor men's real wages) and cultural changes (such as the emergence of expressive individualism and the decline of familism) in the larger society proved particularly potent for African Americans because of the poisonous legacy of slavery and Jim Crow. When the family revolution swept across the nation in the 1960s and 1970s, African Americans were most likely to be caught up in its currents. As this revolution has continued to advance, African Americans continue to be most likely to get pulled into its undertow.

Latinos and the Family Revolution

In the midst of the contentious 2006 debate about immigration, *New York Times* columnist David Brooks weighed in to argue that Latino "immigrants themselves are like a booster shot of traditional morality injected into the body politic," holding up Latino immigrants as paragons of traditional family life.[50] Brooks pointed to lower divorce rates, more support of elderly parents, and frequent family dinners as signs of familism among Latino immigrants. In these respects, the Latino community would seem to be a bastion of traditional family values, standing strong against the currents of the contemporary family revolution.

The reality is more complicated. Brooks is correct to contend that Latino immigrants, especially women, generally lead family-centered lives.[51] But this is markedly less true for Latinos in subsequent generations. As we have seen, nonmarital childbearing, single parenthood, divorce, and cohabitation are higher among second- and third-generation immigrant Latinos than among those of the first generation.[52] Indeed, Latinos now experience higher rates of nonmarital childbearing, single parenthood, and cohabitation than do whites. So the evidence suggests that the family revolution has eroded the familistic traditions of Latinos coming to the United States from a range of different Latin American countries.

What social forces have made Latinos vulnerable to the family revolution? As with blacks, both structural and cultural factors have played important roles. First, like African Americans, Latinos are much more likely than whites to be poor. In 1975, the first year adequate data are available, 23 percent of Latinos were poor.[53] Although fluctuating over time, this figure was almost the same thirty-one years later: in 2006, 21 percent were below the poverty line, compared to 8 percent of whites.[54] Latino men do not suffer from the same levels of unemployment as do black men, but they are much more likely than whites to be undereducated and consequently working in low-skill jobs in construction, agriculture, manufacturing, and the restaurant industry.[55] Latina women are also disproportionately concentrated in low-wage service sectors of the economy.[56] As marriage becomes increasingly defined as a luxury good in the larger society, Latinos—especially more acculturated Latinos—may be marrying in lower numbers simply because they feel they cannot afford to meet the marriage bar.[57]

Second, because of their skin color, customs, language, legal status, and public concerns about undocumented immigration, many Latinos face discrimination in their workplaces, neighborhoods, and encounters with government officials ranging from police officers to state social workers.[58] Discrimination is stressful, and it can strain relationships and marriages.[59] Discrimination can also produce an adversarial outlook toward mainstream institutions—including marriage, education, and work—that adversely affects the likelihood of marriage.[60]

There are also cultural forces at work here. Two are indigenous to many Latin American countries: *machismo* and consensual

unions. Some Latino men are shaped by a *machismo* ethic characterized by displays of masculine strength and power, promiscuity, and alcohol abuse.[61] Studies suggest that Latino men in the
United States are more likely than white men to engage in domestic violence and infidelity.[62] Women in relationships with *macho*
men, or women whose social networks include large numbers of
such men, are probably less likely to get married or stay married.

Nonmarital cohabiting unions are common in many Latin
American societies. More than 50 percent of all unions involv-
ing women of reproductive age (15 through 49) in much of
the Spanish Caribbean and Central America, including the
Dominican Republic, El Salvador, Honduras, and Nicaragua, are
nonmarital. In Mexico, more than 20 percent of women in intimate relationships reside in a cohabiting union.[63] Much of the
increase in nonmarital childbearing among Latinos has occurred
in these cohabiting relationships, which are less stable than marriages in both Latin America and the United States.[64]

Like all Americans, Latinos are affected by the individualism
and hedonism found in the larger culture, notably the popular
culture, of the United States. Like African Americans, Latinos
are more likely to be consumers of popular culture than whites;
for instance, Latinos, especially second- and third-generation
Latinos, watch more television than do whites.[65] Exposure to the
live-for-the-moment and individualistic ethos fostered by popular culture may be one reason why many Latinos are experiencing
"downward assimilation," as evidenced by the fact that second-
and third-generation Latinos do worse than first-generation
Latinos on family outcomes ranging from divorce to nonmarital
childbearing.[66] Journalist Roberto Suro, a long-time observer
of Latinos in the United States, has recently pointed out that
familism is strongest among Latinos who speak mostly in Spanish
and weakest among Latinos who speak mostly in English; in his

estimation, "a powerful process of acculturation is taking place among immigrants and their offspring which produces an erosion of the strong sense of family evident among recent immigrants in favor of attitudes similar to those of non-Latinos in the U.S. population."[67]

For Latinos, as for African Americans, these structural and cultural forces work in tandem. For instance, downward assimilation seems to be most common among the children of Latino immigrants with low levels of education.[68] That is, Latinos who are most likely to experience poverty, discrimination, and bad neighborhoods are also the ones who seem most likely to eschew the family values of their forebears.[69] The negative aspects of the family revolution seem to have the most power among precisely the Latinos who have the fewest resources to escape its grasp.

CHAPTER BY CHAPTER

The family revolution of the last half-century has played an outsized role in the lives of Latinos and, especially, African Americans. But we do not want to suggest that black and Latino relationships and families do not have unique family strengths. African Americans have been celebrated for close-knit kinship ties and for the powerful relationships between mothers and their children;[70] similarly, Latinos are known for the strength of their extended families and their love of children.[71] Churches have historically played a crucial role in lending religious, moral, and social support to black and Latino families.[72] This leads to our fundamental research question: Is religion achieving success in creating the conditions where relationships, marriages, and families can flourish in black and Latino communities?

This broad question has four components. First, are black Protestant, Catholic, and Latino Protestant churches supporting what sociologist Elijah Anderson has called a "code of decency"—encompassing hard work, temperance, and personal responsibility[73]—which lends strong indirect support to happy and stable relationships in black and Latino communities? We take up this question in chapter 2, showing that religious faith is indeed connected to the code of decency; for instance, churchgoing African Americans and Latinos are more likely to be employed, to avoid falling prey to drug or alcohol addiction, and to steer clear of crime. This code of decency is particularly important for minority men, who are more likely than their female peers to engage in street behaviors (e.g., dealing drugs) that can harm their relationships.[74] By adhering to this code of decency, churchgoing black and Latino men have a better chance of thriving, economically and socially; equally important, they also make better husbands and partners.

How does religion influence sexual activity and childbearing among African Americans and Latinos? Chapter 3 finds that faith makes a difference: churchgoing African Americans and Latinos are more likely to hold traditional views about sex and childbearing, and they are less likely to have sex outside of marriage or a child outside of wedlock. However, religion seems to influence white sexual and childbearing behavior more than that of blacks and Latinos.

Does religion foster marriage in black and Latino communities? Chapter 4 shows that religion is indeed linked to pro-marriage attitudes and, for the most part, to higher marriage rates among African Americans and Latinos. The link between religion and marriage is partly a consequence of the emphasis that churches attach to family life, as well as to living in accord with the code of decency. We also speculate that minority men and women with an interest in marriage tend to seek out churches, knowing that they will provide social and normative support to their relationships. This is what social scientists call a selection effect.

Chapter 5 takes up our final question: How does religion influence the quality and stability of married and unmarried relationships among Latinos and African Americans? Surprisingly, we find that both married and unmarried couples benefit from religious faith and participation. Couples who are religious are more likely to enjoy happy relationships. This is the case not because churches spend a lot of time talking about marriage; indeed, they do not. Rather, we attribute our findings to the fact that couples are exposed to the code of decency and the Golden Rule when they attend church. Also, couples do not typically benefit from religion when only the woman is religious, but there are modest benefits if just the man attends services regularly. We argue that shared faith supplies moral, social, and spiritual solidarity and that religion seems especially important in turning men's hearts and minds toward their wives or partners.

Marital stability itself is a different question. Frequent church attendance substantially reduces the likelihood that a married couple will call it quits, but only if they are white. Religious participation has no effect, positive or negative, on the stability of Latino or African American marriages. This comes as a surprise to us, given how consequential religion is for nonwhite behavior in other contexts. However, it is consistent with the findings presented in chapter 3, which show that religion has a much stronger negative effect on the nonmarital fertility of whites than on that of blacks or Latinos. The absence of religious effects on black and Latino marital stability also drives home the point we make elsewhere in this book: religion is not a silver bullet. It produces many benefits for regular churchgoers, but not everyone will benefit from participating.

This book poses timely questions, because social scientists have reached a sobering conclusion: although recent changes in American family life have benefited some, especially adults, others face new challenges, most often children. Compared to children raised in an intact, married family, children raised in single-parent or cohabiting homes are significantly more likely to suffer psychological problems such as depression, to get into trouble with the law, to become pregnant as teenagers, and to drop out of high school.[75] Adults have also paid a price for the family revolution, although the outcomes are more varied. Specifically, the retreat from marriage of the last fifty years has been accompanied by less marital happiness,[76] fewer investments made in spouses,[77] more divorce,[78] and rising levels of instability among couples who cohabit.[79] Finally, communities with extensive divorce, single parenthood, and cohabitation are more likely to experience economic, social, and psychological ills such as poverty, crime, suicide, and low social mobility.[80] Given their disproportionate exposure to the family revolution, Latino and especially African American children, couples, and communities have paid the biggest social, economic, and psychological costs for the retreat from marriage associated with the family revolution of the last half-century.

DATA

This book is based upon a combination of quantitative and qualitative data that allows us to paint a sweeping picture of religion and family life among African Americans and Latinos. We rely on six national surveys. First, we use data from both the 1979 and 1997 cohorts of the National Longitudinal Surveys of Youth (NLSY). Both NLSY cohorts contain large numbers of respondents who have been reinterviewed annually or biennially. Second, we draw on the National Longitudinal Study of Adolescent to Adult Health (formerly known as the National Longitudinal Study of Adolescent Health, and still referred to by its common name, Add Health), another large panel study. Panel data such as these provide the optimal means for studying family transitions like marriage, divorce, or having a child. Third, we use the 1972–2012 General Social Surveys (GSS).[81] A cross-sectional sample of 1,500 to 3,000 English-speaking households within the continental United States, the GSS has been conducted annually or biennially since 1972. Its consistency over time makes it an ideal data set for studying trends. Fourth, we employ the National Survey of Religion and Family Life (NSRFL), a 2006 sample of approximately 2,400 adults. The NSRFL contains extensive questions on religion, as well as oversamples of African Americans and Latinos. Unlike the GSS, NSRFL interviews were conducted in both English and Spanish. Fifth, we use data from the 2006–2010 National Survey of Family Growth (NSFG).[82] The NSFG has been conducted periodically since 1973 by the National Center for Health Statistics to study family life, fertility, and health. The 2006–2010 survey contains data on over 20,000 men and women aged 15 through 44. It therefore offers a large sample of Americans in their peak years of union formation and fertility.

We also draw on a qualitative sample of 25 clergy and 60 ordinary adults (both religious and nonreligious) drawn from Harrisonburg, Virginia; New York, New York; and San Diego, California. Aided by research assistants, we posed to these respondents a range of questions about family, religion, economics, and culture. We also explored these topics with more than 70 African Americans and Latinos aged 20 through 40 in focus groups in Atlanta, Dallas, Los Angeles, and New York. These interviews and focus groups provided us with rich insights about contemporary relationships, family life, and religion among minorities, and they helped us to understand the patterns we discovered in our six national data sets. Finally, we conducted a year of ethnographic fieldwork in Harlem, Brooklyn, and the Bronx, during which time we visited churches and spoke with clergy and parishioners.

WHY THIS BOOK?

Scholars have spent decades exploring the contours of black and Latino relationships, pondering how poverty, discrimination, national origin, welfare policy, and segregation influence marriage and family life. Perhaps because the ivory tower is one of the more secular arenas in contemporary America, scholars have largely overlooked the role of religion in shaping relationships, marriage, and family life.[83]

This is a striking omission, given that 36 percent of African Americans and 29 percent of Latinos attend church frequently (several times a month or more), 70 percent of African Americans and 61 percent of Latinos deem themselves moderately or very religious, and an estimated 50,000 congregations serve blacks and Latinos around the United States.[84] This book speaks to this omission by shining a spotlight on how religion is shaping the relationships and marriages of blacks and Latinos.

Our book is timely, because African Americans and Latinos now make up more than a quarter of the American population; by 2050 they will compose 42 percent of all Americans.[85] Buffeted by social forces like poverty and racism, black and Latino families have lost ground in recent years. Marriage is down, cohabitation is up; children are spending less time in stable married families and more time in fragile households headed by cohabiting or single parents. Acculturation among Latinos is linked to fewer and less stable marriages. All in all, the family revolution has exacted a toll on African Americans and Latinos that shows little sign of abating.

But this is not the whole story. Our book shows that churches are achieving an important measure of success in fostering lower rates of nonmarital childbearing, more marriage, and happier relationships among blacks and Latinos. Religious faith is linked to higher marriage rates and happier relationships in large part because churches foster an ethic of care and reinforce a code of decency among their members. Churches are helping African Americans and Latinos keep up with America's changing families. However, the religious faith of blacks and Latinos does not seem to make much difference when it comes to divorce. Moreover, the impact of religiosity on sex, marriage, and divorce is stronger and more consistent for whites than it is for minorities. This may be partly because many churches serving black and Latino communities do not squarely address issues related to marriage and nonmarital childbearing for fear of offending the nontraditional families that fill their pews on Sunday.

Given the importance of marriage and family life for Latino and African American children, couples, and communities, clergy and lay religious leaders, as well as others interested in promoting healthy marriages, should use our findings to retool their efforts to strengthen families and relationships. Obviously, they cannot strengthen marriage in black and Latino communities by themselves. Public policy, economic opportunity, and cultural renewal are all needed to revitalize marriage and family life for the nation's two largest minority groups, as for the nation as a whole.

Our book suggests that churches and other groups working with black and Latino families can improve their efforts to strengthen relationships, marriages, and family life with a mixture of realism, grace, and idealism. This is because many of the biggest challenges facing Latino and African American children, couples, and communities revolve around issues related to the sequencing, stability, and quality of intimate relationships—from nonmarital childbearing to multiple-partner fertility. We also think that churches and other groups can do more to address the economic challenges facing their members—with, for instance, employment ministries connecting the unemployed or underemployed to apprenticeship or job opportunities. Obviously, the road they must walk to stronger black and Latino relationships, marriages, and families runs through some of the most difficult and controversial terrain in our culture. Given the integral connection between the health of marriage and the welfare of black and Latino children, as well as the communities they live in, this is a journey worth taking.

Chapter 2

Steering Clear of the Street

Leroy comes across as a poster boy for bad behavior. On a warm summer evening in 2006, this handsome, 33-year-old African American man is riffing on his love life in metropolitan Atlanta. "I've always been known to have one main girl, and then I keep a basketball team. I like my starting lineup. I keep a summer league team, and I have a winter league team. I have one main girl, and then the rest of them is like my little friends."

Leroy speaks with equal measures of pride and nonchalance about his success with women. By his reckoning, it is easy to meet women in clubs, the neighborhood, or the supermarket. Sexual fidelity does not appear to be important to him, though he is currently living with a woman. After all, "everybody cheats."

But as Leroy keeps talking it becomes clear that his story is more complicated than his demeanor would lead us to expect. He arrived in Atlanta in 2002 with his wife and daughter to take a job with a local phone company after his previous employer, WorldCom, let him go after filing for bankruptcy. Within four months of arriving in Atlanta, the phone company downsized and Leroy was out of work again.

After he lost his second job in less than six months, his marriage fell apart. "I came home, told my wife [I was laid off]," recalls Leroy. "I woke up the next day, and she had her bag packed. Her and my daughter was like, 'You don't got a job; I'm leaving.'"

His next serious relationship was even more disastrous. After his marriage fell apart, Leroy began dating a single mother. For over a year, things went very well. "She was the person I could honestly say I got to know her more than I had ever gotten to know anyone in my entire life, even my ex-wife," reports Leroy, adding, "in the beginning when we started dating, it was great." As things turned out, the relationship was not as blissful as Leroy had thought.

After a year and a half, Leroy became concerned because his girlfriend, whom he was putting through nursing school, was staying out late with her girlfriends. He later found out that she was hooked on cocaine. "I had to let her go, because she got so strung out on cocaine, and it was just amazing to see somebody that went from being such a positive role model—everybody loved her, everybody thought she was so intelligent. To go from that person, to just totally turn into a drug addict, and now I hear she's a prostitute. It's so sad to see this."

RESISTING THE STREET'S SIREN CALL

Leroy's current outlook on relationships, on the surface so cavalier, turned out to be shaped by a complicated history of loss, break-ups (including a divorce), unemployment, deception, and drugs—all of which have made it difficult for him to put much faith in relationships in general or any one woman in particular. To him, the only alternative would be a union based on "a strong religious foundation, and agreement and understanding." But right now Leroy does not enjoy such a relationship with his current girlfriend, perhaps because he skips church more than he goes.

As this chapter will make clear, Leroy's experience is emblematic of the challenges facing a noteworthy minority of African

American and Latino families. African Americans and Latinos, especially black and Latino men, are more likely than whites to get caught up in behaviors or situations that put their relationships at risk. For instance, male infidelity and conflict over infidelity are more common among African Americans and Latinos than they are among whites.[1] Substance abuse is comparable across racial and ethnic lines, but perhaps more consequential for African Americans and Latinos (middle-class abusers have greater access to treatment and rehabilitation).[2] Although the scholarly literature does not indicate that the mental health of minorities is consistently worse, Latinos and blacks are more likely than whites to suffer from stress and some forms of depression.[3] Criminal activity and rates of incarceration are also higher among minority males.[4] Black men are markedly more likely to be unemployed or underemployed than their peers, and Latinos are more likely to be working in low-wage jobs.[5] Finally, blacks and Latinos, especially men, are more likely to get caught up in what sociologist Elijah Anderson has called the "code of the street," a lifestyle marked by violent self-assertion, criminal activity, off-the-books work (e.g., hustling), and infidelity.[6] Sociologist Mary Patillo-McCoy observes that a minority of African American young adults experiment with "street" behaviors or hang out with friends or family members involved in street activities even if they do not fully conform to the code of the street.[7] Our own interviews revealed a similar dynamic among some young Latinos, who sometimes characterize it as "del mundo"—that is, of the world.

As this chapter makes clear, only a minority of African Americans and Latinos are drawn into these destructive behaviors. Nevertheless, the fact that these two minority groups are more likely to be affected by these social problems is an important reason why they have more troubled relationships, more out-of-wedlock births, and, in the case of African Americans and native-born Latinos, higher divorce rates than do whites.[8]

In the face of the challenges posed by the street to African American and Latino communities, local churches stress a "code of decency," an ethic of right conduct that runs counter to the code of the street and to what these churches view more generally as destructive, sinful, or street behavior.[9] By Anderson's account, this code of decency encompasses temperance, hard work, honesty, respect, law-abiding behavior, and dedication to family. Although Anderson does not much focus on the role that religious institutions play in fostering the code of decency, our interviews and analysis of national surveys indicate that churches, and religious faith more generally, are bulwarks of decent behavior in many black and Latino communities. Indeed, most African Americans and Latinos abide by this code of decency, in part because they receive support from community churches.

By fostering decent behavior, religion plays a crucial role in creating a personal and social context where individuals and their relationships can thrive. Sociologist Émile Durkheim observed this about one hundred years ago, writing that religion's true function is "to make us act and to help us live."[10] Some of the contributions that religion makes to the stability of relationships and family life among Latinos and African Americans are indirect: religion supplies social, moral, and religious resources that help women and especially men live decent lives. In other words, religion helps sustain Latinos and blacks in their efforts to be hard-working, temperate, law-abiding members of their communities who steer clear of the temptations of the street.

Decent people make better spouses, partners, and friends. Men who avoid trouble with the law and are gainfully employed are more likely to get married and stay married.[11] Spouses who remain faithful to one another enjoy happier and more stable marriages.[12] Men and women who steer clear of drug and alcohol abuse have better relationships.[13] Thus, even if churches do not often focus explicitly on marriage and relationships, they shape the context of black and Latino relationships in important ways by lending support to a decent way of life.

Our organization proceeds as follows. First, we explore racial and ethnic differences in decent behaviors that have implications for the quality and stability of relationships and family life. Next we examine the association between religion and these behaviors and outcomes. Our focus is on understanding racial and ethnic differences in the code of decency, and the role that religion plays in fostering decency among African Americans and Latinos. We follow the same organizational scheme in chapters 3 through 5.

LIVING OUTSIDE DECENT SOCIETY

Four patterns place some blacks and Latinos outside the mainstream of decent society and often undermine their relationships and marriages: (1) male unemployment or underemployment; (2) criminal behavior and incarceration; (3) substance abuse; and (4) infidelity. Individually and especially together, these maladies strain relationships, reduce marriage rates, and increase the odds that spouses will end up calling it quits. How common are they among African Americans, Latinos, and, for that matter, whites, especially men?

Work

Employment is important for at least two reasons. First, unemployment dramatically increases the odds that families suffer from poverty and the hardships—financial, physical, and emotional—it entails.[14] Second, male unemployment tends to be particularly difficult for relationships and marriages.[15] Unemployment undercuts a man's ability to provide for his family, robs him of self-worth, and makes him more likely to withdraw from family life or explode in anger at family members. He may lose the respect of his girlfriend or wife. For all these reasons, unemployment, especially male unemployment, reduces the odds that a couple will get married, stay married, and enjoy a high-quality, low-conflict relationship.[16]

Figure 2.1 displays levels of unemployment (including being out of the labor force entirely) among blacks, Latinos, and whites. About one in five black men is not working, compared to just one in seven white men and one in ten Latino men. Forty-five percent of black men are not employed full-time, compared to just over one-quarter of whites and Latinos. Among women, the black-white employment gap is not as marked. Just over one-third of all women work full-time; indeed, white and African American women are equally likely to work full-time. About one in seven of all women do not work, with Hispanic women being more

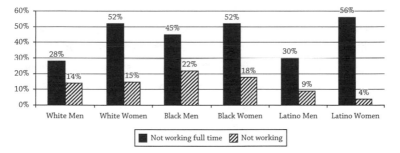

Figure 2.1 Employment for Adults Aged 18–60, by Race/Ethnicity and Sex.
Source: General Social Survey, 2012, respondents aged 18 to 60. We count students as working. N = 1,340.

likely to work than their black or white peers. More notably, both African Americans and Latinos earn markedly less than whites. In 2012, the median black household income was $33,321 and the median Hispanic income was $39,005, compared to $57,009 for non-Hispanic whites.[17]

These trends in employment and income have troubling implications for relationships among blacks and Latinos. Sociologist William Julius Wilson has long noted that high rates of male unemployment make black men less "marriageable"—that is, less appealing as potential husbands in the eyes of women, and indeed in their own eyes.[18] More generally, a large body of research indicates that unemployment, underemployment, and low incomes are associated with lower marriage rates, more marital problems, and more divorce, especially when the partner with job problems is a man.[19] The bottom line is that unemployment and money problems often cast a cloud over relationships and marriages.

Not surprisingly, African Americans report that job and money-related issues are particularly salient in their relationships. We have already seen how Leroy's wife left him after he lost his job in Atlanta. Another woman, Angela, reports that her marriage fell apart shortly after she had her first baby, in part because her husband's salary was not large enough to absorb the financial strain associated with her taking time off to care for their child. "You're used to two paychecks; now you have one [paycheck] and so you're not having enough money to probably even meet all of the bills," recalls this 40-year-old mother from suburban Atlanta. In her words, financial difficulties "put a strain on our marriage" and ultimately brought about its demise.

One sensitive issue, most common among blacks, is when women earn more, or enjoy more stable employment, than the men in their lives.[20] Brittany, a 30-year-old mother from Atlanta,

notes that the fact that she did better than her husband financially was a thorn in his side during their marriage: "He said it
didn't bother him [that I made more] but when certain things
came about, I can tell it bothered him. He didn't feel like he was
really the man of the house, because he wasn't able to take care
of everything, and I think that was his dream [to take care of the
family financially]." He eventually divorced her.

The comparably poor economic performance of their male
partners can be a sticking point for wives and girlfriends, insofar
as they come to view their relationships as inequitable. Linda,
a 42-year-old African American woman living in metropolitan
Atlanta, makes more than her boyfriend and also does more
around the house than he does. "It bothers me because I feel like
I'm always putting out more," she says. For instance, when they
take vacations, "the majority of it [expenses] falls on me, and
I don't like that." Other women who earned more than their husbands or boyfriends expressed similar sentiments.

Latinos also face problems related to work and money, but
they revolve less around male unemployment or underemployment and more around the challenge of low-wage, low-status
jobs. For instance, Claudia, 31, reports that she and her husband
do not have enough time to unwind and enjoy one another, in
part because she works seven days a week so that they can afford
a modest apartment in East Los Angeles. "Not having enough
money to go out causes problems. You need to have money to go
out and have a drink, not just work," Claudia informed us, adding that she has not had a child yet because they cannot afford
daycare, nor can she and her husband afford to have her cut back
on her work hours. Guillermo, a 37-year-old truck driver from
the Los Angeles suburb of Montebello, said that he has frequent
"money problems with my partner." He notes that one of the challenges facing immigrants, both legal and undocumented, from

Mexico and Central America is that they have to spend a lot of money getting to the United States and settling in, and that this can be a real drain on their household finances. Many American Latinos also send regular remittances back home to Mexico or elsewhere.[21]

Long work hours, not to mention irregular work hours, take a toll on many Latino couples. Gabriela, 34, complains that her husband works too much, often late into the night. "I know we need the money financially, but he also needs to be with the children and me," says this stay-at-home Latina from the Los Angeles area. "It's better to not work so many hours so he can have more time with us." Her complaint is significant, as time spent with family generally translates into better relationships between spouses, as well as between parents and children.[22]

No racial or ethnic group has a monopoly on job-related challenges. Nevertheless, Latinos and African Americans face more of these challenges, with African Americans more likely to suffer from underemployment and Latinos more likely to face long and irregular work hours. This is important because a large body of research suggests that stable employment and decent incomes, especially for men, play a crucial role in fostering high-quality, stable relationships and marriages.[23]

Crime

Criminal activity and incarceration, particularly among men, pose major risks to relationships, especially among Latinos and African Americans. Crime is often accompanied by street behaviors such as abusing drugs and alcohol, or multiple sexual relationships. All of this is hard on relationships. When they do end up in jail, men and women cannot support their families or spend much time with them. Once they leave jail, men and women face great difficulties in landing a good job.[24] For these reasons, criminal activity and incarceration do not bode well for marriages and relationships.[25]

The sad reality is that minorities, especially African Americans, are more like to have been charged with a serious crime or to have been incarcerated, in part because the criminal justice system often targets minority offenders.[26] According to figure 2.2, 54 percent of black men and 36 percent of black women in their early or mid-twenties report they have committed a serious crime, compared to slightly less than half of white and Latino men and slightly less than one-third of white and Latina women. Perhaps these figures seem high because criminal activity most often takes place in adolescence or young adulthood.[27] Rates of incarceration also vary by race and ethnicity, as figure 2.3 shows. African American men are almost twice as likely as white men to have done time, with

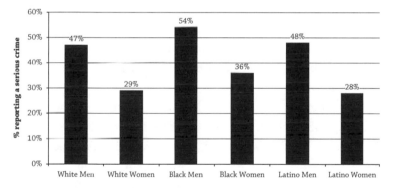

Figure 2.2 The Percentage of Young Adults Aged 22–26 Who Report Having Ever Committed a Serious Crime, by Sex and Race/Ethnicity.

Source: Calculations using data from the National Longitudinal Survey of Youth 1997 cohort, 1997–2002. N = 8,649. Results reflect self-reported measures of criminal behavior in 2001 and 2002. Participants were counted as having committed serious crime if they ever reported having engaged in assault, selling drugs, or stealing something worth more than $50.

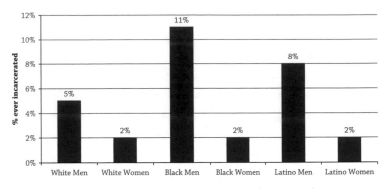

Figure 2.3 The Percentage of Young Adults Aged 22–26 Who Have Been Incarcerated, by Sex and Race/Ethnicity.

Source: Calculations using data from the National Longitudinal Survey of Youth 1997 cohort, 1997–2002. N = 8,649. Incarceration is measured in 2001 and 2002. Participants were counted as having been incarcerated if they ever reported having been in jail or a youth corrections facility.

about 11 percent of black men and 5 percent of white men in their mid-twenties reporting they have ever been incarcerated; Latino men fall in the middle, with 8 percent reporting time in jail or prison. Women are much less likely to have done time, and there are no racial or ethnic differences in female incarceration.

Criminal activity often accompanies other street behavior, including substance abuse and violence, that corrodes relationships. Luis, 31, and Maria, 23, are a Dominican couple living in Washington Heights in New York. Luis has no legal job but hangs out with men who are involved in a range of off-the-books work, from day labor to selling things on the street and the drug trade, and he often engages in these activities himself. In his view, one of the biggest challenges he and Maria face is "getting out of the hood with its crime, drugs." He adds, "There's all type of stuff. We live in it everyday, you know." According to both of

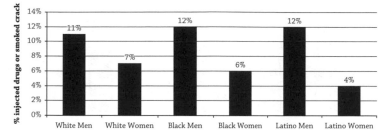

Figure 2.4 The Percentage of Adults Aged 18–60 Who Have Ever Injected Illicit Drugs or Smoked Crack Cocaine, by Sex and Race/Ethnicity.
Source: General Social Survey, 2000–2012, respondents aged 18 to 60. N = 10,862.

them, the "stuff" his peers do includes drinking, violence, and infidelity—all behaviors that spill over into their relationship. Even though she values Luis's interaction with their son and thinks Luis is a good father, Maria fears their relationship does not have much of a future: "Living with someone who still hasn't got the reality check [about getting his life together] isn't gonna work." Her comments are indicative of how a street lifestyle makes relationships difficult to sustain.

Drugs and Alcohol

Drug and especially alcohol abuse plague a minority of blacks and Latinos, although the data do not indicate that blacks and Latinos use drugs and alcohol at consistently higher rates than whites (indeed, white men report the highest level of alcohol abuse). But note that there are subtleties in racial and ethnic patterns of drug and alcohol use. For instance, African Americans do more crack and less meth than whites.[28] Figure 2.4 indicates that about 12 percent of black, white, and Latino men aged 18–60 have shot drugs or smoked crack. Women are less likely to do hard drugs. When it comes to alcohol, figure 2.5 indicates

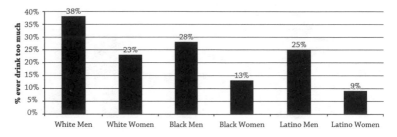

Figure 2.5 The Percentage of Adults Aged 18–60 Who "Ever Drink Too Much," by Sex and Race/Ethnicity.

Source: General Social Survey, 1990–1994 (data on excessive drinking have not been collected more recently), respondents aged 18 to 60. N = 1,925.

that men, especially white men, are more likely to drink to excess. Women, especially Latina women, are less likely to report excessive drinking. Indeed, the gender gap in substance abuse is higher for Latinos.

Substance abuse is problematic because it often leads to domestic violence and infidelity.[29] Abusers have frequent encounters with law enforcement and can struggle to hold down a job, both of which also take a toll on relationships.[30] It is noteworthy that the gender gap in substance use is larger among minorities. For blacks there is a marked gender gap in drug use, and for Latinos there is an equally pronounced gender gap in alcohol use. These disparities probably translate into trouble for couples, with conflicts emerging about drug or alcohol abuse. And the effects of substance abuse may be more consequential for low-income minorities without ready access to treatment for drug and alcohol addiction.

African Americans are more likely than Latinos to mention drug problems when talking about how substance abuse affects their relationships. Leroy's experience with his most recent girlfriend, who developed a cocaine addiction, is just one example of how drug use can destroy a relationship.

Angela had a similar experience. Her last relationship broke up when she discovered that her boyfriend of nine months was doing drugs in the middle of the night. "He had good qualities, a good family background ... and [yet] in the middle of the night I get up to go use the restroom and he's in there doing coke, and it just blew me away because this is a pastor's son," she reports. Angela was particularly concerned that he would "bring this into [her] house" because she has a son who she does not want to be exposed to drugs. Although she was emotionally attached to her boyfriend, she says the relationship is over: "I know this is it. No way that I will have you around—I have a 5-year-old son. There is no way I will have you around my son doing something crazy like this."

More generally, blacks report that drugs have a baleful impact on their community, and relationships and family life in their communities. Brandon, a 37-year-old black man, had this to say about the consequences of drug use for African Americans:

> Drugs have a big impact I think on the community in general, and I think specifically the black community. I know plenty of friends, male and female that have got into [drugs] and they start recreational, and they kept on, and then one thing that tends to happen is now you wanna move and find a drug that gets you to a higher level, then a higher level. Then the next thing you know is you're hooked ... and you forget about all the other things in life. You're only looking for the next high. And you will do anything to get it, and it destroys you, and everybody around you.

Latinos are more likely to say that alcohol, rather than drugs, plays a negative role in their family lives. Luis, from Washington Heights in New York, reports that he deals with the stress in his life by drinking: "Every weekend, I go to the liquor store. I get some bottle of something and just drink my sorrows away." Luis's drinking seems to be linked to his propensity to fight, both verbally and physically, with his partner Maria over money and their mutual concerns about infidelity. Understandably, Maria does not like it when he gets like this. "I'd say he is abusive—physically, mentally, and verbally. So that's what really puts me in the unhappy stage." Marisol, a Latina from San Diego, told us how drinking affects her community and family life: "Well, there is a lot of alcohol in the [Mexican American] community, for sure. And I really, I personally do think it does affect it [the community]. It destroys families."

Yet given the data described in figures 2.4 and 2.5, we do not think substance abuse helps to account for any racial or ethnic differences in marriage and family life. That is because, on average, blacks and Latinos do not abuse drugs and alcohol at higher rates than whites.

Infidelity

Infidelity can be a major source of strain for Latino and especially black relationships. Cheating threatens the expectations of fidelity, commitment, and permanence that undergird most relationships and virtually all marriages in this country (93 percent of Americans view adultery as always wrong or almost always wrong).[31] Not surprisingly, infidelity breeds conflict, distrust, and often violence. In fact, infidelity is one of the strongest predictors of divorce and relationship dissolution.[32] Moreover, unmarried men who are involved in multiple, concurrent relationships are less likely to get married in the first place: they are manifestly less interested in settling down with one woman (recall that Leroy talked about having "one main girl" and then a "basketball team" on the side).[33] Finally, infidelity and the related phenomenon of having multiple sexual partners both increase the odds of what demographers call multi-partner fertility; that is, having children with more than one person. This is problematic because it creates complex financial, social, and emotional obligations that run across households, thereby making it more difficult for adults to maintain a single sustained relationship or marriage and to invest in the children that come from these relationships.[34] For all these reasons, infidelity and multi-partner fertility present a threat to the quality and stability of relationships and family life.

Our research indicates that blacks and Latinos are especially likely to experience or perceive infidelity and multiple sexual partnerships. According to the data shown in figure 2.6, almost twice as many black and Latino men (18 and 16 percent, respectively) report that they have committed adultery, or suspect adultery on the part of their partner, than do white men (9 percent). The trends are even more striking for women, where

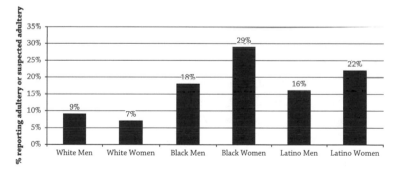

Figure 2.6 The Percentage of Adults Aged 18–60 Reporting Infidelity in Their Relationship, by Sex and Race/Ethnicity.

Source: National Survey of Religion and Family Life, 2006. N = 1,489. Results are weighted. The figure measures whether married or partnered respondents report either cheating on their partners or suspecting their partners of infidelity.

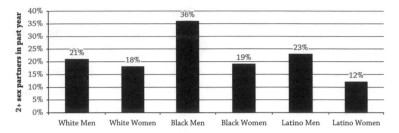

Figure 2.7 The Percentage of Never Married Adults Aged 18–44 Who Have Had Two or More Sex Partners in the Past Year, by Sex and Race/Ethnicity.
Source: National Survey of Family Growth 2006–2010. N = 20,725. Results are weighted. Unfortunately, the data do not allow us to determine if these are serial or concurrent relationships.

more than one in five black (29 percent) and Latina (22 percent) women report adultery or, especially, concerns about adultery in their relationships, compared to just 7 percent of white women.

Figure 2.7 explores recent sexual partnerships among never-married adults. Men, notably black men, are more likely to have multiple partners, while Latinas are the least likely. The gender gap is largest between black and Latino men and women. These findings are consistent with other research that indicates that black men are especially likely to be involved in patterns of sexual behavior that undercut the quality and stability of their relationships.[35]

Our interviews suggest that infidelity begets distrust and oftentimes more infidelity, as spouses and partners resort to retaliatory cheating or just come to conclude that infidelity is inevitable. Take Brittany, the 30-year-old African American woman from Atlanta. Her marriage ended after her husband cheated on her. She has dated since her divorce and admits that she has occasionally cheated on boyfriends: "There have been incidences where I've been unfaithful because for one, I think once you've been hurt, I don't value relationships as much as I [used to]," she says, adding that infidelity has usually occurred when there was an "attraction with someone else" and she "didn't value the relationship" she was currently in. Predictably, this cycle of infidelity seems to have dimmed her interest in any particular relationship. Linda, also African American and from Atlanta, says she has given up on marriage because she caught two different fiancés cheating. "Well, I live with somebody [now], and it works for me, because I've been engaged twice, and both times, I caught my man cheating," she reports, adding with a note of bewilderment, "And they couldn't come up with a reason why, because they had everything they needed at home."

Infidelity also affects some Latino couples, although it is much more common among men than women. In the words of one Mexican American woman from Los Angeles, "If a Latino hears that a woman was unfaithful, we can't believe it. When it is a man, we do believe it. It is expected of a man, but not of a woman." Other respondents reported that infidelity is more common among native-born Latinas and more acculturated Latinas. This same woman observed that women are more likely to engage in infidelity in the United States than in Latin America because "women have more freedom" in the States. Her views were echoed by other men and women in our interviews.

Lucia is a 29-year-old Puerto Rican living with her boyfriend, David, in the Bronx. David continued to fool around even after they got together; indeed, he fathered a child with another woman after their relationship began. This has caused obvious pain to Lucia, who worries about his relationship with the mother of his second child. Noting he is often out during the weekend, she says, "I guess he's with his baby's mama or some other girl because he's always coming home with glitter on him." His infidelities have taken a toll on their relationship and her sense of happiness and self-worth. "I'm not too happy either [with our relationship]," she says, adding, "because he'll be going around with other girls." Lucia has no interest in marriage because her experience with relationships has led her to conclude that "there's always going to be cheating."

Needless to say, the consequences of extramarital sex are usually jealousy, conflict, and ultimately the dissolution of relationships and marriages. One San Diego Latina reports that she often hears neighborhood couples fighting about infidelity:

Q: Is marriage doing well in your community?
A: No, not where I live. There are a lot of couples who fight. I wake up in the middle of the night, because I sleep with my window open, and I hear them arguing all the time. "You're cheating on me. I want to leave you. I've asked you for a divorce before." There's all that stuff going on.

Claudia echoes this concern about infidelity. For this immigrant from Guatemala, now living in Los Angeles, adultery has cast a pall over her friends' marriages. "I can stand a lot of things," she says. "But I won't forgive it [infidelity] and I won't forget it. I know couples with that problem who come back together and get married again. But somewhere or another it comes up again. It will be there for the rest of their lives. It's not something you forget." Claudia hopes she and her husband can stay faithful, but a note of worry runs through our interview. "That's what I say now [about infidelity], but I don't know what I would do if I were in that situation."

This chapter suggests that Latinos and especially African Americans are more likely than whites to get caught up in behaviors that undercut the quality and stability of their marriages and relationships. Even though most black and Latino men and women do not experience the challenges addressed here (and whites outpace both groups when it comes to heavy drinking), it is also true that many of the problems covered in this chapter, especially unemployment, incarceration, and infidelity, are more common among minority men. Broadly speaking, black and Latino men appear to be more likely than white men to get caught up in street-like behaviors that interfere with their participation in mainstream American life. Finally, the misbehavior of these men is problematic not just because it places them outside the mainstream of decent society, but also because it diverges from the behavior of their wives and girlfriends, who are less likely to be unemployed, abusing drugs or alcohol, incarcerated, or unfaithful. In other words, within many couples a divide opens up between a man lured by the call of the street and a woman trying to maintain her place in decent society. For all these reasons, black and Latino couples face greater challenges in forming relationships built around mutual respect, fidelity, trust, and affection.

EXPLAINING THE STREET

What accounts for these racial, ethnic, and gender differences in behaviors and circumstances? In particular, why are Latino and especially black men more likely to have difficulty with work, crime, and infidelity? Comprehensive answers to these questions are beyond the scope of this book. Nevertheless, we can detail a few of the most important structural and cultural causes of street behaviors. Some apply to both sexes, others just to men.

First, on the job front, shifts since the 1970s away from manufacturing and toward information and services in the US economy have made it especially difficult for men with less education to secure remunerative employment or sometimes any employment at all.[36] From 1979 to 1991, the real wages of men with a college degree dropped by 2 percent but those of high-school educated men dropped by 16 percent.[37] This trend is particularly important because blacks and Latinos tend to have less education than whites.[38] This economic shift has proved particularly debilitating for black men, who often enjoyed good industrial jobs for much of the postwar era until the 1970s. Furthermore, employers are also more likely to discriminate against minorities, especially black men, when making hiring decisions.[39] Employers tend to pay undocumented immigrants less than they do American citizens.[40] For all these reasons, minorities, especially black men, are more likely to have trouble finding good jobs, or jobs scheduled during regular hours. These work-related difficulties are consequential not only because they can affect men's and women's ability to make financial contributions to their families but also because they can undercut one's sense of self-worth and personal happiness. This affects their capacity to successfully engage with their families.

Second, since the 1960s American popular culture has taken an increasingly hedonistic turn, such that consumers of popular television shows, movies, and music are exposed to an ethic of immediate gratification, individual assertion, and hedonism that encompasses a range of behaviors, from drug use to sexual infidelity. These changes may be more consequential for blacks and Latinos both because minorities spend more time consuming popular culture and because minorities are more likely to be depicted in a negative light on TV.[41] For instance, one recent study found that black youth spend nearly six hours daily watching TV and Latinos spend 5:21 hours, compared to 3:36 hours for whites.[42] And what youth are watching is important. Students of popular culture note that minority men in particular are often depicted in a negative light. In the words of sociologist Orlando

Patterson, the African American male often serves as a "symbol of Dionysian liminality and the repressed pleasure principle"[43] for the larger culture; this is particularly problematic because

> Athletes and entertainers are now the dominant exemplars of Afro-American achievement and the role models that set the tone, style, ideals, and moral standards of most Afro-American youth and young men. Alas, their way of life reflects the worst aspects of underclass Afro-American street culture, especially in relation to women.[44]

Media studies suggest similar dynamics are in play for Latinos, who are more likely than whites to be depicted in the popular culture as hot-tempered, sexual, and criminally inclined.[45] Thus cultural shifts since the 1960s may have encouraged Americans, and especially minority men, to dismiss or flout norms of decency related to hard work, drug use, criminal activity, and sexual restraint.

Third, discrimination contributes to the behavioral trends among blacks and Latinos noted in this chapter, both because racial, ethnic, and xenophobic discrimination is a source of personal stress and because it can become a self-fulfilling prophecy. Latinos and especially blacks are more likely than whites to report that they have been the victim of employment discrimination, racial or ethnic police profiling, housing discrimination, or discrimination in a social situation.[46] The experience of discrimination can engender feelings of anger, depression, distress, and hopelessness.[47] Moreover, the experience of discrimination can lead men and women to lose faith in society and conventional morality, turn away from education and gainful employment, pick up drugs or alcohol, or otherwise embrace the code of the street.[48] When this happens, discrimination becomes a kind of self-fulfilling prophecy where blacks and Latinos engage in precisely the behaviors that were attributed to them in the first place.

Fourth, we note the strong role of family origins in shaping people's lives. Despite the commonly held perception of America as a land where people create their own destiny, social science has convincingly demonstrated that people's families of origin play a powerful role in determining how far they get in life. People who grow up in poor families, notably many African Americans and Latinos, start out life with profound disadvantages. They do not get as far in school as do children from educated, middle-class families.[49] Family structure also plays a role in determining life chances. People from unstable families of origin are less likely to finish high school and, if women, are more likely to get pregnant out of wedlock.[50] They are also far more likely to have trouble in their own relationships. Living with divorced parents or a mother who has never been married has substantial effects on adult children's romantic relationships, including lower marriage rates and higher divorce rates.[51] African Americans and Latinos are more likely to come from poor, unstable families, and this confers many disadvantages right out of the starting gate.

Finally, as noted in the previous chapter, we believe that two different subcultures influence blacks and Latinos in the contemporary United States. For African Americans, a street subculture emerged in the cultural and social tumult of the late 1960s that stressed an adversarial posture toward the norms of larger society; this subculture, exacerbated by the loss of good jobs since the early 1970s, encompasses criminal activity, violence, sexual conquest, alcohol and drug abuse, and other deleterious behaviors.[52] This street subculture has proved to be particularly salient for some poor African Americans, especially men, in large part because the greater society has proven to be less welcoming to them. As noted above, aspects of this subculture have been amplified in the popular culture.[53] The end result is that a small but noteworthy minority of African Americans take their cues from a street subculture that encourages them to reject the norms, beliefs, and behaviors of decent society.[54]

For Latinos, a "macho" subculture that evolved over centuries in Latin America has had an ambiguous impact on their communities. On the one hand, machismo continues to be linked to a strong work ethic and the sense of "providership" on the part of men. This helps to explain why Latino men have relatively high rates of employment, even though their access to well-paying jobs is limited, they often do not get far in school, and they face greater language and cultural barriers than do whites or blacks. On the other hand, machismo can be associated with an ethic of male domination, alcohol abuse, domestic violence, and promiscuity on the part of some Latino men.[55] Indeed, the findings detailed in this chapter suggest that a minority of Latino men are influenced by this macho ethic, which tends to undercut stable and high-quality relationships and marriages, especially in a society such as the United States where women are relatively free to leave an unhappy relationship.

These structural and cultural features of American life, together with the street and macho subcultures found within black and Latino communities, have made it difficult for some Latinos and blacks to conform to the norms and behaviors associated with decent society. Taken together, they may help explain why Latinos are more likely to be incarcerated or unfaithful, and why black men are more likely to be unemployed, engaged in criminal activity, incarcerated, or unfaithful in their relationships, compared to their white peers.

The social, economic, and cultural challenges blacks and Latinos face can manifest themselves in psychological distress. As figure 2.8 indicates, minorities are almost twice as likely as

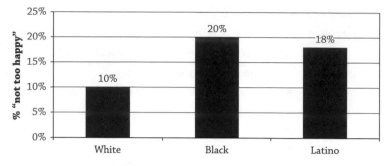

Figure 2.8 The Percentage of Adults Aged 18–44 Who Report Being "Not Too Happy," by Race/Ethnicity.

Source: General Social Survey, 2000–2012. N = 6,557. There are not significant gender differences in happiness.

whites to report being unhappy. Specifically, 20 percent of blacks and 18 percent of Latinos report that they are "not too happy" in life, compared to only 10 percent of whites. Because psychological distress is linked to a range of problem behaviors,[56] it may help to account for why blacks and Latinos are more likely to fall prey to self-destructive or antisocial activities such as crime or infidelity. Psychological distress also affects relationships and marriages, insofar as men and women who are unhappy are less likely to be affectionate and engaged with their partners, and more likely to succumb to conflicted, violent, or critical patterns of behavior in their relationships and marriages.[57]

DECENT DISCOURSE

Since the sexual and family revolutions of the late 1960s and 1970s, churches, especially black Protestant and Catholic denominations, have spoken out less about sex, childbearing, and marriage. In a word, many churches have backed away from taking a strong stand for what many think of as the traditional family. But this does not mean that churches serving black and Latino communities lack a normative agenda. By and large, they have remained stalwart supporters of a code of decency that encompasses hard work, temperance, responsibility, sexual fidelity, and the Golden Rule. Moreover, churches provide a religiously grounded message of hope and comfort, as well as the religious rituals and the social networks that make this message plausible in men and women's lives by helping to protect them from worldly or street temptations.

Sermons provide clear cues to blacks and Latinos looking for temporal guidance. In Catholic and Protestant churches serving predominantly black and Latino congregations, sermons often touch on right conduct. For instance, Rev. Josiah Wilson, the pastor of Olivet Baptist Church in Harlem, one of the most prominent pulpits in the city, offered this admonition to his congregation in a sermon entitled, "The Recovery of Righteousness":

[Most civilizations] are destroyed from within. The outward manifestations of this inner decay have been threefold. Three things that you see outwardly. One is drunkenness. . . . Break it out—getting high. I don't mean a sip here and there; I mean getting high all the time. [Another is] idleness. . . . And finally, immorality. This means that strong civilizations, those that are able to endure, and withstand attacks from without [have] sobriety, industry, and clean moral living. . . .

So, Beloved, I am suggesting to you that there is no greater need before us today than the recovery of plain old-fashioned righteousness. . . . who among us would . . . eschew drunkenness, idleness, and immorality? Who would dare to stand in the face of the onslaught of the culture of sin that has enveloped our nation and say, "I refuse to succumb. I will not yield to the temptation. I will stand like a tree planted by the water. I will not move"?

Clearly Rev. Wilson is seeking to motivate his congregation—which ranges from working- to upper-class blacks from Harlem and around metropolitan New York—to steer clear of the code of street and the vices of substance abuse, idleness, and "immorality." Although he never defined immorality in his sermon, we suspect it is an oblique reference to sexual infidelity.

Wilson is careful to make his pitch for righteousness accessible and credible to his congregation by humorously acknowledging that his own past is not pristine, that members of the church still struggle to live decently, and that he needs spiritual encouragement in his own effort to live right. In his words:

It ain't no secret that Rev. Wilson ain't always been Rev. Wilson. You know that. I had my season in the far country too. I was deep in the far country [laughter] . . . [But] each one of us has a commitment to God. That commitment is that, through Christ, we will lead lives worthy of God's grace. I will not get high . . . I'm sure there is nobody in the congregation who gotta get high all day. [laughter]. No drinkers here [laughter]. No reefer smokers here [laughter]. There are no freebasers [of cocaine] here . . .

Ask God to have mercy on me. Because you got it together; you know what is happening [in our community]. You in the street every day. You saw the preacher from around the corner in the bar. You know what is happening. I don't go for that. Then pray for me. I need prayer so that I can try to the best of my ability to walk the straight and narrow and to appear before men and women as perhaps an example.

Rev. Wilson is typical of many black and Latino Protestant clergy in his acknowledgment of his own prodigal period, his struggles to live up to his calling, and his recognition that members of his congregation also struggle to steer clear of the street or of vices that stand in opposition to his church's code of decency. His sermon makes the church welcoming to members and visitors who spent their lives struggling with substance abuse, criminal activity, or other forms of street lifestyles, or who are still struggling to put these vices behind them.

Churches encourage decent behavior in a variety of other implicit and explicit ways. In New York and Los Angeles, we noticed that Catholic churches serving predominantly Latino communities often posted the Ten Commandments in Spanish and English in a prominent place inside or outside the church. Religious education and youth programs for black and Latino churches typically stress the importance of the Ten Commandments and the Golden Rule as guides to good behavior. These programs influence the children, young adults, and the parents who send their kids to them.

David Hernandez leads a youth group at Victory Chapel in the Bronx. He argues that his youth group helps steer teenagers and young adults clear of the street, both through the substance of its message and by providing alternative activities to young African Americans and Latinos in his community. His group addresses a number of challenges facing adolescents and young adults in the Bronx: "We go into all those things (that affect our teens)—peer pressure, violence, drugs, gangs," Hernandez says. "And then we lead them to Christ." According to Hernandez, the Gospel's message of hope and liberation, combined with the community found at Victory, helps steer many of the youth in his church clear of the street and helps others leave temptations behind.

Churches, especially black and Latino Protestant churches serving low-income communities, provide numerous activities, from Bible studies to socials on Wednesday nights and throughout the weekend. These activities provide members with spiritual succor, social support, and help protect them from the siren song of the street. "We have fellowship breakfasts, dinners, and lunches and all that kind of good stuff," notes Rev. Sanford, a black Baptist pastor of a low-income congregation in Harlem. "All that becomes very important to us because we have a fear of even going into other social settings [e.g., a bibulous social event] that we once went into ... I find that we are challenged to provide more opportunities for [our members] to do things here at the church to keep them out of the settings they used to frequent."

Churches do more than provide preaching, teaching, and fellowship intended to reinforce the code of decency in their members. Many also preach financial responsibility, offer classes on financial management, or connect parishioners to job opportunities in the community. For instance, Rev. Henry Sanford reports that he addresses credit card debt and personal saving from the pulpit. Rev. Juan Emilio Lopez, the pastor of a Pentecostal church serving Latinos in Brooklyn, says that job placement is an important part of the work his church does on behalf of its members. "Anyone here without a job, it's a given that we have responsibility to find them a job," he says, adding, "we will make [their need for a job] known among the church."

Finally, black and Latino churches often provide a message of hope, acceptance, and comfort as well as opportunities for enthusiastic worship that can be therapeutic for attendees. In the face of difficulties related to poverty, discrimination, legal status, substance abuse, or simply the quotidian challenges of family life, religious messages related to redemption, unconditional acceptance, and a new life of faith can be comforting and inspiring to church attendees. Equally important, churches, especially Pentecostal and charismatic churches, often serve up a diet of dynamic preaching, uplifting singing, and intense, personal prayer in worship that affords attendees a cathartic spiritual experience. The message of hope and the experience of worship in many of these churches can help attendees remain psychologically resilient in the face of the ordinary and extraordinary challenges they confront. In short, many blacks and Latinos find worship to be therapeutic.[58]

Black and Latino churches thus provide preaching, teaching, and social networks that reinforce the code of decency. They also provide a religious *nomos*—a panoply of beliefs—that affords black and Latino attendees a sense of meaning, purpose, and hope that can buffer against the stressors they confront in their lives, stressors that lead some blacks and Latinos to pick up drugs and alcohol, engage in other forms of risky behavior, or succumb to depression.[59] Indeed, one study finds that African Americans who frequently attend religious services live almost fourteen years longer than do African Americans who never attend.[60]

Let us be clear. Religion is not a silver bullet that provides blacks and Latinos (or anyone else) with perfect protection against bad behavior. Nevertheless, judging by the preaching, teaching, and pastoral programming of black and Latino churches, we expect religion to foster adherence to the code of decency among African Americans and Latinos in the United States. The questions, then, are (1) to what extent does religion foster decent behavior among blacks and Latinos; and (2) what are some of the factors that affect the efficacy of religion in fostering decency in the lives of minority men and women?

RELIGION AND THE CODE OF DECENCY

When it comes to religion and decency, religious tradition does not matter that much but religiosity does.[61] Across all denominations, black and Latino men and women who are more religious—who attend church more, who pray more, and who socialize more with religious friends and family—tend to behave more decently than their peers who do not regularly engage in religious practices and are not embedded in strong religious networks. (Still, it is important to note that black and Latino Protestants tend to be more religious than their Catholic peers.)

Work

Religious attendance is consistently associated with less idleness among black and Latino men. Figure 2.9 indicates that twenty-something men who attend church regularly (several times a month or more) are significantly less likely to be

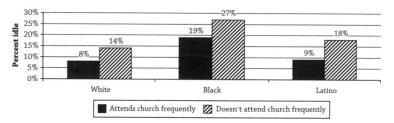

Figure 2.9 The Adjusted Percentage of Young Men Aged 22–26 Idle in 2002 (Out of Work and Out of School), by Race/Ethnicity and 2000 Church Attendance.

Source: National Longitudinal Survey of Youth 1997 cohort, 1997–2002, men only. N = 3,964. We controlled for religious denomination, marital and cohabiting status, education, age, urban residence, region of residence, and whether they lived with their biological parents as teenagers. Results are expressed as predicted probabilities computed via logistic regression. The effects of religious attendance are statistically significant.

idle, out of both school and work, compared to their peers who are not regular churchgoers. After controlling for a range of socio-demographic factors, data from the National Longitudinal Survey of Youth's 1997 cohort indicate that 19 percent of black churchgoing men in their mid-twenties are currently idle, neither working nor enrolled in school, compared to 27 percent of black men who are unchurched. Nine percent of Latino churchgoing twenty-something men are neither working nor enrolled in school, compared to 18 percent of their less religious or secular peers. Eight percent of white churchgoing twenty-something men are idle, compared to 14 percent of their less religious or secular peers.

These trends are echoed by the men we interviewed. One 33-year-old African American reported that his church provided him and his peers with practical assistance and a theological perspective on work, both of which have proved valuable in motivating him to find employment and stick with it: "Knowing God's purpose [through prayer and counsel from fellow believers] helps you to understand what it is you're supposed to do in your professional life, which is also part of a calling, and knowing that you've been called along a certain path does give you a certain amount of commitment and confidence" in your work, says Steven, a resident of Harrisonburg, Virginia. He adds that his black Protestant church has a job board and makes an active effort to "[find] out about jobs [and] it does make them [congregants] aware so that people know."

Steven is not alone. As noted above, many churches make deliberate efforts to connect their members to jobs in their community. Equally important, congregants often make informal efforts to connect their friends to jobs. This is important, because men's stable employment improves their lives in numerous ways. In particular, employment fosters higher quality relationships, paves the way for entry into marriage, and reduces the odds of divorce for all couples, black, Latino, and white alike.

Crime

Criminal activity and incarceration pose serious risks to the quality and stability of family life among Latinos and especially African Americans. As we might expect, there are noteworthy differences by religious attendance. As figure 2.10 indicates, men and women in their early to mid-twenties who regularly attended church in 2000 were between 2 and 12 percentage points less likely to report having committed a serious crime in 2001 or 2002. The effect of religious attendance is weaker for blacks than for whites and Latinos. Regular religious attendance reduces the odds of criminality by slightly more than 15 percent for African Americans and by more than 30 percent for Latinos and whites.

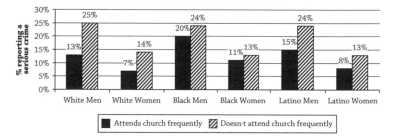

Figure 2.10 The Adjusted Percentage of Young Adults Aged 22–26 Who Reported Having Ever Committed a Serious Crime, by Sex, Race/Ethnicity, and Church Attendance.

Source: National Longitudinal Survey of Youth 1997 cohort, 1997–2002. N = 7,714. Reported are self-reported measures of serious criminal behavior in 2001 and 2002, based on religious attendance in 2000. We controlled for religious affiliation, marital and cohabiting status, education, age, urban residence, region of residence, and whether they lived with their biological parents as teenagers. Results are expressed as predicted probabilities computed via logistic regression. The effects of religious attendance are statistically significant, as is the interaction between race and religious attendance for African Americans.

When it comes to criminal activity, religion appears to be less protective for blacks than for members of other population groups.

There is also a strong link among twenty-something adults between attending church in 2000 and having been incarcerated in 2001–2002, as figure 2.11 shows. Religious attendance is associated with a reduction in the odds of imprisonment that varies from about 20 to 80 percent, though absolute levels of incarceration are low. Also, the association between religion and imprisonment is stronger for men. More specifically, only 4 percent of black men who attend church have been incarcerated, compared to 6 percent who attend infrequently or not at all. Only 1 percent of Latino men who attend regularly have been imprisoned, compared to 5 percent who do not attend regularly, and only 1 percent of white men who currently attend have been incarcerated, compared to 3 percent who do not attend regularly. Clearly religious attendance is linked to lower rates of subsequent incarceration.

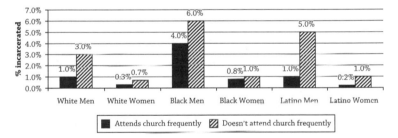

Figure 2.11 The Adjusted Percentage of Young Adults Aged 22–26 Who Have Been Incarcerated, by Sex, Race/Ethnicity, and Church Attendance.

Source: National Longitudinal Survey of Youth 1997 cohort, 1997–2002. N = 7,714. Reported are self-reported measures of incarceration measured in 2001 and 2002, based on religious attendance in 2000. We controlled for religious affiliation, marital and cohabiting status, education, age, urban residence, region of residence, and whether they lived with their biological parents as teenagers. Results are expressed as predicted probabilities computed via logistic regression. The effects of religious attendance are statistically significant; the interactions between race and religious attendance are not.

Arthur, a 32-year-old African American from Harrisonburg, Virginia, has done time in prison, yet is emblematic of how religion can help men and women steer clear of criminal activity. Arthur became a Christian while incarcerated. "I only came to know Christ when I got locked up," he reports, adding, "God met people like Paul on the Damascus road. He met other men on the crack pipe. He met me when I was selling drugs in prison. So, you know, that was a big thing for me, knowing that I have a relationship with God."

Since Arthur has gotten out of prison, he has avoided further criminal activity, including drug use. He credits his local Baptist church and regular prayer with keeping him away from temptations like drugs and his old friends. He attends church every Sunday, helps lead the men's group at his church, and attends a Wednesday night Bible study. Personal prayer is also important to him. "I get a prayer in every day," he says. "Prayer is my safety valve. It's my seat belt." From Arthur's perspective, his faith protects him from falling into a life of sin so long as he makes a regular effort to stay in touch with God. "I'm delivered on a daily basis and my delivery is like this: 'Lord, get me through the next 30 minutes. Lord, get me through the next hour. Lord, get me through this day.'"

Arthur is now thinking about finding a good woman. Given the changes he has made in his life recently, his prospects for a successful marriage are much better than they were five years ago, when he was in prison for selling drugs.

Drugs and Alcohol

Drugs and alcohol often play a central role in derailing relationships and marriages. Religious attendance reduces substance abuse, but less so for African Americans than for Latinos.

Figure 2.12 shows the association between church attendance and excessive alcohol consumption among adults in their

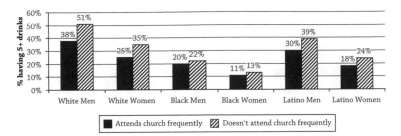

Figure 2.12 The Adjusted Percentage of Young Adults Aged 22–26 Who Have Had 5+ Drinks in the Past 30 Days, by Sex, Race/Ethnicity, and Church Attendance.

Source: National Longitudinal Survey of Youth 1997 cohort, 1997–2002. N = 7,714. Reported are self-reported measures of consuming more than five drinks in one sitting in the past thirty days in 2002, based on religious attendance in 2000. We controlled for religious affiliation, marital and cohabiting status, education, age, urban residence, region of residence, and whether they lived with their biological parents as teenagers. Results are expressed as predicted probabilities computed via logistic regression. The effects of religious attendance are statistically significant, as is the interaction between race and religious attendance for African Americans.

mid-twenties. Regular church attendance is associated with a reduction in the odds of binge drinking of between 10 and 28 percent for young adults.[62] The effect of religion is equally powerful for whites and Latinos. Specifically, whites and Latinos, more prone to binge drinking than African Americans, are about 25 percent less likely to abuse alcohol if they attend church on a regular basis. The effect of churchgoing on binge drinking among blacks is weaker: regular church attendance only reduces their odds of having five or more drinks in one sitting by about 10 percent.

Religion has similar effects on illicit drug use among twenty-somethings. As figure 2.13 indicates, churchgoers are less likely to report that they have used illicit drugs in the past thirty days. Again the association between religion and drug use is weakest for African Americans. Churchgoing whites are about half as likely as their less religious peers to have used drugs in the

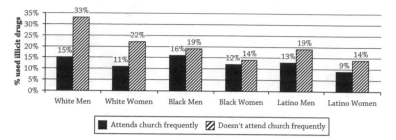

Figure 2.13 The Adjusted Percentage of Young Adults Aged 22–26 Who Have Used Illicit Drugs in the Past Thirty Days, by Sex, Race/Ethnicity, and Church Attendance.

Source: National Longitudinal Survey of Youth 1997 cohort, 1997–2002. N = 7,714. Reported are self-reported measures of using illicit drugs within the past thirty days in 2002, based on religious attendance in 2000. We controlled for religious affiliation, marital and cohabiting status, education, age, urban residence, region of residence, and whether they lived with their biological parents as teenagers. The effects of religious attendance are statistically significant, as is the interaction between race and religious attendance for African Americans.

last month, compared to about one-third less likely for Latinos, and approximately 15 percent less likely for African Americans.

Take Jorge, a 48-year-old Mexican American youth leader at a Catholic church in San Diego. He reports that he was living a "very wild life: drugs, alcohol, and all that" and attending church intermittently. But after deciding to take his faith more seriously by attending his local parish regularly and teaching religion there, he renounced his libertine ways. "When I dedicated time to teach, I realized I can't be teaching one thing and living another," he recalls. "So to me, the church helped me a lot to get away from that." Now Jorge no longer uses drugs, only drinks alcohol on occasion, and steers clear of old friends who party.

Infidelity

For obvious reasons, infidelity often proves toxic to existing relationships and marriages, and interferes with the formation

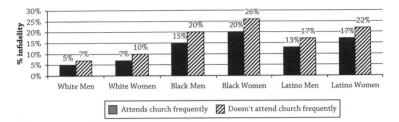

Figure 2.14 The Adjusted Percentage of Adults Aged 18–60 Reporting Infidelity in Their Relationship, by Sex, Race/Ethnicity, and Church Attendance.

Source: National Survey of Religion and Family Life, 2006. N = 1,304. Results are weighted. The figure measures whether married or partnered respondents report either cheating on their partners or suspecting their partners of infidelity. We control for denomination, employment status, marital status, sex, presence of children, education, age, and geographic region. The effects of religion are statistically significant.

of new ones. Christianity proscribes adultery and most churches encourage their adherents to abide by the Golden Rule, so we expect religion to be associated with decreased infidelity and fewer sexual partnerships among African Americans and Latinos. Frequent church attendance also brings congregants into contact with happily monogamous couples, which should further instill the importance of fidelity to a good relationship.

Our expectation is confirmed, as regular church attendance is associated with fidelity.[63] Figure 2.14 uses data from the National Survey of Religion and Family Life (NSRFL) to examine the relationship between regular church attendance and reports of infidelity in a marriage or cohabiting union after controlling for broad demographic differences. For the purpose of this analysis, we consider a relationship unfaithful either if the respondent acknowledges infidelity or suspects his or her partner of infidelity. African Americans are most likely to report infidelity, followed by Latinos; whites have by far the lowest rates of infidelity (or suspicions of an unfaithful partner). For all three groups, regular church attendance makes infidelity less likely. Twenty percent of black men who do not attend regularly report being in adulterous relationships, compared to 15 percent of those who go to church several times a month or more. The comparable figures for black women are 26 and 20 percent. For Latino men, 13 percent report being in adulterous unions if attending church frequently, compared to 17 percent for infrequent attendees and the unchurched. The comparable figures for Latinas are 17 and 22 percent. The association between religious participation and fidelity is roughly similar across racial and ethnic lines.

It should be remembered that the NSRFL is cross-sectional, so we are unable to determine if the relationship between frequent religious attendance and infidelity is causal. It is possible that an adulterous spouse or partner seeks to mend a damaged relationship through renewed faith. It is equally likely that religious doctrine and instruction discourages adultery while simultaneously ameliorating the unhappiness that might lead to infidelity in the first place.[64] A third possibility is that religion exposes congregants to happy couples. These might serve as role models for good relationships, as well as creating social pressure not to stray from one's partner.

The NSRFL data allow us to explore this last possibility. We reexamined the relationship between regular church attendance and infidelity while accounting for how many of the respondent's friends attend church regularly with him or her. After controlling for church friendships, the association between regular church attendance and being in an adulterous relationship lost statistical significance. This leads us to conclude that an important reason why religious participation decreases infidelity is because it exposes congregants to models of healthy relationships. Alternately, people who attend church with their friends might think twice about cheating on their partners given the opprobrium, and perhaps even ostracism, that might occur.

Figure 2.15 indicates that religion is linked to lower levels of multiple sexual partnerships among adults aged 18–44. These data allow us to look at patterns of such partnerships over the course of one year among unmarried adults but do not contain direct measures of infidelity among unmarried adults who are currently in a relationship. Regular churchgoers are between 30 and 60 percent less likely to have had two or more sex partners in the past year compared to their peers who attend church infrequently or not at all.

Recall that Leroy from Atlanta has been burned by infidelity in the past, yet is currently seeing a number of women at the same time. In his experience, "everybody cheats." But he does see a way out. From his perspective, religious couples have a chance at fidelity. "[If] your relationship has been based on a religious foundation, where you all have a strong religious foundation, and

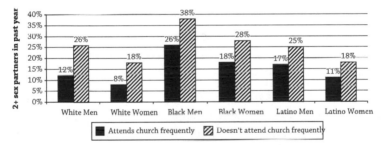

Figure 2.15 The Percentage of Never Married Adults Aged 18–44 Who Have Had Two or More Sex Partners in the Past Year, by Sex, Race/Ethnicity, and Church Attendance.

Source: NSFG 2006–2010. N = 14,469. Results are weighted. We controlled for denomination, education, age, urban residence, work status, income, and whether they lived with their biological parents as teenagers. Results are expressed as predicted probabilities computed via logistic regression. The interaction between race and religious attendance is statistically significant, as is the coefficient for respondent sex. Results are weighted. As the NSFG is a cross-sectional data set, we cannot be sure that the reduced number of sex partners is a consequence of religious participation.

agreement and understanding, then I see that being a possibility of working that way [without infidelity]," observes Leroy.

The evidence suggests that religious spouses and partners do indeed have a greater chance at forging faithful, monogamous relationships. One reason this is the case is that they are more likely to be embedded in a network of religious friends who take their relationships seriously, hold their peers accountable, and monitor their social life. Another reason may be that the messages and rituals associated with religious life reinforce the norm of fidelity.[65]

Depression

Although emotional health is not a primary component of decency, a growing body of literature suggests that mood does play a role in fostering good behavior, and in helping men and women steer clear of vices such as substance abuse and infidelity. In particular, a number of studies suggest that people are apt to drink more, start using drugs, or look for another sexual partner when they are stressed out or depressed.[66] Moreover, research by sociologist Christopher Ellison and his colleagues indicates that religion often acts as a buffer against psychological distress, both by providing people with social support and by lending their lives meaning and purpose—even in the face of problems like poverty, discrimination, unemployment, and so forth.[67] Accordingly, it is useful to consider how religion protects African Americans and Latinos from depression.

We find that people who attend church regularly are less likely to report being unhappy. Figure 2.16 shows data on happiness by church attendance and race/ethnicity from the 2000–2012 General Social Survey (GSS), controlling for basic social and demographic differences between respondents. Latinos and

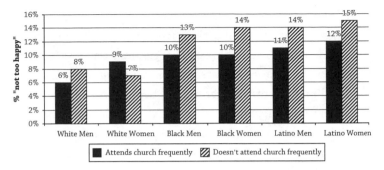

Figure 2.16 The Percentage of Adults Aged 18-44 who Report Being "Not Too Happy," by Race/Ethnicity, Sex, and Church Attendance.

Source: GSS 2000–2012. N = 5,883. Controls include denomination, education, age, survey year, city size, geographic region, marital status, inflation-adjusted income, employment status, and whether respondent came from an intact family. The effects of race and religious attendance are statistically significant. There are no meaningful gender differences in happiness.

African Americans are more likely to report being "not too happy" (as opposed to being pretty happy or very happy) than are whites. For all three population groups, attending regularly decreases unhappiness by several percentage points. There are no gender differences in happiness. Although the GSS data are cross-sectional, we suspect that religious participation plays a role in fostering better mental health among African Americans and Latinos. As noted above, the psychological benefits of religion—both in terms of social integration and in terms of lending meaning to people's lives—are well documented.[68]

CONCLUSION

This chapter shows that religious faith plays an important role in fostering a code of decency in black and Latino communities. This code encompasses hard work, lawful behavior, temperance, and sexual fidelity in married and unmarried relationships. We find that African Americans and Latinos who are regular churchgoers are more likely to abide by this code of decency and less likely to fall prey to the code of the street. Churchgoing minorities are also more likely to enjoy better mental health, which we suspect helps them to identify with and abide by the code of decency.

Religion is not a magic bullet when it comes to protecting blacks and Latinos from the lure of the street, or what some Latinos call "del mundo." For instance, more than one in ten churchgoing blacks and Latinos report drug use, excessive drinking, infidelity in their relationships, or, for men, a history of serious criminal activity. More than one in ten churchgoing black young men report that they are currently idle (that is, not working or attending school). Furthermore, this chapter suggests that African Americans are sometimes less likely to benefit from religious attendance than are Latinos and whites.

Be that as it may, regular religious attendance is associated with a number of positive outcomes for blacks and Latinos. Churchgoing Latinos and African Americans are significantly more likely to be gainfully employed, to steer clear of criminal activity or substance abuse, to be faithful, and to be happy, compared to their peers who don't attend church, or attend only infrequently. It is noteworthy that religion appears to play a valuable role in steering black and Latino men in positive directions; this is important because minority men are much more likely than minority women to get caught up in the code of the street.

The association between religion and the code of decency is significant because there are many economic, policy, and cultural forces conspiring against a decent way of life for minorities, especially minority men. Discrimination, xenophobia, poverty, machismo, and a popular culture that often depicts minorities in an unflattering light can all steer blacks and Latinos away from decency. In contrast, this chapter suggests religion is one force pushing black and Latino men and women in a decent direction. Indeed, in many communities, religion is the only multigenerational and familial force for decency on the ground. As we shall see in the following chapters of this book, this makes men and women into better husbands, wives, partners, and, by extension, better parents.

Chapter 3

Religion, Sex, and Childbearing

We interviewed David and Maria Rodriguez in their Bronx townhouse in 2006. Shortly after immigrating to the United States from, respectively, Guatemala and Peru as young adults, they met at a family party in the United States and went on to have two children, a 14-year-old son and a 9-year-old daughter. David pulls in a decent income working full-time for the postal service, while Maria is a stay-at-home mom. "The purpose of life [is] having a family," David told us. At this, Maria nodded in agreement, adding, "To me . . . [family is] very important, especially as I'm very close to my side of my family, my mother and my brother, and my kids are important to me." The couple attends Mass at their local Catholic church about once a month, though Maria goes more often than David. She also attends social events and religious programming at the church, but David does not. In all these ways, they seem like a traditional Latino couple: family-oriented, moderately religious (especially Maria), and living the American dream.

But as our interview progressed, it became apparent that David and Maria's family life is not as traditional or harmonious as it first seemed. They are not married. Although they have been dating on and off for fifteen years, they had only been living together for five years when we spoke to them. David only moved in after he noticed their son acting up. Both of them have had sexual relationships with other partners since the time they first started dating. What's more, their own parents had had tumultuous relationships that ended in separation or divorce.

When we asked Maria how happy she was in their relationship, her response was underwhelming: "He's not a bad person. [Laughter]. I . . . he's a good dad. I cannot say bad things about him. [Laughs]. Not now anyways. [Laughs]." Maria wishes they were married, but David does not seem interested. He puts their chances of getting married at about 40 percent, dismissing marriage as "just a piece of paper." Given their history, the ambiguous quality of their relationship, and David's qualms about marriage, we left the interview concerned that their relationship would not go the distance, and that their two children would experience the same kind of instability that they themselves had experienced growing up.[1]

The fact that David and Maria's family started with a nonmarital birth is emblematic of trends among Americans, especially Latinos and African Americans. According to data collected between 2006 and 2010, 51 percent of Latino births occur outside of marriage, mostly to women who are living with the fathers of their children (see figure 3.1). Among African Americans, 63 percent of children are born to unmarried mothers, a majority of whom are not living with the fathers of their children. The bottom line is that most African American and Latino children are born outside of marriage.

This is noteworthy for at least two reasons. First, families formed outside of marriage tend to be less stable, affectionate, and safe than families formed in marriage. Although some unmarried families do just fine, the latest research suggests that children born to cohabiting couples—as is the case for most Latino children born to unmarried mothers—are, compared to children born to married families, more than twice as

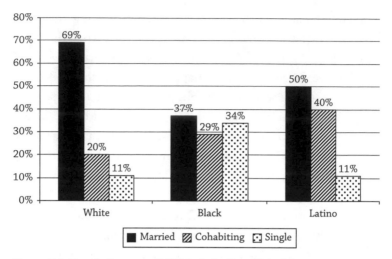

Figure 3.1 Family Status at Childbirth, by Race/Ethnicity.

Source: National Survey of Family Growth, 2006–2010. N = 5,142. Results are weighted. Numbers may not add to 100% due to rounding error.

likely to see their parents break up by the time they turn 12 and are about twice as likely to suffer from delinquency, depression, or child abuse.[2] Likewise, children born to single unmarried mothers—as is the case for just over half of the black children born to unmarried mothers—are several times more likely to experience family instability—at worst, a series of father figures coming and going—as well as the kind of social or emotional difficulties often experienced by children in cohabiting families.[3]

Lacking the stability and legal recognition afforded by marriage, not to mention the twin challenges of discrimination and poverty, most African American and Latino families formed outside marriage do not last, and many do not provide an ideal context for childrearing. Having children outside of marriage also reduces the odds of having a stable marriage down the road, whether unwed parents marry each other or someone else.[4]

The lack of legal, social, and familial clarity associated with a nonmarital birth can foster confusion, conflict, and ambivalence among couples, especially when parents break up and bring children from a previous union into a new relationship. Colloquially speaking, "baby mama drama" is more likely to follow in the wake of a nonmarital birth. Thus, nonmarital childbearing is risky not only for the children who come into the world without the benefit of married parents but also to the adults who bring them into the world.

Second, the prevalence of nonmarital childbearing among African Americans and Latinos is surprising because both of these groups are more religious and more traditional than their Anglo peers in a number of ways. For instance, blacks and Latinos attend church more often than whites and are as or more likely to voice opposition to premarital sex than are whites. These beliefs and behaviors tend to be associated with lower rates of childbearing outside of wedlock. This leads to a curious paradox regarding childbearing among minorities in the United States: blacks and Latinos are both more religious yet prone to high rates of nonmarital childbearing.

This chapter explores this religion–nonmarital fertility paradox in two ways. First, do structural factors (such as poverty) and cultural factors (like attitudes toward sex) aside from religion account for the distinctive racial and ethnic patterns of nonmarital childbearing found in the United States? Second, does religion, and the beliefs and behaviors associated with religious faith, reduce nonmarital childbearing among blacks and Latinas, or are religious effects simply swamped by other cultural and structural dynamics? Conversely, might religion and, notably, its effects on family culture among blacks and Latinos, actually foster comparatively high levels of nonmarital childbearing in these communities?

THE ECONOMIC CONTEXT OF BLACK
AND LATINO CHILDBEARING

Racial and ethnic differences in the timing of marriage and child-bearing play a role in accounting for comparatively higher levels of minority nonmarital childbearing. One important explanation for high levels of nonmarital childbearing among African Americans is that black women are postponing or foregoing marriage in much greater numbers than are whites. This trend puts black women at risk of having a child outside of marriage, especially since they often first give birth in their late teens or early twenties. Latinas are also prone to having children outside of marriage, but this is linked to early childbearing, not comparatively late marriage. At age 20, 95 percent of black women, 80 percent of Latina women, and 86 percent of white women have not yet gotten married, though 32 percent of blacks and 26 of Latinas will have had a child out of wedlock (the figure for white women is 11 percent). By age 25, 76 percent of black women, 50 percent of Latina women, and 52 percent of white women have never been married, even though 58 percent of blacks, 46 percent of Latinas, and 25 percent of whites will have had a child out of wedlock.[5]

One reason that African American women are postponing or foregoing marriage is money. In the next chapter, we will discuss in detail how economic factors contribute to the race gap in marriage formation. For now, three points are worth noting. First, despite the modern emphasis on a "soulmate" union that emphasizes a strong emotional relationship between spouses, most Americans continue to see marriage as an economic enterprise as well, and are less likely to get (and stay) married when they do not have the means to do so.[6] Because African American couples in their twenties and thirties are significantly less likely than their white peers to have a middle-class income or assets, they are less likely to marry even when they have children.[7] Second, since the 1970s black men have seen their real wages fall, even as black women have seen their real wages rise; this means that black women are more economically independent of black men and are less likely to feel like they need to marry a man for economic support, even if they are having children with him.[8] Finally, both African Americans and Latinas are more likely than whites to have grown up poor. This increases, at least for women, the likelihood of having children out of wedlock.[9] People growing up without money are more likely to have children earlier and prior to marriage because they lack educational or vocational prospects that might otherwise motivate them to avoid a non-marital birth, and because the stresses of growing up poor make them more likely to fall into unstable relationships that are liable to result in an unplanned pregnancy.[10]

The experience of Nicki Brown, 34, an African American church secretary and unmarried mother of two living in Harlem, is emblematic of the socioeconomic barriers to marriage confronting black parents. She has been with her boyfriend Joe, the father of her two children, off and on for twelve years. Currently they live together. According to Nicki, the "main issue" in their relationship is money: Joe does not earn enough on a consistent basis to make her feel ready for marriage, especially since she pulls in a steady income.

In her lifetime, Nicki has seen many friends and family divorce, sometimes for economic reasons, and worries that marriage might be followed by a financially ruinous divorce. This is a particularly salient issue for her since she has more money than Joe. "If you get divorced and you have to split all your stuff, there's this big emphasis, at least in my age group, on assets," she reports. "[I]f we break up [now], we don't have to divide anything up. What's yours is yours, and what's mine is mine, and that's it."

Partly for economic reasons related to her boyfriend's employment history, not to mention marriage-destroying fights over money in her circle of family and friends, Nicki has steered clear of marriage to the father of her children.

To explore the role of economic factors in accounting for premarital fertility, we conducted multivariate analysis of the National Longitudinal Survey of Youth 1997 cohort (NLSY97). Our results indicate that economic factors, including parental wealth, maternal education, respondent education, and respondent employment history, account for a substantial portion of the disparity in premarital fertility between African Americans and whites. Before adjusting for economic differences between respondents, black men are three and a half times more likely than white men to father a child out of wedlock; after adjusting for economic differences, this figure declines to 142 percent, or just shy of two and a half times more likely. For black women, accounting for economic differences between individuals also decreases the black–white divide in the likelihood of having a child out of wedlock, from 178 percent to 93 percent. These results are shown in figure 3.2.

Economic factors also account for a considerable portion of the Latino–white divide in nonmarital childbearing. Our baseline model shows that Latino men are 117 percent more likely than white men to father a child out of wedlock. After adjusting for economic differences between respondents, this disparity is reduced to 49 percent. For Latinas, the increased likelihood of a nonmarital birth declines from 115 percent (before controlling for economic factors) to 35 percent (after including economic controls).

But money isn't everything. As our findings and the experience of David and Maria Rodriguez (who have a middle-class income) illustrate, economic factors do not entirely explain the

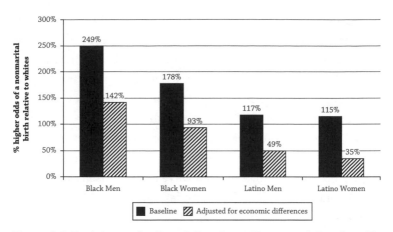

Figure 3.2 Explaining the Racial Divide in Nonmarital Fertility: The Economic Explanation.

Source: National Longitudinal Survey of Youth 1997 cohort, 1997–2009. N = 4,310 (men), 4,040 (women). Respondent education and work history are time-varying independent variables. See the appendix for more information about this analysis. We control for region, urbanicity, and age at the first wave of the NLSY97. Given that nonmarital births typically occur in the late teens or early twenties, we do not use respondent income as an independent variable.

contemporary racial and ethnic divides in nonmarital childbearing. Indeed, a distinctive set of cultural beliefs, behaviors, and experiences make minority couples especially vulnerable to having a birth outside of marriage.

THE CULTURAL CONTRADICTIONS OF MINORITY CHILDBEARING

Some conservative commentators contend that high rates of nonmarital childbearing among minorities can be attributed to a crisis in values in black and Latino communities. For instance, Heather MacDonald of the Manhattan Institute writes that "[m]arriage is clearly no longer one of [the] family values" held by Latinos in the United States.[11] But the evidence does not bear this charge out. Latino values about sex and family are similar to those of whites, while blacks tend to hold more traditional values. Table 3.1 suggests that 41 percent of female and 27 percent of male African Americans think premarital sex is often or always wrong; for Latinos, the comparable figures are 24 percent and 20 percent, and for whites, 22 percent and 15 percent. These national data are consistent with how Nicki and her friends view premarital sex: "We all know that we're not supposed to [have sex outside marriage]." Or take attitudes toward children. Latinos are more likely than whites (or blacks) to opine that people cannot be happy unless they have children. Eight percent of African American men and 6 percent of the women feel this way (see table 3.1). The numbers are much higher for Latinos: 26 percent of the men, and 22 percent of the women view having children as essential to one's happiness; for whites the corresponding figures are 6 and 4 percent. Only when it comes to single motherhood do African Americans and Latinos take a more accommodating view of contemporary families. Sixty-three percent of black men, 81 percent of black women, 64 percent of Latino men, and 76 percent of Latinas think that single mothers do just fine, compared to 49 percent of white men and 70 percent of white women.

What's going on here? People often subscribe to a range of values that are not always consistent with their behavior. In this case, we think that attitudes toward sex are nominally held among blacks and Latinos, but are not salient for personal behavior, whereas the salience of pro-child attitudes among Latinos makes them more open to having children regardless of their marital status. Like sociologists Kathryn Edin and Maria Kefalas, we suspect that comparatively more African American women and, especially, more Latino women than white women welcome the arrival of a child even when their personal or

Table 3.1 ATTITUDES TOWARD SEX AND PARENTHOOD, BY RACE/ETHNICITY AND SEX

Survey Question	White		Black		Latino	
	Men %	Women %	Men %	Women %	Men %	Women %
Premarital sex is often or always wrong[1]	15	22	27	41	20	24
People can't be happy unless they have children[2]	6	4	8	6	26	22
Single parents can raise children just as well as two parents[3]	49	70	63	81	64	76
Respondent would be happy if she got pregnant/impregnated a woman[4]	32	27	42	35	55	43
A woman should be able to have an abortion for any reason[5]	48	48	51	49	38	29

Note: Respondents aged 18–44 only for all data sets.

Sources:
[1] General Social Survey, 2010–2012. N = 360 (white men), 413 (white women), 63 (black men), 110 (black women), 82 (Latino men), 97 (Latina women).
[2] National Survey of Family Growth, 2006–2010. N = 3,513 (white men), 4,118 (white women), 1,169 (black men), 669 (black women), 1,550 (Latino men), 1,844 (Latina women); weighted.
[3] National Survey of Religion and Family Life, 2006. N = 180 (white men), 220 (white women), 142 (black men), 319 (black women), 181 (Latino men), 382 (Latino women); weighted.
[4] National Survey of Family Growth, 2006–2010. N = 1,703 (white men), 1,686 (white women), 666 (black men), 831 (black women), 818 (Latino men), 775 (Latino women); weighted.
[5] General Social Survey, 2010–2012. N = 323 (white men), 375 (white women), 63 (black men), 110 (black women), 82 (Latino men), 97 (Latino women).

romantic circumstances are not ideal.[12] Indeed, 35 percent of unmarried black women and 43 percent of Latinas aged 18–44 say they would be happy if they got pregnant, compared to 27 percent of unmarried white women in this age group. Table 3.1 also indicates that Latinos are more likely to register opposition to abortion, which probably makes them more likely to carry a nonmarital pregnancy to term. Moreover, there is less stigma surrounding nonmarital childbearing among blacks and Latinos than there is among whites. According to our data, 55 percent of black female teenagers and 57 percent of Latino female teenagers would be embarrassed by a pregnancy, compared to 68 percent of white teenagers.[13] Thus, pro-child attitudes and accommodating social norms related to nonmarital childbearing trump attitudes toward sex for many black and Latino couples and women. Ultimately culture is more than abstract values; it is also about the immediate experiences, expectations, and norms that shape people's lives.

One reason that cultural support for postponing childbirth until marriage is markedly weaker among blacks and Latinos is that many Latinos and, especially, many blacks grew up or currently live in homes and neighborhoods where nonmarital childbearing, cohabitation, and single parenthood are common.[14] Among today's young adults, 70 percent of African Americans and 49 percent of Latinos were not living with both parents when between 12 and 18 years old, compared to 44 percent of whites.[15] These statistics are echoed by Nicki Brown, who reports that "all [of my friends] had kids out of wedlock." Moreover, nonmarital childbearing and long-term cohabitation are more common among Latinos in part because "consensual unions" are a long-standing tradition in Latin American countries.[16] This could be one reason why David Rodriguez looks at marriage as "just a piece of paper."

The prevalence of nonmarital childbearing, single parent-hood, and cohabitation in minority communities is both cause and consequence of distinctive expectations regarding sex, contraception, and childbearing. For instance, after noting that most of her friends view nonmarital sex as wrong in principle, Nicki says, with a laugh, "We do it anyways," adding, "In the community, I think dating is real relaxed, you know. You date who you date; you see who you see, when you want to see him. You have sex with who you want to have sex with."

The Latinos we talked to generally echoed Nicki's sentiment. First- and second-generation Mexican respondents pointed out that American sexual mores are more permissive than those back in Mexico, especially in its conservative rural or small-town regions. They attribute this in part to the anonymity afforded by life in metropolitan America, as well as a popular culture that is more free-wheeling in its treatment of sex. In the words of one 29-year-old immigrant from Mexico living in Los Angeles: "[Compared to] what your parents gave you in Mexico, it's different here. Everything is more liberal here." In his view, second-generation Mexican Americans, in particular, are habituated to a more permissive American outlook on sex and relationships.[17] "Those who are born here of Mexican parents—it's very few who continue with the same family and cultural traditions [that can be found in Mexico]."

Whatever blacks and Latinos might think about nonmarital sex in the abstract, in the real world there is generally tacit acceptance. Sex before marriage is common among African Americans and Latinos, slightly more so than for whites. Table 3.2 shows that among unmarried adults, 80 percent of African American women and 83 percent of African American men, 81 percent of Latino men and 76 percent of Latino women, compared to 72 percent of white men and 72 percent of white women, have had sex in the last year. Moreover, African Americans and Latinos are

Table 3.2 SEXUAL AND RELATED BEHAVIORS,
BY RACE/ETHNICITY AND SEX

Survey Question	White		Black		Latino	
	Men %	Women %	Men %	Women %	Men %	Women %
Has had nonmarital sex in the past year[1]	72	72	83	80	81	76
Used birth control at first and last sex[2]	70	68	54	51	51	44
Have ever aborted a pregnancy[3]	14	19	21	27	9	14

Source: National Survey of Family Growth, 2006–2010; [1]N = 3,077 (white men), 3,219 (white women), 1,147 (black men), 1,764 (black women), 1,392 (Latino men), 1,485 (Latino women); [2]N = 2,624 (white men), 2,334 (white women), 1,063 (black men), 1,436 (black women), 1,242 (Latino men), 1,120 (Latino women); [3]N = 2,149 (white men), 3,417 (white women), 942 (black men), 1,675 (black women), 1,286 (Latino men), 1,851 (Latino women). Weighted.

much less likely to use contraception than are unmarried whites, perhaps in part because they hold more welcoming attitudes toward children and because nonmarital childbearing is less stigmatized than it is among whites. Table 3.2 shows big disparities in contraceptive use at first and last sex among unmarried adults: 51 percent of African American women and 44 percent of Latinas used contraception at first and last sex, versus 68 percent of their white peers.

Note that racial and ethnic differences in abortion do not appear to account for comparatively higher rates of nonmarital childbearing, at least among blacks. This is because African Americans—but not Latinos—are more likely to have had an abortion than their white peers.[18] Table 3.2 shows that among women who have ever been pregnant, 19 percent of whites, 27 percent of blacks, and 14 percent of Latinos have had an abortion. There are similar disparities in the rates of men who have ever had a partner who terminated a pregnancy.

Thus, even though African Americans and Latinos do not have more liberal or permissive values related to sex and family, they are more likely to hold beliefs such as a strong pro-child ethic and tacit acceptance of premarital childbearing that almost certainly increase their chances of having a child outside of wedlock. These chances are only heightened by high rates of both nonmarital sex and unprotected sex.

Finally, insofar as some behaviors associated with the code of the street—e.g., criminality and infidelity are more common among minorities, especially black and Latino men, these behaviors may also reduce the odds that minority couples feel secure enough to marry before they have children. We will address this subject in more detail in the next chapter, but suffice to say that street-like behavior appears to be one more factor accounting for comparatively higher levels of nonmarital childbearing among black and Latino couples.

Our multivariate analysis suggests that cultural factors also account for a noteworthy portion of the racial divide in nonmarital childbearing. The National Longitudinal Survey of Youth provides few measures of culture, so we turn to a different data set, the National Longitudinal Study of Adolescent to Adult Health (Add Health).[19] At baseline, the Add Health data show that African American men are 137 percent more likely than white men to father a child out of wedlock, while Latino men are 42 percent more likely than whites to become fathers prior to marriage. For women, the corresponding figures are 112 and 34 percent, for blacks and Latinas respectively.[20] Our cultural model includes attitudes toward

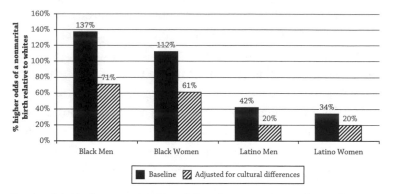

Figure 3.3 Explaining the Racial Divide in Nonmarital Fertility: The Cultural Explanation.

Source: National Longitudinal Study of Adolescent to Adult Health, 1994–2008. N = 8,552 (men), 9,258 (women). See the appendix for more information about this analysis.

sex, pregnancy, and single parenthood, as well as contraceptive use, media consumption, delinquency, multiple sexual partners, and whether respondents were raised in two-parent families. These factors substantially reduce racial/ethnic differences in premarital fertility. After controlling for cultural differences between respondents, black men are 71 percent more likely than whites and Latino men are 20 percent more likely than whites to father a child before marriage. For women, the corresponding figures are 61 and 20 percent. These results, summarized in figure 3.3, suggest that cultural factors play a key role in explaining racial and ethnic disparities in nonmarital fertility. Still, noteworthy differences persist.

IS RELIGION A BARRIER TO NONMARITAL CHILDBEARING?

Religious faith may be a barrier to nonmarital childbearing among blacks and Latinos, insofar as it both proscribes premarital sex and single parenthood and increases the odds that couples marry. Alternately, religious faith among minorities might increase the odds of nonmarital childbearing by promoting generativity (an emphasis on the importance of children) and proscribing contraception and abortion. We now turn to the role that religious attendance among Latinos and African Americans plays in fostering these beliefs and behaviors, as well as religious attendance's direct and indirect effects on nonmarital childbearing.

Take Roberto Calderon and Lila Valdez, a dating couple who attend Victory Chapel, a Pentecostal church in the Bronx. Thirty-year-old Roberto admits that he had casual flings when he first began attending the church but gave them up after being drawn more deeply into Victory's community and confessing his sexual behavior to a church pastor. Now, he is committed to "living holy," which includes treating Lila, 27, with respect and consideration, while forsaking premarital sex. "You know, I don't want to mess this up. And I want the Lord to be pleased with the way we conduct ourselves. So that's the motivation to not engage in anything before marriage."

Roberto is also worried about fathering a child outside of wedlock, both because it is discouraged at Victory and because he thinks families begun outside of marriage often end with one parent raising the child. "You know, I think it'd be very difficult for the child as well as the mother or father, whoever's going to raise the child. It's not the ideal situation." On the advice of the church leadership, he and Lila minimize their risk of becoming sexually active by not spending time alone in one another's apartments late at night. In these ways, their religious faith fosters beliefs and behaviors that discourage premarital sex and, as a consequence, nonmarital childbearing.

How representative are Roberto and Lila? Figure 3.4 indicates that minority men and women who attend church

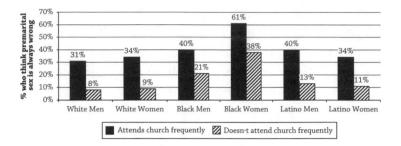

Figure 3.4 The Percent of Adults Who Think Premarital Sex Is Always Wrong, by Race/Ethnicity, Sex, and Church Attendance.

Source: General Social Survey, 2000–2012. N = 1,310 (white), 492 (black), 275 (Latino). Racial/ethnic differences are statistically significant, so the analysis was conducted separately by population group. Sex differences are significant only for African Americans. Respondents over age 44 are excluded, as are married respondents. Results based on all respondents are similar. We control for denomination, education, inflation-adjusted income, age, survey year, urbanicity, region, employment status, and whether respondents hail from intact families.

regularly (that is, at least several times a month) are about 20 to 30 percentage points more likely to believe that premarital sex is wrong, although the effect of religious attendance is somewhat weaker for African Americans and Latinos than it is for Anglos. Figure 3.5 suggests that religious attendance is linked to greater concern with single parenthood across the board, with women much more approving of single parenting than are men. Based on these findings religion does appear to play a role in fostering a cultural climate that is less conducive to nonmarital childbearing.

Religious attendance is associated with less premarital sex, but the effect is again weaker for minorities than it is for whites. Figure 3.6 shows that unmarried churchgoing Latinas are 12 percentage points less likely to have had sex in the last year, compared to their unchurched peers. The effect of church attendance on the sexual behavior of black women is, at 16 percentage points,

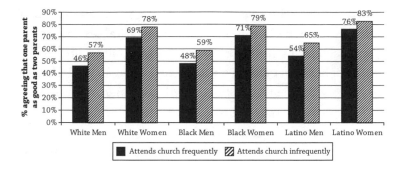

Figure 3.5 A Single Mother Can Bring up a Child Just as Well as Two Parents, by Race/Ethnicity, Sex, and Church Attendance.

Source: National Survey of Religion and Family Life, 2006. N = 2,277. Results are statistically significant for differences by sex and church attendance but not by race/ethnicity. We control for denomination, age, education, income, and employment status. Results are weighted.

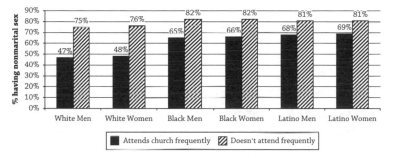

Figure 3.6 Nonmarital Sex in the Past Year, by Race, Sex, and Church Attendance.

Source: National Survey of Family Growth, 2006–2010. N = 14,469. Racial/ethnic differences are statistically significant and vary significantly by church attendance. Sex differences are not significant. We control for denomination, education, income, age, survey year, urbanicity, marital status, employment status, and whether respondents hail from intact families. Results are weighted.

a bit greater. For white women, churchgoing is associated with a 28-percent-point decline in the odds of premarital sex. Figure 3.6 suggests similar patterns for unmarried men, although attending church has larger effects on the sexual behavior of black and, especially, white men than it does for Latino men. Overall, religion and premarital sex are more loosely coupled for minorities than for whites.

Nicki's experience is suggestive. At her Baptist church in Harlem, she reports that her pastor "doesn't talk about [sexual conduct] often" and that when he once brought up the topic in the church, which has many single mothers and unmarried couples, "there was some shiftin' in seats and there was discomfort." Since talk of nonmarital childbearing and single parenthood rarely occurs, she thinks that the single mothers in her church generally "feel comfortable here because they're not judged." By her reckoning, while most members of her church know that premarital sex and nonmarital childbearing are not viewed as the ideal by the pastor and church leadership, her church does not provide a clear message to its members about sex or nonmarital childbearing. Her view was echoed in many of our conversations with clergy and ordinary lay members of black and Latino churches around the country (except for a minority of Catholic parishes and Pentecostal churches). A large share of evangelical Protestant churches, which serve a substantial share of whites and a growing number of Latinos, do confront these topics on a more regular basis.[21]

Other beliefs and behaviors underscore the complexity of the relationship between religion and childbearing. African Americans and Latinos, especially the latter, are also less likely than whites to regularly use contraception, though religion does not have consistent effects on birth control usage (figure 3.7). Next, figure 3.8 indicates that religion is linked to less acceptance of abortion among unmarried men and women as a whole;

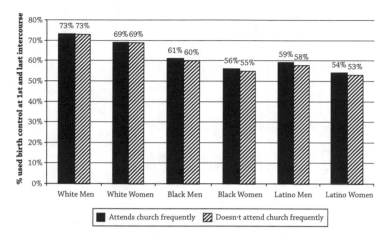

Figure 3.7 The Percentage of Respondents Who Used Birth Control at First and Last Intercourse, by Race/Ethnicity, Sex, and Church Attendance.

Source: National Survey of Family Growth, 2006–2010. N = 10,529. Sex and racial/ ethnic difference are statistically significant, but birth-control use does not vary by church attendance. We control for denomination, education, income, age, survey year, urbanicity, employment status, and whether respondents hail from intact families. Results are weighted. Married respondents are excluded.

church-attending Latinas are the group that is least supportive of abortion. Figure 3.9 suggests that religious attendance is linked to less abortion, a result that holds across the board. Consistent with their professed beliefs, churchgoing Latinos have the lowest abortion rates. Finally, figure 3.10 indicates that Latinas and Latinos, especially churchgoing ones, are more likely to endorse the notion that people cannot be happy unless they have children. Taken together, these findings suggest that regular religious attendance, combined with familism—the Latino orientation toward family observed by many scholars—may make Latinos more likely to embrace children and to eschew behaviors, such as abortion and regular contraception, that would prevent them from having children, even outside of marriage.[22]

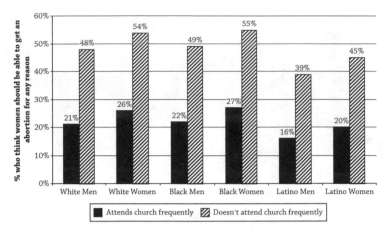

Figure 3.8 The Percent of Respondents Who Think Women Should Be Able to Get an Abortion for Any Reason, by Race/Ethnicity, Sex, and Church Attendance.

Source: General Social Survey, 2000–2012. N = 14,452. The difference between whites and blacks is not statistically significant. Respondents over age 44 are excluded. We control for denomination, education, inflation-adjusted income, age, survey year, urbanicity, region, employment status, and whether respondents hail from intact families.

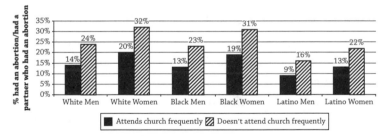

Figure 3.9 The Percentage of Respondents Who Have Aborted a Pregnancy/ Had a Partner Who Aborted a Pregnancy, by Race/Ethnicity, Sex, and Church Attendance.

Source: National Survey of Family Growth, 2006–2010. N = 6,129. Sex difference and difference between Latinos and whites are statistically significant. We control for denomination, education, income, age, survey year, urbanicity, employment status, and whether respondents hail from intact families. Results are weighted. Married respondents are excluded.

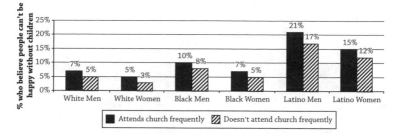

Figure 3.10 The Percentage of Respondents Who Believe that People Cannot Be Happy without Children, by Race/Ethnicity, Sex, and Church Attendance.

Source: National Survey of Family Growth, 2006–2010. N = 15,654. Sex and race differences are statistically significant. We control for denomination, education, income, age, survey year, urbanicity, employment status, and whether respondents hail from intact families. Results are weighted.

This chapter makes it clear that religious attendance does not uniformly promote beliefs and behaviors that might reduce the incidence of, or racial disparities in, nonmarital childbearing. In particular, churchgoing Latinas who are unmarried are less likely to rely on contraception and abortion than other women, but they are also less likely to be sexually active. Clearly the links between religious faith, sexual and reproductive beliefs and behaviors, and nonmarital childbearing are more complex than one might initially expect.

What, then, is the bottom-line association between religion and nonmarital childbearing among black and Latina women, and how much does the greater religiosity of African Americans and Latinos affect racial and ethnic gaps in nonmarital childbearing? Figure 3.11 provides some answers.

African Americans, Latinos, and whites who regularly attend services are less likely to have children outside of wedlock. The effects vary by sex and race/ethnicity, but generally speaking regular religious participation decreases the odds of

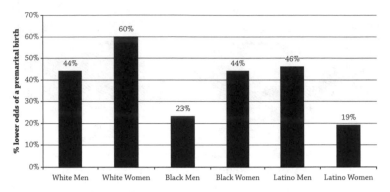

Figure 3.11 The Reduction in the Odds of a Premarital Birth Associated with Frequent Church Attendance, by Race/Ethnicity and Sex.

Source: National Longitudinal Survey of Youth 1997 cohort, 1997–2009. More information about this analysis appears in the appendix. All differences by race/ethnicity, sex, and church attendance are statistically significant, except for the gap in premarital fertility between white women and Latinas. Religious variables are time-varying. Results based on Add Health are similar. N = 2,207 (white men), 2,042 (white women), 1,161 (black men), 1,110 (black women), 955 (Latino men), 888 (Latina women).

a nonmarital birth by at least one-fifth, compared to people who do not attend regularly. In general, the effects are stronger for whites than for blacks or Latinos, and stronger for women than for men. Still, for minority couples like Roberto and Lila, religious faith and integration into the life of a religious community reduces their chances of premarital sex and nonmarital childbearing.

Many factors help to explain the relationship between church attendance and premarital fertility. Socioeconomic conditions like education and employment, adherence to the code of decency, and, especially, differences in sexual culture like having multiple partners all help explain why religious participation decreases the likelihood of having a child out of wedlock.

When we incorporate socioeconomic variables (i.e., education, work history, parental education, parental income) into our models, there is no longer any statistically significant association between church attendance and nonmarital fertility for black men. For whites, black women, and Latino men, accounting for these differences between respondents attenuates the effects of church attendance on nonmarital fertility but does not totally explain them away. Adding measures of sexual history to our statistical models further attenuates the effects of religious participation, as does adherence to the code of decency. Religion appears to reduce nonmarital childbearing in part by fostering related behaviors—fewer sexual partnerships, less cohabitation, less substance abuse, less criminality. Even after controlling for all of these differences—socioeconomic, cultural, and those related to the code of decency—between respondents at the same time, regular church attendance continues to have a substantial impact on the nonmarital fertility of white women, African American women, and Latino men. In our earlier research we have speculated that some of the benefits of regular religious participation appear to be direct and not mediated by social differences between individuals.[23] This appears to be the case here. Perhaps consistent involvement with organized religion promotes social norms, social control, or religious beliefs not measured in our data analysis that may account for the robust association between religion and nonmarital childbearing for these groups.

Still, it is clear that many churchgoers, especially Latinos and African Americans, do have children outside of marriage. Religion is not a silver bullet for couples like Nicki and Joe, who are familiar with, yet ambivalent toward, traditional Christian teachings regarding sex and nonmarital childbearing, teachings that seem unrealistic and largely foreign to the world that they and their friends occupy. Furthermore, as noted earlier, figure 3.11 indicates that religious attendance is less likely to serve as a bar to nonmarital childbearing among Latinas and African Americans than it is among whites.

On balance, religion plays a noteworthy role in minimizing the racial and ethnic differences in nonmarital childbearing, and the level of black and Latina nonmarital childbearing, in the United States. Yet it is also no panacea, insofar as a large minority of churchgoing black and Latino parents are having children outside of marriage.

CONCLUSION

Nonmarital childbearing is markedly more common among blacks and Latinos than it is among whites in the United States. This is partly because blacks and Latinos are more likely to have nonmarital sex and less likely to use contraception consistently. More broadly, this chapter indicates that cultural factors (such as pro-children attitudes and more positive sentiments toward the possibility of a teen pregnancy) and socioeconomic factors (such as parental wealth and respondent education) both play a role in accounting for racial and ethnic differences in nonmarital childbearing. Our findings suggest that progressives are right to argue that racial and ethnic differences in poverty and exposure to a climate of disadvantage help account for the racial and ethnic differences documented here in nonmarital childbearing. But they also suggest that conservatives are right to argue that cultural factors play a role in accounting for racial and ethnic differences in nonmarital childbearing.

Religion also makes a difference, as Anglos, blacks, and Latinos who regularly attend church are substantially less likely to have a baby outside of wedlock. This is partly because unmarried, regular attendees are less likely to be sexually active and more likely to abide by the code of decency (for instance, they are more likely to be gainfully employed).

However, not every aspect of religious faith and community life in the Catholic, Pentecostal, and black churches that serve Latinos and African Americans reinforces the norm of childbearing within marriage. In fact, the pro-child and pro-life ethos found in many of these churches probably means that more pregnancies are brought to term than would otherwise be the case, particularly for Latinos. More important, these churches do not clearly and consistently reinforce the belief that childbearing should occur within the bonds of marriage. This is partly why many of the single mothers and cohabiting couples who attend Catholic and Protestant churches serving black and Latino communities do not report much tension between their personal and religious lives. For all these reasons, strong religious faith is not necessarily a deterrent to premarital sex and nonmarital childbearing among African Americans and Latinos. This may help explain why religion seems to exert less of an influence on many beliefs and behaviors related to sex and nonmarital childbearing among minorities than among whites.

Still, it is the case that blacks and Latinos who regularly attend Catholic and Protestant churches in their communities are more likely to believe that premarital sex is wrong, somewhat less likely to have premarital sex, and less likely to have children outside of wedlock, compared to their peers who do not regularly attend services. Religion plays a role in integrating sex, marriage, and parenthood in black and Latino communities across the United States. Indeed, were it not for the power of religion in these communities, a markedly larger percentage of black and Latino children in the United States would be born to their parents outside of marriage.

Chapter 4

Wandering Toward the Altar

Eduardo and Graciela Valdez met close to midnight on the dance floor of a New York salsa club in 2000. A single mother, Graciela had returned to her childhood Catholicism after giving birth to a son out of wedlock. The only reason she had gone dancing that night was to humor her cousin, who was celebrating her 24th birthday. Having quickly tired of the men she met at the club, she recalled praying to God, asking "'Why? Why I am I here?' And I knew in my heart I did it to please my cousin." She added, "So I was saying to God, 'Help me through this.'" Then Graciela felt a tap on her shoulder. It was Eduardo, asking her to dance. She initially rebuffed him, but he persisted. She then "saw something in his face and in his eyes, just like such kindness, and I just saw a lot of things that I don't see in too many people." Eduardo turned out to be graceful, courteous, and not overly forward, all things that she was looking for in a man at that point in her life.

This initial meeting led to a few years of intense on-and-off dating. Both ambitious professionals who put in long work hours—he is now an assistant school principal in the Bronx, and she is a radio producer—Graciela and Eduardo were struggling to balance their careers, their relationship, and Graciela's responsibilities as a single mother, all of which caused, in her words, "a lot of arguments, a lot of debating, a lot of discussions." Beneath the concerns about juggling priorities lurked deeper issues. Both

Eduardo and Graciela were children of divorce and had experienced fractious family lives. "I was scared of marriage, the whole concept of giving yourself completely and unconditionally, like tying yourself to another person, which obviously takes a lot of trust, a lot of compromise" recalled Graciela.[1]

Eventually this Mexican American couple from Spanish Harlem was able to get help from a priest friend of Eduardo's, Father Ron, in navigating their apprehensions. Father Ron encouraged them to make their relationship their top priority, guided them through Pre-Cana (the Catholic Church's wedding preparation program) after they became engaged in 2003, and told them to live their faith. His counsel and the example of other Catholic friends gave them hope. "Luckily, because of the church and the people that we've met [at church], I realized . . . that there are happy marriages, and that even if [some] weren't, it doesn't mean that we can't have [a happy marriage]," said Graciela, now 28. Eduardo, 32, adds that he had been pursuing a vocation to marriage (Catholics believe that marriage is one way to live out God's will) when he met Graciela and became convinced that she had the qualities he was looking for in a wife: faith, intelligence, beauty, and a zest for life. As they got to know one another, his religiously grounded commitment to marrying Graciela grew. "This commitment came from that faith in God," recalled Eduardo, adding, that he had faith in marriage "despite all my brokenness, despite all my flaws . . . [She was] the only person that I believe, that I know, that loves . . . not just the good Eduardo, but also the broken Eduardo. And I felt called also to do the same thing for her," that is, to love her, faults and all.

The Valdez's faith-driven capacity to appreciate one another's strengths and weaknesses, their sense that God was present in their relationship, and the support and counsel they received from Catholic laity and clergy played a key role in helping them navigate the often conflicting priorities of romance, career, and parenthood. Their faith also strengthened their confidence in marriage, a confidence that was initially fragile because of their own experiences while growing up. Indeed, the Valdezes, who are happily married today, are living proof that the past need not always be prologue to the future. They attribute their decision to get married and their quality family life in large part to the power of their religious faith and their involvement in the Catholic Church.

In Harrisonburg, Virginia, James Johnson and Stephanie Carter are active members of Mt. Zion Baptist Church. James credits his newfound faith with helping him to steer clear of drugs, move past a checkered relationship history, and with bringing Stephanie into his life. God is the "foundation" of his relationship with Stephanie: "[W]ithout Him, you know, you really don't have a foundation [for your relationship]. So, well, my thing is about that, though, I always say a house with no floor or no roof won't stand. You could build and build, but without a roof or without a floor, it would never stand. . . . So basically without Jesus, it's gonna fall." Stephanie and James pray regularly together, believe that marriage is ordained by God, and by James's reckoning enjoy an exceptionally strong relationship. James says he is the "happiest person in the world" because "I feel like a new man when I'm with her. Now that I'm with her, I feel like a different person and feel like my life is finally moving forward and not just stuck in a circle like a little hamster in a wheel just going like this [gestures in a circle]."

James, 26, and Stephanie, 24, have a good relationship but are not married. These two young African Americans are living together because both James and Stephanie are fearful of divorce, do not wish to repeat the mistakes they made in the past, and look at cohabitation as a good way to test their relationship before making a permanent commitment to one another. Their reluctance to marry also seems to be colored by the fact that they do not have a lot of money.[2] James is earning minimum wage at a local carwash, while Stephanie works part-time at James Madison University as a cashier at a food court. Right now, they are barely covering their basic expenses of food, rent, and a car payment.

"I want to wait a year [to get married]," reports James. "I want to make sure all my ducks are in a row before I say, 'I do,' and there is no way out. There's no back door . . . because in the Bible it says you're not supposed to get a divorce. Got to stay together 'til death do you all part, and that's the way I want it to be." Ironically, James's commitment to a religiously grounded ethic of marital permanence is one reason why he is opting for cohabitation over marriage with Stephanie, at least for the time being. The precarious nature of their finances seems to be another.

James Johnson's experience is suggestive of the limits of contemporary faith when it comes to fostering marriage, especially in the black community. It is clear that his faith is sincere, that it helps him to steer clear of the siren call of the street, and that it is strengthening his relationship with Stephanie. These are all developments that increase the likelihood that he and Stephanie will eventually marry.[3] Indeed, they have a wedding date on the calendar for the next year. But their religious faith has not guaranteed a straightforward march toward the altar, just as it has not done so for many Latinos and, especially, many African Americans. As this chapter makes clear, even though religious faith increases the likelihood of marriage, various economic, cultural, and interpersonal obstacles still stand in the way of African Americans, Latinos, and other Americans as they ponder matrimony.

The fact that Americans face roadblocks to marriage like the ones noted above can be unfortunate, insofar as marriage typically advances the welfare of adults almost as much as it does that of children. Certainly not everyone needs to be married, can marry, or should marry, but most adults benefit from getting and staying married.[4] These benefits extend to African Americans and Latinos in much the same way as they do to white Americans. For instance, African Americans who marry enjoy markedly higher incomes and less poverty than their unmarried peers, and Latinos who marry are less likely to be in poor health, to smoke, or to suffer from psychological distress than their unmarried peers.[5] In general, married people are healthier, have more money, and enjoy better sex lives.[6] Not surprisingly, the majority of blacks and Latinos aspire to marriage, even though not all of them will ultimately tie the knot.[7] However, it is important to note that many of the benefits of marriage, especially for black women, are contingent upon a happy relationship, a subject to which we will return in the next chapter.[8]

THE RETREAT FROM MARRIAGE AMONG BLACKS AND LATINOS

The last half-century has witnessed dramatic changes in marriage in the United States. Fewer Americans are marrying, and those that do are waiting longer. The age at first marriage rose from 23 for men and 20 for women in 1960 to 29 for men and 27 for women in 2010.[9] Over this same period, the percentage of Americans in early middle age (35–44) who were married fell from 88 to 65 percent.[10] Another sign of the retreat from marriage is the skyrocketing rise in nonmarital births. The overall rate has more than doubled since 1980, with 40 percent of children now born out of wedlock.[11]

These trends are stronger for nonwhites. As we observed in the previous chapter, nonmarital fertility is especially common among blacks and Latinos. It increases their odds of poverty and reduces their chances of marriage down the road.[12] There are also noteworthy racial and ethnic differences in when people first get married. In 1960, both black and white men married at the median age of 24. By 2010, black men were marrying at 31, a full three years later than whites.[13] The trend is even stronger for women. In 1960, African American women, with a median marriage age of 22, were only a year ahead of white women. By 2010, the gap was six years (31 for blacks, 25 for whites), as figure 4.1 indicates. Latino men now marry two years later than white men, while Latinas marry at the same age as white women (historical data are not available for Latinos). Divorce, although down over the past thirty years, is still much more common than it was a half-century ago.[14] The bottom line is that people will spend less of their lives married than in years gone by. For adults between the ages of 40 and 45, 43 percent of African Americans

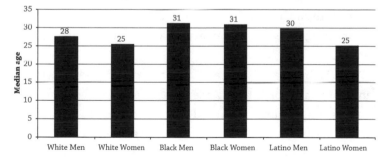

Figure 4.1 Median Age at Marriage, by Race/Ethnicity and Sex.

Source: Calculations from life tables based on the National Survey of Family Growth, 2006–2010. N = 5,275 (white men), 6,156 (white women), 1,752 (black men), 2,142 (black women), 2,409 (Latino men), 2,722 (Latina women). Results are weighted.

are married, compared to 65 percent of Latinos, and 66 percent of whites.[15] Fifty years ago these figures were much higher.[16] This holds especially true for blacks, whose marriage rates have fallen disproportionately.

It is important not to overstate the magnitude of this retreat from marriage. Almost 90 percent of Americans will still wed at some point in their lives, although this figure is dramatically lower for African Americans.[17] And as this chapter makes clear, Latinos are currently about as likely to marry as are Anglos. Furthermore, the majority of Americans continue to evince a preference for marriage over single life.[18]

These trends have numerous consequences for American family life. We certainly recognize that people unsuited for marriage, who in years past might have been pressured into forming ill-fated unions, now have the freedom to remain single. It is also the case that adults in abusive marriages can now exit those unions more easily. But for many other Americans, the retreat from marriage has been less than positive. Single people miss out on the numerous benefits of marriage already noted. Marriage, assuming it is not rife with conflict, is better for children than is single parenting.[19] All in all, the retreat from marriage has had a variety of adverse consequences for children.

What is driving this retreat from marriage? And why has it been so dramatic for African Americans in particular? Many progressive social scientists contend that structural changes to the American economy have been the primary drivers of this family revolution, whereas many conservative commentators and scholars argue that cultural and policy shifts in the post-1960s era ended up undercutting marriage and family life.[20] We do not accept this dichotomy, suggesting instead in chapter 1 that a confluence of economic, policy, and cultural currents came together in the last half-century to produce a profound retreat from marriage in the United States.

African Americans and the Retreat from Marriage

The retreat from marriage proved particularly consequential for African Americans.[21] Why have African Americans been especially likely to delay marriage or forego it altogether? As we have suggested, we believe there are both structural and cultural factors at work here.

Structurally, African American couples have markedly less income and fewer assets than do white couples. Figure 4.2 shows that among twenty-something cohabiting and married couples, over half of African American couples have incomes of less than $30,000, compared to just 34 percent of white couples. This is one reason why blacks are more likely to postpone or forego marriage, insofar as they do not reach the bar of a decent middle-class income that most Americans think is a prerequisite

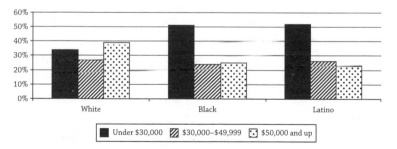

Figure 4.2 Family Income for Married and Cohabiting Twenty-Somethings, by Race.

Source: National Survey of Family Growth, 2006–2010. N = 1,536 (white), 356 (black), 803 (Latino). Results are weighted. Percentages may not sum to 100% due to rounding error.

for marriage today.[22] The fact that African American couples have less money also makes it more difficult for them to go ahead and have a big-ticket wedding—a noteworthy stumbling block, given that the average wedding now costs more than the eye-popping figure of $25,000.[23] In fact, couples often reference the expense of a modern wedding in explaining why they are not married.[24]

From a structural perspective, one key issue is that the supply of "marriageable" black men has declined since the 1970s. Due to a host of social factors that include discrimination, deindustrialization, and a criminal justice system run riot, black men have suffered from high rates of unemployment, underemployment, and incarceration since the early 1970s.[25] As of 2010, the median individual income of twenty-something black men was $11,800, whereas among white men it was $20,403.[26] Consequently, fewer black men qualify as attractive marriage partners to black women looking to wed.[27] Over this same time, black women's earnings have risen, making them less economically dependent upon marriage.[28] These trends have reduced the incentives for black women to get married.

Recall one major reason that Nicki Brown, introduced in the previous chapter, is not married to her long-running boyfriend, Joe: she out-earns him, and her job as a church secretary is more stable than his work as a musician. Although currently working, Joe has experienced bouts of unemployment in the course of their relationship, a source of evident concern to Nicki. She remains bitter about the time when she was pregnant and he was unemployed, and "he just stayed home sleeping." Nicki believes her financial position is better than Joe's and is clearly worried that his job prospects are precarious. She is not willing to put her own assets at risk of a divorce settlement by marrying him.

Judging from our interviews, many black women have a similar view of their comparably stronger financial position. Among Nicki's friends, there is "much negativity placed upon the institution of marriage," in part because they associate marriage with "having to have these joint bank accounts" that place their individual assets at peril. They would rather be in a committed relationship and avoid the financial "drama that comes with marriage," especially in case the marriage fails.

National data shown in table 4.1 tell the same story. Forty-two percent of unmarried black women report that the single men they know are not making enough money to marry, compared to just 28 percent of white women.

Nicki and Joe's experience suggests that the economic forces undercutting marriage among blacks concern more than just overall family income. They are also about the gendered shifts in earnings and employment that have occurred in the last forty years. As minority men, especially less educated black men, have seen the real value of their income decline and their spells of unemployment increase, they have become less attractive as potential husbands.[29] Indeed, William Julius Wilson has pointed out that there are fewer marriageable men in many minority communities than there were a half-century ago.[30] Not surprisingly, most studies suggest that socioeconomic factors explain part of the black–white gap in marriage patterns.[31] We come to the same conclusion based on our analysis of the National Longitudinal Survey of Youth 1997 cohort (NLSY97). At baseline, black men are 53 percent less likely to get married than are white men, and black women are 68 percent less likely to get married than are white women. After adjusting for various socioeconomic differences between respondents, including education, employment history, and income, the marriage gap is a bit smaller for black men at 48 percent, but nevertheless still noteworthy. For African American women, economic factors in

Table 4.1 ATTITUDES TOWARD MARRIAGE AMONG THE
UNMARRIED, BY RACE/ETHNICITY

Survey Question	Percent Agreement		
	White	Black	Latino
My job or education comes before marriage at this time in my life.			
MEN	45	50	61
WOMEN	41	50	48
I would lose my freedom (if I married)			
MEN	42	36	39
WOMEN	21	21	36
Asked of Men			
Most of the single women I know are not responsible enough.	25	35	48
I am not earning enough money to get married.	53	47	41
Women cannot be trusted to be sexually faithful.	18	30	39
Asked of Women			
Most of the single men I know are not responsible enough	47	56	48
Most of the single men I know are not earning enough money	28	42	39
Men cannot be trusted to be sexually faithful	34	55	40

Source: National Survey of Religion and Family Life, 2006. N = 130 (white), 302 (black), 192 (Latino). Results are weighted.

the NLSY97 data make almost no difference, at least not directly. (Keep in mind that people usually marry within their own population group, so if economic factors are keeping black men from marrying, they are indirectly affecting black women.)[32] These results are summarized in figure 4.3. They are not too far out of line with research by sociologists Robert Mare and Christopher Winship that indicates about 20 percent of the decline in black marriage rates can be attributed to declines in the labor force position of black men. Economic factors make a difference, but they are only one reason why African Americans are less likely to get married than are whites.

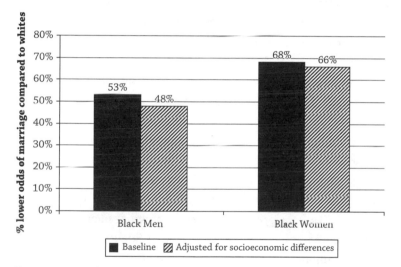

Figure 4.3 Explaining the Black–White Marriage Gap: The Economic Explanation.

Source: National Longitudinal Survey of Youth 1997 cohort, 1997–2009. N = 4,290 (men), 4,075 (women). Socioeconomic differences include the educational attainment of respondents and their mothers, wealth in respondents' families of origin, respondent employment history, and respondent income. Analyses control for region, urbanicity, and age at the first survey wave. All variables measuring respondent characteristics except age are time-varying. See the appendix for additional information on this analysis.

As sociologist Orlando Patterson has argued, culture also plays a role here, because even middle-class blacks are less likely to get and stay married than are middle-class whites.[33] As we noted in chapter 1, his central claim is that African American relationships and family life have been compromised by the poisonous legacy of slavery—a legacy of gender distrust, single motherhood, and male infidelity—over the last century and a half. From Patterson's perspective, slavery continues to haunt modern black relationships and marriage patterns. We would further add that contemporary racism can be a strain on black relationships and family life.

Whatever their historical roots, the behaviors highlighted by Patterson stand in the way of marriage for some African Americans. Concerns about infidelity, multiple-partner fertility, and distrust come up frequently in our interviews. For instance, Keisha, a 28-year-old Atlanta woman, expresses hesitation about entering into marriage because she was cheated on by her long-standing boyfriend. "I was in a relationship for a long time," she said. "It ended because I was cheated on; so I don't think I don't [sic] really value relationships anymore either." Consistent with Keisha's assessment, concerns about infidelity are higher among blacks than among whites. Table 4.1 indicates that 30 percent of black men and 55 percent of black women express concern about fidelity, compared to 18 percent of white men and 34 percent of white women.[34] As we have seen, infidelity is indeed more common among African Americans, especially black men, than among whites.

As reported in chapter 2, blacks are somewhat more likely to be affected by the ethos of the street, especially as it bound up with male idleness and incarceration, and this may also help to account for why African Americans are less likely to marry than whites. Indeed, table 4.1 shows that black men and women are more likely than their white peers to view the opposite sex as "not responsible enough" to get married.

Still, African Americans and whites both value marriage. Fifty-six percent of blacks feel that it is better to be married than to be single, compared to 54 percent of whites and 68 percent of Latinos.[35] Nevertheless, blacks are more likely to have a history of family instability, discord between the sexes, exposure to a popular culture that depicts black men in a negative light, and experience with the criminal justice system that make it more difficult for them to realize their dreams of marriage.

We explored some of these ideas using data from the NLSY97. Our analysis, shown in figure 4.4, adjusts for various differences

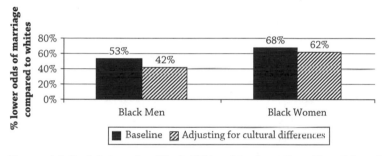

Figure 4.4 Explaining the Black–White Marriage Gap: The Cultural Explanation.

Source: National Longitudinal Survey of Youth 1997 cohort, 1997–2009. N = 4,290 (men) and 4,075 (women). All measures of culture except family structure of origin are measured as time-varying independent variables. The analysis controls for region, urbanicity, and age at the first survey wave. We conducted a similar analysis using data from the National Longitudinal Study of Adolescent to Adult Health (Add Health). The Add Health design is weaker than NLSY97's—it has fewer waves of data spread out over more time, with most independent variables only measured once—but Add Health contains superior measures of culture: one tapping family background, sexual partnerships, and premarital fertility; another measuring television viewing in adolescence; and a third capturing attitudes regarding sex and pregnancy. These variables accounted for less of the racial/ethnic marriage gap than did the NLSY culture variables, except for Latino men. Finally, analysis that includes both structural and cultural factors suggests that each group of variables makes a contribution to the racial marriage gap.

between respondents, including family structure of origin, numbers of sex partners, use of birth control, cohabitation history, and premarital fertility. Accounting for these cultural differences can explain a small portion of the black–white gap in marriage rates, but substantial differences remain.

Our results suggest that distinctive beliefs and behaviors related to sex and relationships found among African Americans help to account for a modest share of racial differences in entry into marriage. Like Patterson, we suspect that many of these beliefs and behaviors arise from the corrosive legacy of slavery, Jim Crow, and discrimination. But this is only part of the answer. Like Wilson, we believe that these cultural developments have been reinforced by structural changes—namely, the decline in men's real wages—that have had a disproportionate impact on poor and working-class African Americans over the last half-century.[36] We also suspect that other structural and cultural factors that we were unable to measure—like local residential segregation—account for some portion of the low marriage rate for blacks. Finally, these trends have been accentuated by the cultural shifts of the 1960s and 1970s, shifts that undercut many of the family- and community-centered norms and behaviors that had stabilized black family life in the century after the end of the Civil War. Today, these cultural factors–manifested in, for instance, comparatively high rates of infidelity and nonmarital childbearing–make it more difficult for African Americans to forge and sustain relationships that lead to marriage.

Latinos and the Retreat from Marriage

Some scholars, such as sociologist David Hayes-Bautista, have argued that Latinos are a bastion of family-centered living. In his words, "They will continue to marry and form families with children at far higher rates than any other population."[37] The reality, as we have seen, is more complicated. Hayes-Bautista is correct to state that Latino immigrants, especially women, often hold strong family values and lead family-centered lives.[38] And Latinos are about as likely to be married as are whites. But nonmarital childbearing, divorce, and single parenthood are higher among native-born Latinos than among foreign-born Latinos.[39] As a matter of fact, Latinos now face higher rates of nonmarital childbearing, single parenthood, and cohabitation than do whites. The obvious explanation is that America's half-century retreat from marriage has eroded some of the family-oriented traditions of Latinos, especially those born and raised in the United States.

Still, our analysis of the NLSY97 data indicates that Latinos and whites are equally likely to get married. The story is a little different when looking at the National Longitudinal Study of Adolescent to Adult Health (Add Health) data. Here there is a weak and inconsistent pattern of slightly lower marriage rates for Latinos than for whites: perhaps Latinos have about 10 percent lower odds of getting married than do whites. We are loath to attach much significance to such a small difference in a single data set, so our broader conclusion is that whites and Latinos have similar marriage rates.

This is striking because Latinos have fewer economic resources than do whites. Among twenty-something cohabiting and married couples, over half of Latino couples (52 percent) have incomes of less than $30,000, compared to just 34 percent of white couples (see figure 4.2).[40] And though Latino men do not suffer from unemployment to the same extent as black men, they tend to work in low-paying industries. This may account for why Latina women have a less than optimistic view of single men's earning power (see table 4.1).[41] Latinas themselves are disproportionately concentrated in the low-wage service sectors of the economy.[42]

We attribute the resilience of Latino marriage in the face of their often shaky economic position to the lingering power of Latino familism and religious faith. When it comes to the former phenomenon, Hayes-Bautista appears to be correct to argue that this familism is a cultural force fostering marriage among Latinos. One pertinent question is how long this familism will continue to shape marriage trends among Latinos. As journalist Roberto Suro has noted, familism is losing ground among native-born Latinos; in his words, "a powerful process of acculturation is taking place among immigrants and their offspring[,] which produces an erosion of the strong sense of family evident among recent immigrants in favor of attitudes similar to those of non-Latinos in the U.S. population."[43] We turn next to the power of religion in undergirding marriage among Latinos and African Americans.

BRIDGING THE MARRIAGE DIVIDE

We have seen how the Valdezes benefited from having a circle of Catholic friends, fellow parishioners who gave Eduardo and Graciela models of successful married life. Their Catholicism also allowed Eduardo and Graciela to accept their own and each other's imperfections, an encouraging portent for a happy marriage.

How much does religious participation increase the likelihood of marriage among blacks, Latinos, and whites? Previous chapters showed that religiosity is associated with greater adherence to the code of decency—temperance, employment, sexual fidelity, and obeying the law—all of which are conducive to marriage.

Table 4.2 THE PERCENTAGE OF RESPONDENTS WHO THINK
IT'S BETTER TO GET MARRIED THAN STAY SINGLE, BY RACE/
ETHNICITY, SEX, AND CHURCH ATTENDANCE

	White		Black		Latino	
	Men	Women	Men	Women	Men	Women
	%	%	%	%	%	%
Doesn't attend church regularly	54	34	56	43	65	51
Attends church regularly	75	51	65	51	76	61

Source: National Survey of Family Growth, 2006–2010. N = 7,556 (white), 3,417
(black), 3,522 (Latino). Unmarried respondents only. Results are weighted. These are
cross-sectional data, so we acknowledge that the causality may be complicated here.

Churchgoing young adults are also more likely to express an
interest in marrying, according to table 4.2. We hypothesize that
religious faith among African Americans and Latinos is associated with a range of behaviors and beliefs, including an ethic of
decency and exposure to happily married friends and fellow congregants, that increase both faith in the institution of marriage
as well as bolster odds of getting married.

Marcos and Clara Martinez, a young Latino couple living in
Harrisonburg, Virginia, provide an example of how religion can
pave the way toward marriage. Marcos, a 29-year-old Catholic
construction worker with a high-school education, recalled
his life of "drugs, alcohol, [and] women" shortly after arriving
in the United States as a 20-year-old immigrant from Mexico.
Four years later Marcos joined St. Veronica's Catholic Church
in Harrisonburg and settled down. The church provided him

with an opportunity to grow in his faith and "a chance for me to get out" of the lifestyle he had embraced as a new immigrant. By his own account, as he became more involved in his faith he came to learn that the Catholic Church viewed marriage as a sacrament—in other words, a holy relationship—and that "marriage is essential for humanity." He started dating Clara, whom he had met at St. Veronica's, but unlike many of their peers they steered clear of cohabitation, because he had learned at church that "marriage has to be sanctioned by the church before God." Finally, the church's messages about marriage and forgiveness, and the good example set by many older married men at church, gave Marcos confidence that he need not follow in the footsteps of his father, who treated his mother "like a total machista [macho man]," acting like he "had the right to go out, have other women, waste money any way he wanted" and otherwise dominate and disrespect his mother. In all these ways, Marcos's faith, frequent church attendance, and his religious peers gave him the encouragement he needed to start a good marriage as a young adult.

Likewise, Clara, whose abusive father abandoned her mother when she was 8, has taken comfort and direction from her faith when it came to marriage. She trusted Marcos more because she met him in church. Like him (but unlike many of her friends) she was determined to steer clear of cohabitation: "To us, marriage is sacred and we wanted to do it right. So we went through the church and took the [premarriage preparation] classes." This 28-year-old nanny reported that these classes addressed the importance of virtues like love, humility, and forgiveness. They taught "us that if you have a family you need to be like Jesus, like Joseph and Mary, be a holy family and we have tried to imitate them." These explicit messages about family life, notably their embrace of beliefs conducive to a happy marriage, helped to prepare her for married life. This was important for Clara, given that her experiences growing up had left her tentative about marriage. Her circle of religious friends and their shared faith also helped her to steer clear of cohabitation and motherhood before marriage, common paths for her fellow twenty-something Latinas.

Clara and Marcos provide a good example of how the Catholic Church can foster marriage among some of its more devout adherents, but in talking to them it becomes clear that some of their friends, including friends who attend church with them, have not taken Catholicism's approach to relationships and marriage to heart. According to Marcos, a number of their friends and acquaintances have a casual approach to dating, cohabitation, and sex. "Now, it's just dating . . . to have someone to go out and have fun and spend time with someone and if they are lucky they have sex," he said, adding, "I think it's [this pattern's] the same in and out of the church." Why does religion exert a strong influence on Marcos and Clara but not some of their churchgoing peers? Marcos attributes high levels of cohabitation, premarital sex, and out-of-wedlock childbearing among even some church-attending Latinos in part to the fact that homilies in the Catholic Church do not often touch on sex, cohabitation, or nonmarital childbearing. "I've hardly ever heard homilies that talk specifically about the family or about practical advice" for people in relationships and families. Practically, this means that many Latinos attending Catholic churches are not regularly exposed to its marriage- and family-related messages.

His assessment was shared by many Catholic lay and religious leaders that we spoke to in Latino communities, and to a lesser extent by Pentecostal authorities serving Latino churches. Based on our interviews, as well as Sunday visits to about a dozen Catholic and Protestant churches in Latino neighborhoods in California, New York, Virginia, and Texas, we conclude that priests, pastors, and lay religious leaders only occasionally mention sex, childbearing, or marriage in their sermons or in other religious venues. Protestant churches serving Latinos are more likely to touch on these themes. Not surprisingly, Protestant Latinos hold more conservative views on family matters than do their Catholic peers.[44]

Many religious leaders, especially Catholic clergy, steer clear of marriage, sex, and childbearing in favor of a kind of Golden Rule Christianity that emphasizes the importance of loving one's neighbor—in this context, children, spouses, and romantic partners—and embracing comparatively noncontroversial Christian virtues like forgiveness, fidelity, and redemption (perhaps this is why churchgoers seem to have happier relationships irrespective of marital status).[45] Thus, many Latinos appear to be pushed to embrace beliefs and behaviors that indirectly foster marriage, but are not always directly encouraged to pursue marriage itself.

Similar sentiments are expressed by black Protestant congregants. Indeed, many black churchgoers and black clergy report that their churches often steer clear of direct discussions of sex, nonmarital childbearing, and marriage, in part because of the extent of single parenthood in the black community. John and Danielle Hudson, members of Trinity African Methodist Episcopal Church in Harlem, observe that these sensitive topics rarely came up in their church. John, for instance, said that sermons in their church touched "more so [on] relationships as opposed to marriage." He speculated that this was because their church has "more single people than married couples" and the pastor did not wish to alienate the unmarried adults and single parents in the congregation. Danielle also noted that the church was initially divided about hosting a baby shower for an unwed mother, but eventually decided to do so as not to be "unfairly judgmental." (We heard similar stories at other black churches, where baby blessings and christenings are regularly held without regard to parents' marital status; according to our respondents, this was unheard of a generation ago.)

The Hudsons, who married in 2004, described their church community as warm and welcoming, a congregation where the message is "God is love," to use Danielle's formulation, and a place where Christian virtues like forgiveness, fidelity, humility, redemption, and second chances were regularly featured. They found this message helpful as they moved toward marriage. For example, John hints that he was not faithful in his previous relationships, but that pattern ended once he started regularly attending Trinity in 2000 and met Danielle. "Infidelity is not an option [for me now,] you know," the 42-year-old African American said, adding, "I mean for a married person, especially if you are growing in God, then you . . . see but you don't look." Shortly after John and Danielle met they started thinking about marriage.

John's growing faith was also important to Danielle when they were first dating each other. Her first husband had not shared her faith. After that experience, Danielle "decided I had to have a man who was evenly yoked with me, who would be willing [to share my faith]." She needed to be "able to pray with my husband, and John is very open to prayer." Their shared faith helped to foster intimacy, communication, and shared values, all of which facilitated the move to marriage.

Like her husband, Danielle, a 39-year-old African American administrative assistant at the New York Board of Education, reports that religion leaves her feeling "strengthened" because "I know that He [God] loves me unconditionally." Her faith also makes her more accommodating of John's faults and failings: "[My faith] allows me to realize that John can't be all in all and that I need to not rely on him and expect him to be perfect," she

said, adding, "I pray for patience [with him] and I pray for understanding and clarity before I react to a situation." This prayer-
ful spirit was particularly important in providing Danielle with
the confidence to move ahead with marriage with John, because
her first marriage had ended in an acrimonious divorce about a
decade before we interviewed her.

The Hudsons' experience in the black church is consistent with many of the interviews we conducted with African
Americans in Georgia, New York, and Virginia. Judging by these
interviews, religious faith, as reflected by regular church attendance, increases the odds that black respondents value marriage,
embrace the code of decency, and receive valuable social support
for their relationships. All of these things increase the likelihood
that African Americans and Latinos alike get married.

The role of faith in promoting marriage is supported by our
analysis of marriage trends for blacks and Latinos in two national
surveys, the NLSY97 and Add Health. The results, shown in figure 4.5, are consistent with our qualitative data: religious participation makes marriage more likely for everyone except Latinas.
African American men who attend church several times a month
or more are 46 percent more likely to get married, while African
American women who attend frequently are 51 percent more
likely to tie the knot. Whites of both sexes also marry more when
they attend religious services regularly. Our analyses suggest
that the black–white divide in marriage would be even larger
than it is were it not for the fact that African Americans are more
likely to attend religious services than whites.

The story is somewhat different for Latinos. Latino men
who attend services several times a month or more are 62 percent more likely to get married than are their unchurched
peers. For Latinas, church attendance has a trifling effect on
marriage rates.

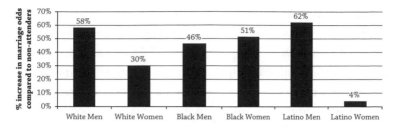

Figure 4.5 Regular Church Attendance and the Probability of First Marriage.

Source: National Longitudinal Survey of Youth 1997 cohort, 1997–2009. N = 2,196 (white men), 2,040 (white women), 1,141 (black men), 1,138 (black women), 953 (Latino men), 897 (Latina women). We control for region, urbanicity, and age at the first survey wave. See the appendix for more information about this analysis. NLSY results are presented here, given the relative strength of the survey design. Results based on Add Health are similar.

What happens to these religious effects when we control for economic and cultural factors? In general, not much. Cultural differences cannot explain the higher marriage rates for people who attend church regularly. We adjusted our results for a wide range of differences between respondents, including socioeconomic variables like income and education, cultural factors like sexual behavior and a history of cohabitation or premarital fertility, and differences in adherence to the code of decency, such as substance abuse and criminal behavior.[46] None of these factors can account for the strong effects of religious participation on marriage rates. Indeed, adjusting for these differences strengthened the relationship between religion and marriage across the board. For men and women of all races and ethnicities, attending church regularly increases the odds of marriage by at least two-thirds. The only exceptions are black women, whose chances of marriage go up by 50 percent with regular attendance, and Latinas, who see a 17 percent increase in marriage rates. On the other end of the spectrum, Latino men are more than twice as likely to tie the knot if they attend religious services several times a month or more. These results suggest that religious, cultural, and social factors that are unmeasured in the NLSY97—such as religious friendship networks, family attitudes, or a strong faith in God's presence in one's relationship—may be driving the association between religion and marriage that we have observed.

Religious faith, as we have seen with James Johnson and Stephanie Carter, is ultimately no guarantee that serious relationships end in marriage. Our earlier research suggested that marriage rates were highest when both partners regularly attend services.[47] Compared to non-churchgoing relationships, marriage rates are still higher among couples in which only one partner attends. Our qualitative data on this point is mixed. Sometimes couples move away from the altar when one partner, usually the woman, is religious and the other is not. Take the case of Nicki Brown and her musician boyfriend, Joe. Although Nicki stresses financial concerns in explaining her decision not to marry Joe, she also believes their failure to pray together, or attend church together, is a "big problem." And she is not sure "how important it [her relationship] is to God." Faith—she is religious, he is not—apparently contributes to their failure to marry after two children and a twelve-year relationship.

CONCLUSION

The retreat from marriage has affected all Americans. Whites, blacks, and Latinos alike will spend less of their lives married than did their forebears. Latinos and whites marry at the same rate. The median marriage age is a bit higher for Latino men, but that is about the only demographic distinction. Things are much different for African Americans. They are far less likely to get married than whites or Latinos. When they do marry, it tends to be much later on.

How can this marriage gap be explained? The results presented here suggest that cultural factors, such as having a child outside of marriage, matter slightly more than structural factors such as income and education. But this only scratches the surface. To date, social scientists have not been particularly successful in explaining why blacks now marry at rates so much lower than do whites. We respectfully add our names to the list of social scientists who have failed to account for the racial divide in marriage.

Our scholarly contribution concerns the importance of religious participation to understanding racial and ethnic differences in marital behavior. For whites, African Americans, and Latinos alike, regular church attendance profoundly increases the likelihood of getting married. Generally speaking, people who attend religious services several times a month or more are at least 50 percent more likely to tie the knot compared to people who attend less frequently. The one major exception to this pattern is Latinas: the effect of church attendance on their marriage rates is marginal at best.

Otherwise, this chapter provides more questions than answers. The two national data sets we analyzed here, the NLSY97 and the Add Health, offer little insight into why religious participation increases marriage rates so profoundly. The structural and cultural factors considered elsewhere in this book cannot explain the association between church attendance and marriage, but our qualitative data provide some insights. Some churchgoing black and Latino couples, such as Marcos and Clara Martinez of Harrisonburg, Virginia, and Eduardo and Graciela Valdez, from New York, attribute their decision to marry in part to their view of matrimony as being integral to their faith.

However, many Latinos and blacks do not hear this message at church. Attending congregations populated by single parents and other fellow parishioners living out of wedlock with their partners, they are more likely to hear their pastors emphasize decent behavior and Golden Rule theology than the importance of marriage. This was the experience of John and Danielle Hudson. For churchgoers like these African American New Yorkers, religion provides a message of love and forgiveness that indirectly encourages couples to move toward the altar.

Although religious participation increases marriage rates for Latino men, it has no such effect for Latinas. More broadly, Latinas and whites are equally likely to tie the knot. These findings raise interesting questions.

We are not the first to observe what has been called the Hispanic Paradox: Latinos marry (and divorce, as we shall see in the next chapter) at the same rate as whites, despite lacking so many of the socioeconomic advantages generally correlated with marriage.[48] Thus, Latino familism somehow encourages marriage in the face of socioeconomic adversity, adversity that leads whites and, especially, African Americans to delay or forego marriage. We are left to speculate that Latinos would have much higher marriage rates than do whites if the former shared the material resources of the latter. We also wonder why blacks are far less likely than Latinos to get married, despite sharing a similar structural position in American society. We will return to this question in the last chapter of this book.

The other question we cannot fully answer concerns why it is that Latinas, uniquely, do not marry at higher rates when they attend church frequently. Some of the results we present in the next chapter, on the benefits of shared religious participation for relationship quality, speak to this question. Latinas who attend regularly may develop higher standards for their prospective mates; they may expect better behavior than their boyfriends are willing or able to provide. Some of our previous research on Latinos using different data offers complementary findings. Specifically, Latino men who have churchgoing girlfriends but do not attend church frequently themselves report being less happy with their relationships compared to similar men whose partners do not attend regularly.[49] As is the case here, we assume that a Latina's religious participation raises the bar, perhaps unrealistically, for her boyfriend's behavior. It remains an open question as to why this pattern seems particularly prevalent among Latinos, although chapter 2 of this book did offer one hint: the gender gap in substance abuse is by far the highest for Latinos (Latinas are the least likely to be substance abusers of any of the population groups we examine). It is not hard to imagine that churchgoing, abstemious Latinas might be disapproving of boyfriends who enjoy a drink.

For most Americans, however, churchgoing boosts the odds that men and women find their way to the altar.

Chapter 5

A Path to Wedded Bliss?

The key to a good marriage, according to Angela, a 38-year-old African American, is having a spouse who has your spiritual back. Angela's first marriage, to a man who did not share her faith, ended badly a decade ago. She is now happily married to 40-year-old Rusty Franklin. The foundation of their marriage is their shared Pentecostal faith. "It's wonderful when you're down and you have a husband, a partner, a friend that can say. . . 'I see that you're going through some things. Let us pray together,'" said Angela, adding, "It's wonderful when my husband can say, 'Baby, I haven't really seen you picking up your Bible the last couple of days. You all right?'"

Angela prays regularly with her husband and enjoys worshiping with him at a large church in the Atlanta suburbs. Together they share a network of Christian friends who encourage them and socialize with them. Her church has ministries dedicated to couples, children, and singles—all of which, in Angela's opinion, play a key role in "strengthening the family" at her congregation. Partly because of her faith and her unsuccessful first marriage, she believes that she has to continuously "work on it [the marriage]." Here Angela mentions frequent small acts of service, as well as regularly kissing her husband. "Whatever it takes to make the other person feel good, that's what you have to continue, as opposed to being selfish, and thinking that I have that person, and that's it," she said. Their shared faith, along with her deliberately generous approach to married life, has helped to create a strong marriage where intimacy, security, and trust are the order of the day.

If Angela and Rusty are any indication, religious teachings, social support, shared rituals, and a commitment to an ethic of marital generosity seem to foster high-quality relationships among many black and Latino couples. Understanding the role that religious faith may play in strengthening black relationships is particularly important because of the religion-family paradox discussed earlier in this book: African American relationships tend to be less happy and dissolve more, compared to whites and Latinos. Yet blacks are more religious than other Americans.[1] Black relationships are subject to many strains, from pervasive discrimination to poverty to higher levels of infidelity. We think that the tragic mistreatment of the African American family, and of African Americans themselves, may limit the influence of the black Church upon some aspects of African American relationships and family life. One way to respond is by posing the counterfactual: what would black relationships and family life look like in the absence of the black Church?

With all this in mind, we wish to understand if religion boosts the quality and stability of African American relationships, much as it appears to do for the population at large.[2] Perhaps religious participation fosters successful relationships by minimizing or protecting against some of the social challenges that confront African American couples. Indeed, it may be the case that black couples who have a strong faith do better than American couples more generally.

We know less about the quality and stability of Latino relationships. Most studies show that whites and Latinos have comparable divorce rates.[3] Some research suggests that second- and third-generation Latinos are more susceptible to divorce than first-generation Latinos, insofar as they are less likely to adopt a family-centered ethos.[4] Indeed, the idea that the family is an important institution for Latinos, and that family roles and responsibilities are accorded a high priority in daily life, has received a fair amount of research attention.[5] This *familistic* orientation may lead to happy relationships for Latinos. On the minus side of the ledger, the *machismo* found among a minority of Latino men, and characterized by alcohol abuse, promiscuity, and the domination of women, may undermine Latino relationships.[6] Accordingly, this chapter seeks to understand how Latino relationships may be distinctive, and to determine what role, if any, religion plays in strengthening or weakening Latino unions.

Given the growing role cohabitation plays in the lives of American young adults, we extend our inquiry to live-in relationships. We do so both because of the prevalence of cohabitation and because the Protestant and Catholic traditions serving black and Latino communities have traditionally frowned on unwed partnerships. Does religious disapproval of cohabitation translate into smaller benefits of religious participation for cohabiting minority couples, compared to their married peers? Our previous research suggests the answer to this question is no—church attendance seems to improve both married and cohabiting relationships.[7] Indeed, the previous chapter of this book indicated that many clergy ministering to African American and Latino parishioners do not spend a lot of time explicitly talking about marriage, sex, or single parenting.[8] Perhaps religion encourages generic norms of good behavior, such as the Golden Rule, that benefit romantic relationships irrespective of marital status.

It is important to understand what makes for good relationships among blacks and Latinos, because research tells us that adults and especially children are more likely to flourish when they live in happy and stable families. We know, for instance, that stable, high-quality family relationships foster better physical health, greater happiness, and better performance at school and work among adults and children, respectively, and that the benefits of a happy family life extend to African Americans and Latinos in much the same ways that they do to whites.[9] Accordingly, this chapter takes up two fundamental questions: (1) How does the quality and stability of relationships vary by race and ethnicity in the United States? and (2) What does religion have to do with relationship quality and stability among black and Latino couples?

RACIAL AND ETHNIC VARIATION IN RELATIONSHIP QUALITY AND STABILITY

A clear majority of blacks, Latinos, and Anglos report that they are happy in their relationship, as figure 5.1 reveals, but there are some noteworthy differences. African Americans are least likely to report high-quality relationships, Latinos fall in the middle, and whites are the most likely to report happy relationships. Much of the racial disparity in relationship quality can be explained by the low quality of black cohabiting unions. Cohabiting African Americans are more than 20 percentage points less likely to be in happy relationships compared to white and Latino cohabiters. The racial/ethnic differences in relationship happiness are smallest among married people, although whites continue to report the highest quality relationships. Consistent with prior research, married partners are happier than their cohabiting counterparts, a pattern that is particularly true for African Americans.[10]

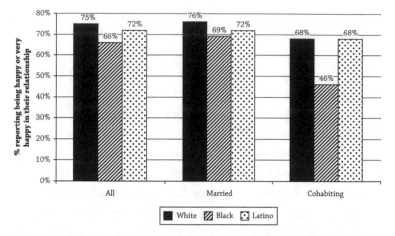

Figure 5.1 Relationship Quality by Race/Ethnicity and Union Status.

Source: National Survey of Religion and Family Life, 2006. N = 558 (white), 328 (black), 483 (Latino). Results are weighted and are statistically significant based on tests performed on the unweighted data.

Marital stability largely parallels relationship quality, with one exception: Latinos enjoy the most stable marriages. Figure 5.2 shows the percentage of marriages expected to be intact after five and ten years, by race. Consistent with prior research, whites and Latinos have roughly similar divorce rates, but blacks are significantly more likely to dissolve their marriages.[11] These differentials hold for divorce levels after both five and ten years of marriage.

Overall our data reveal that white and Latino relationships enjoy similar levels of quality and stability. This is striking, because Latinos have less income and education than do whites and yet do as well as their Anglo peers when it comes to intimate relationships. The obvious conclusion is that other factors are driving relationship outcomes for Latinos and Anglos. As noted in the last chapter, we think that Latino familism, especially among first-generation immigrants, offsets the socioeconomic challenges facing Latino couples.

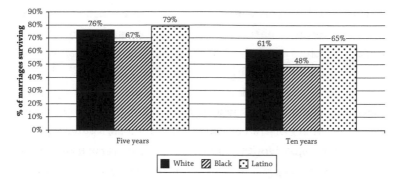

Figure 5.2 Life Table Estimates of the Percent of Marriages Surviving to Five Years and Ten Years, by Race.

Source: National Survey of Family Growth, 2006–2010. N = 5,190 (white), 1,190 (black), 2,139 (Latino). Results are based on life tables of first marriage survival probabilities for women. Results are unweighted.

African Americans are less likely to enjoy high-quality relationships and are markedly more likely to divorce than are whites or Latinos. Based on our data on relationship quality from the National Survey of Religion and Family Life, it is difficult to know what to make of the racial divide in relationship quality. In previous chapters we saw that economic and cultural differences could explain part of the differences between whites, blacks, and Latinos in nonmarital childbearing and marriage rates, but this doesn't seem to be the case here. Adjusting for socioeconomic differences between respondents, including income, education, employment, and the presence of work-related stress, has only a very small effect on the black–white disparity in relationship quality.[12] Compared to whites, African Americans make less money, have less formal education, and are more likely to be unemployed. Although all these factors tend to undermine relationships, they cannot explain the big racial divide in relationship quality.[13]

Cultural differences between blacks and whites, including attitudes toward marriage, commitment, and divorce, also don't do much to explain racial differences in relationship quality. Nor does prior marital history (in other words, whether respondents have ever been divorced). These differences are important, because couples who share a family-centered orientation to marriage, who are highly committed to one another and are averse to divorce, are more likely to invest in their relationship, enjoy a high-quality marriage, and to avoid divorce.[14] Likewise, adults who are in their first marriages enjoy more stable relationships.[15] Still, adjusting for cultural differences between respondents has no meaningful effect on the racial divide in relationship quality.

Factors that are unmeasured in our analyses, such as racial segregation or local economic conditions, may help account for the racial differences we document here.[16] Be that as it may, our analysis includes most of the factors generally used in studies of marriage and divorce. More generally, social scientists have not had a great deal of success in accounting for why blacks have lower marriage rates and higher divorce rates than do members of other population groups.[17]

Despite differences in overall relationship quality, blacks, whites, and Latinos mostly behave in similar ways in their intimate partnerships. Table 5.1 displays differences in several different relationship-related behaviors. Although African Americans express a bit less love and affection in their relationships, there are not noteworthy differences in two other relationship behaviors: criticism or the incidence of small acts of kindness. But as we noted in chapter 2, there are big racial and ethnic differences in one key measure of relationship behavior: infidelity. The last row of numbers in table 5.1 measures whether either a survey respondent or his or her partner has been unfaithful. Eight percent of

Table 5.1 DIFFERENCES IN BEHAVIOR IN ROMANTIC
RELATIONSHIPS, BY RACE/ETHNICITY

Survey Question	White %	Black %	Latino %
My spouse/partner often expresses affection or love	82	76	82
My spouse/partner often performs small acts of kindness	74	74	65
My spouse/partner often criticizes or insults me	6	6	7
There is infidelity in my relationship	8	21	19

Source: National Survey of Religion and Family Life, 2006. N = 583–585 (white), 372–378 (black), 525–528 (Latino). Results are weighted. The data measure respondent's infidelity and their perceptions of their partner's infidelity.

whites report adulterous relationships, compared to 21 percent for blacks and 19 percent for Latinos. That is a big difference.

Can racial differences in these relationship behaviors, notably infidelity, explain the racial divide in overall relationship quality? Prior research by sociologists Kathryn Edin and Maria Kefalas suggests that they might matter. Their discussion of challenges facing poor couples indicates that these behaviors, along with departures from the code of decency, often are more salient than economic factors in threatening the quality and stability of contemporary relationships.[18] But our data offer a different finding. Despite higher levels of infidelity in Latino and black unions, adjusting for infidelity and other relationship behaviors does not explain the racial gap. This notwithstanding, for whites, blacks, and Latinos alike infidelity is predictably associated with less happy relationships.

When it comes to marital stability, how do structural and cultural factors help account for the racial difference in divorce rates between blacks and whites? Here we rely on divorce data from respondents from the National Longitudinal Survey of Youth 1979 cohort.[19] This survey has followed young people originally interviewed in 1979 into middle age, and therefore provides an excellent opportunity to understand how church attendance affects marital stability. At the same time, keep in mind that many of these respondents were marrying (and divorcing) in the 1980s and 1990s, so our findings may not reflect current conditions.

Figure 5.3 indicates that structural factors, such as income and work history, play a modest role in explaining racial differences in marital stability. Cultural factors, such as being raised in a non-intact family or having a premarital birth, account for a somewhat larger share of the black–white divide in divorce.

Although our data indicate that African Americans are less happy in their relationships and more likely to divorce than are whites or Latinos, the reasons for this divide are not entirely clear. The only factor we can point to with any certainty is the low quality of black cohabiting relationships (see figure 5.1). The race

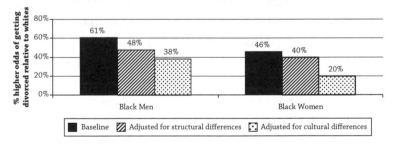

Figure 5.3 The Racial Divide in Divorce: Structural and Cultural Explanations.

Source: National Longitudinal Survey of Youth 1979 cohort, 1979–2008. See endnote 19 and the appendix for more information on this analysis.

gap in relationship quality cannot be explained by economic differences, key cultural differences, or several meaningful differences in behavior within relationships, such as expression of love
and affection, or the absence of criticism or infidelity. All of these
factors have substantial effects on relationship quality in and of
themselves. In contrast, we find evidence that economic and cultural factors account for a small portion of the racial divide in
divorce. Ultimately, the causes are less important than the consequences: African Americans are less likely to enjoy high-quality,
stable partnerships than are whites or Latinos.

IS FAITH A BULWARK OF HAPPY, STABLE RELATIONSHIPS?

Do these average differences in union quality and stability
conceal variation by religious adherence? Latino and African
American couples who regularly attend church may enjoy particularly happy and stable relationships. Moreover, the racial gap
in relationship quality and divorce might be even larger if not
for the fact that African Americans attend church at higher rates
than do whites. We explore these issues by profiling two couples,
then taking a look at national data on relationship quality and
stability.

Consider Michael, 33, and Latisha Brown, 34, the African
American couple we first encountered in chapter 1. When they
met in their early twenties in Brooklyn, they had a lot going
against them: they both came from families headed by single
mothers, they were partying every weekend at clubs, they had
accrued substantial debt on fourteen different credit cards, and
were both working low-wage jobs at McDonalds. Since marrying, they have endured their share of additional trials, including

emotional struggles (for her) and unemployment (for him). Many people would not have been able to forge or sustain a marriage under these circumstances. But after ten years of wedlock, they are now thriving. Their story is suggestive of how shared church attendance and prayer can undergird a strong, stable, and happy marriage.

When Latisha was a child, her mother had a revolving door of live-in boyfriends. One of those men molested Latisha, an experience that impaired her relationships with the opposite sex over the years. Before she met Michael, she gravitated toward "bad boys." This left her disillusioned with men. When she met Michael, she initially struggled to trust him. Once they got married, Latisha's childhood experiences caused difficulties in their sexual and romantic life.[20] Michael did ordinary things that were hard for Latisha to endure: "He couldn't hug me from behind. He couldn't whisper to me in a certain way. And one time he laughed and I just wanted to choke him, because he laughed the same as the guy who molested me laughed," she recalled.

Latisha did not know how to deal with these feelings, and the challenges they brought into her marriage, until the subject of molestation came up in a marriage enrichment class she took with Michael at their place of worship, Faith Deliverance Church. The class stressed how childhood sexual abuse could cause difficulties in adult relationships. At that point, she realized that had to confront her past head on. Latisha began to pray for deliverance and sought counseling from a female minister at her church. Consequently, when experiencing negative thoughts about her husband when he was physically affectionate with her, she would pray, "God, I refute that, I refute that. And God was trying to show me that I needed to get over this emotion."

Talking with her church counselor, Rev. Angela McClain, was also helpful. During counseling, Rev. McClain suggested that Latisha and Michael take a break from physical intimacy. So Latisha asked Michael to avoid all physical contact, even hugging, for a time. This was hard for him, but he consented, and prayed with her for healing. Of this time, Michael said, "Okay, I know I'm used to touching [Latisha], I'm used to this, you know. But I pulled back and I just said, 'God, you're gonna do this. She's going to be all right when you say so.'" After a few months, the prayers, counseling, and support from her husband allowed her to turn a corner: now, she only feels uncomfortable about physical encounters with Michael on occasion. "I feel so free now," she said. According to Michael, "we've really gotten a lot closer through that [experience]."

Michael has also faced hurdles during their marriage, including job troubles that might have derailed some couples. After 9/11, he lost a good job as an office manager at a financial firm that was based in the World Trade Center. He is now working as a taxi dispatcher for about half what he used to make, and less money than Latisha makes at her job with the fire department. Still, their shared faith has made a challenging situation endurable.

Michael's work as a taxi dispatcher was difficult, especially since he labored long hours to earn a fraction of what he had made at his previous job. Michael was frustrated, because he felt like he was failing to be a good provider for Latisha. "But I did the job as unto the Lord, and so I took that to mean I'm doing the job as if Jesus Christ himself was signing my paycheck. I worked really hard and because of that I was elevated to dispatcher in three years," he said. "If I didn't work as hard, I don't know where I would be. You know, I probably would have been fired, 'cause they had no problems firing [laughs] people."

After Michael's travails with making a living, some of Latisha's friends disparaged him. "[They were] like oh, you know, [he's] becoming like a 'no good black man,'" she said. But Latisha responded quite differently to his employment difficulties than did some of her peers. "Because we don't have the money [we used to], he feels kind of down. But I don't mind that. I told him that what every woman, and what every Christian woman wants, is security in their marriage. And to hear you pray every night and pray as you do, and to see you studying [the Bible] . . . how you love God, that's good enough for me." Her confidence in him, as well as the support he received from men in his "Brother to Brother" group at church, allowed him to keep his head up. Of the men at his church, Michael said, "[I] have all these people around and they help us out and they do keep us in line. . . . So, we know we can call some people if we're really going through [difficulties], you know. It's just comforting to know that God's provided that kind of thing for us."

What is evident from the Browns' marriage is that their shared faith has buffered them from many of the challenges that have destroyed other relationships in the African American community. Their social and emotional connections to a church community help them weather difficulties, be they the emotional fallout of childhood molestation or a job loss. The ritual power of shared and individual prayer, which fosters a sense of intimacy, perspective, and trust in their marriage, has also been comforting to them. And their faith has given them the willingness to compromise and forgive, something that has been crucial in keeping their marriage strong in the midst of the trials and tribulations that they have experienced.

Clearly their faith has been more than a buffer. Indeed, it has helped them to build a strong and happy marriage. Michael reports that he prays every night, and that Latisha is "always first" in his nightly prayers. Latisha knows this and has clear admiration for Michael's faith. This allows her to trust him in ways that she could not trust the previous men in her life. Finally, their faith gives their relationship a sense of purpose that fosters heightened intimacy, meaning, and stability. "When you attach God to the equation [of marriage], all of a sudden now, you know that you're born for a purpose and she's born for a purpose. Now, your marriage is for a purpose and that, all of a sudden, the idea of divorce becomes even that much more crazy because now you have this Godly reason to be together," he said. "Once you really understand that [purpose] . . . you really do see yourself as one. You're together because you can't see yourself apart."

Roberto, 37, and Marcia Flores, 35, who immigrated to the United States from Mexico when they were children, are representative of some of the unique challenges and opportunities facing churchgoing Latino couples. These San Diego residents met in their early twenties, lived together for a number of years, and had their daughter prior to getting married. In 1997, they wed and had a son shortly thereafter. For most of the early years of their relationship, Roberto struggled with drugs and alcohol, and spent many a weekend away from his family. "Before, I used to be in the world ('del mundo'); I used a lot of drugs, I drank a lot, I didn't care for my family, not my wife, my brothers, mother and father, I didn't care about them," he said, also noting, "when the weekend came I left my wife and I would go play soccer with friends . . . and then go drinking and that was my whole weekend."

He also says he took a "macho" approach to family life, leaving domestic responsibilities to Marcia. "You come home and you boss people around," he said, describing his macho ethic. "You force your wife and your kids to do things for you. And the woman had to take care of all the house one way or another, the man did nothing." If he had kept up this approach to family life, an approach characterized by intoxication and machismo, Roberto thinks his family would have fallen apart: "I'm sure my wife would have left me. I wouldn't have my wife or kids anymore if I had stayed in that path."

In 2000, Roberto took a detour. Some friends suggested that he and Marcia attend a charismatic retreat for couples at a local Catholic church, and, after some prodding from her, he decided to go. Much to his surprise, Roberto was overcome at the retreat, filled with remorse over his failings as a husband and father. What happened next was powerful: "That's when I met God," he said, adding, "I cried before God, which was something I never did. I never cry. But a lot of things I never did before I did on that day." Besides crying at the retreat, Roberto felt "all the presence of God," and decided to stop using drugs, alcohol, and treating his family so poorly.

In the wake of the retreat, Roberto and Marcia have seen a marked upturn in the quality of their marriage. "Until I started going to church and they taught me that the family is important and you have to care for it," he said, "I never knew that before, I really didn't think I had to put family first before." At church, he has learned that God "has a plan for marriage," that he must live "unity in all aspects" of his marriage. In practice, this meant temperance, and coming to embrace the notion that "you need a lot of love to raise a good family."

This has translated into big changes in their marriage and family life. Roberto stopped abusing drugs and alcohol, curtailed his involvement with friends and soccer on the weekends, and took a more engaged approach to "helping in the house." A religious perspective and religious rituals became more common for Marcia and Roberto. Now, Roberto says, "time with my family is something spiritual to me," and he and Marcia pray with their kids on the weekends. The changes he has experienced in his marriage and family, in turn, have further deepened Roberto's faith: "That's why I know there's a God."

The Flores' experience is suggestive of how a shared faith can help a couple dealing with male misbehavior and other challenges. Their charismatic faith enabled Roberto to experience powerful, life-changing religious rituals and to become integrated into a religious community that embraces a positive, family-oriented ethos. Their faith—especially Roberto's—has given the couple a sense of hope in helping to make the changes needed to strengthen their marriage and family life. As suggested in Elizabeth Brisco's *The Reformation of Machismo*, men's religious faith can counter some of the misogyny associated with machismo in the Latino community; in this case, Roberto has jettisoned his expectation that he could devote all his free time to friends, soccer, and drinking, and leave Marcia with full responsibility for the caretaking and housework that is part and parcel of family life.[21]

The Flores' and Browns' experience of faith and family life is emblematic of many couples, as figure 5.4 indicates. Couples in which both partners attend church regularly are substantially more likely to report being happy in their relationships than are couples in which neither partner attends regularly. This result holds equally for whites, blacks, and Latinos.

Figure 5.4 indicates that couples are happier if they both attend. What about couples where only one partner attends? According to the National Survey of Religion and Family Life, if only the male partner attends, the relationship generally is somewhat happier compared to those in which neither partner attends (but less happy than when both attend). There is no benefit when just the female partner attends.[22] Indeed, the least happy relationships for Latinos occur when just the woman goes to church often.[23]

And if only one partner attends, it is indeed usually the woman.[24] Angela Franklin, the woman introduced at the beginning

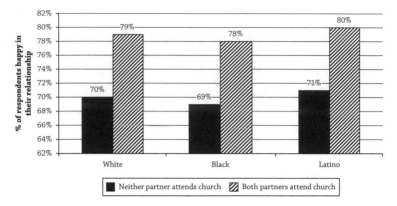

Figure 5.4 Relationship Quality, by Race/Ethnicity and Frequent Church Attendance.

Source: These results are based on a logistic regression standardization of data from the National Survey of Religion and Family Life, 2006. N = 1,691. Results control for denomination, region, income, education, stress at work (or being out of the labor force), marital status, respondent sex, age, and the presence of children. Racial/ethnic differences in relationship happiness become nonsignificant after religious variables are added to the model. Results are weighted.

of this chapter, thinks that one major reason her first marriage ended was that she and her ex-husband were "unequally yoked": she was religious, he was not. Specifically, she and her ex did not socialize together at church, did not pray together, and, more broadly, did not share a commitment to a Christian lifestyle. According to Angela, a devout Baptist, this lack of common religious ground made it hard for them to deal constructively with difficulties over money (she earned more than her ex) and communication. They ended up divorced after eight years of marriage. For this couple, religion was not a source of connubial solidarity.

We are not surprised by the gendered effects of church attendance on relationship satisfaction. Indeed, we have written about it at length in our previous work.[25] Compared to women, men are less likely to focus on relationships, but are more likely to do so when grounded in formal institutions.[26] Marriage is one example, while religion appears to be another.[27] These dynamics may explain why men's church attendance is especially beneficial to relationships. Conversely, there are good reasons to suspect that relationships will suffer when only the woman is active in her faith. Perhaps religious women in relationships with secular men demand more from them, which ultimately results in less satisfied husbands and partners. We observed in previous chapters that men are more susceptible to the code of the street. This may prove more problematic to churchgoing wives and partners than to women with a more secular orientation. It is also possible that churchgoing women, especially churchgoing Latinas, are neglecting their partners for their faith.

Why does shared religious attendance lead to happiness? In previous chapters we have suggested that religion fosters cultural norms that are conducive to good, stable relationships. Our data indeed show that adjusting for a range of cultural differences between respondents, most notably a commitment to the institution of marriage and a rejection of the acceptability of divorce (or breaking up) as a solution to relational difficulties, explains about one-quarter of the association between joint religious participation and relationship quality. In other words, religion encourages people to take the long view in their relationships, and therefore view them more positively. On the other hand, relationship-related behaviors, such as those detailed in table 5.1, like infidelity, surprisingly cannot account for the association between religious participation and relationship quality (though all these behaviors have predictable effects on happiness).[28]

Data from the National Survey of Religion and Family Life afford direct insight into two specific mechanisms, one social and one devotional, that link relationship quality with religious participation. First, almost half of jointly attending couples enjoy the lion's share of their friendships with fellow parishioners. Attending religious services with your friends accounts for more than half of the association between church attendance and relationship quality, which means that couples who have many shared friends at their church are happier than other couples.[29] Attending church with your friends exposes you to many role models of happy, healthy relationships. Recall, for instance, that Angela and Rusty have taken comfort from their church friends. These friends can also offer support when an intimate relationship hits the inevitable speed bump, and such friends may encourage each other, by example or the threat of stigma, to resist the temptation of an affair.[30]

Second, couples in which both members attend church are more likely to say that they often pray together, and shared prayer completely accounts for the association between church attendance and a happy relationship. Previous studies show that prayer helps couples deal with stress, and allows them to focus on shared beliefs and hopes for the future, and deal constructively with challenges and problems in their relationship, and in their lives.[31] In fact, we find that shared prayer is the most powerful religious predictor of relationship quality among black, Latino, and white couples, compared to denomination, religious attendance, or shared religious friendships.[32] As Émile Durkheim reminds us, religious rituals have real power in people's lives.[33]

What is interesting about these findings is that they apply equally to married and cohabiting couples. This is consistent with our earlier research on urban couples.[34] Although churches once stigmatized and otherwise sanctioned couples for "living in sin," our results suggest the benefits of shared religious attendance do not vary by marital status. This finding is consistent with our qualitative data, which show that most lay and clerical leaders serving black and Latino churches minimize the importance of marriage in their preaching and teaching related to family life. Instead, they emphasize more generic tenets of good behavior, such as the Golden Rule.

Finally, we consider whether religious participation actually leads to less divorce. Our results from the National Longitudinal Survey of Youth 1979 cohort are somewhat inconsistent with the other findings presented in this book. Frequent church attendance substantially reduces the likelihood of dissolving a marriage, but only for whites. White men who attend religious services several times a month or more are 28 percent less likely to get divorced compared to people who do not attend regularly, while white women who attend frequently are 31 percent less likely to terminate a marriage. Also, our results suggest that white couples who attend together are least likely to divorce.[35] There are no statistically significant attendance effects for blacks or Latinos. Some of the previous studies identifying a relationship between church attendance and enduring marriage have analyzed people of all races and ethnicities together, and we suspect that in these studies the strong effects of church attendance for whites concealed the absence of effects for blacks or Latinos.[36]

Why does religion, which generally has strong effects on the beliefs and behaviors of blacks and Latinos, fail to have any impact on their divorce rates? We cannot know for sure, but one possibility is that white congregants are more often exposed to sermons and other church teachings about the inviolability of marriage.[37] Moreover, churches serving predominantly white communities are more likely to offer family ministries targeting traditional families than are churches focusing on African Americas.[38] In any event, the absence of religious effects for blacks and Latinos underscores the complexity of the relationship between religion and well-being. More generally, marital happiness is not perfectly correlated with marital stability. Certainly unhappy marriages are less likely to endure, but many other factors ultimately help to determine which marriages last and which do not.[39] This seems to be the case here. Although church attendance produces happier marriages for people of all races and ethnicities, the benefits of religious participation for marital stability are limited to whites.

CONCLUSION

A majority of black, Latino, and white Americans are happy in their relationships, and among those who are married over one-half will make it to their tenth anniversary. Clearly many couples of all races and ethnicities are flourishing in America.

At the same time, this chapter indicates that African Americans are less likely to be happy in their relationships and more likely to divorce than are whites or Latinos. The reasons for this racial divide are not entirely clear: differences in structural factors such as income and cultural factors like family structure of origin can only account for a portion of black relationship quality and marital behavior. The African American propensity to be in less-than-happy cohabiting partnerships also plays a part in the lower overall quality of black relationships. Perhaps de facto racial segregation, a lack of marriageable men, or local economic conditions, factors that we do not explore in this book, contribute to racial differences in relationship quality and stability. At the same time, we note that we are not alone in our inability to account for racial differences in marriage and relationships. Many have tried to provide an explanation, and so far social science has come up short when it comes to being able to offer a comprehensive explanation for racial differences in relationship quality and stability.

Couples who attend religious services together are happier in their relationships than are their peers who do not regularly attend church. This finding holds for whites, African Americans, and Latinos alike. It is true that most people are happy in their relationships irrespective of church attendance, but black, Latino, and white couples who attend together enjoy an added boost here. Moreover, this holds for married and cohabiting couples alike. Our ethnographic fieldwork suggests that pastors ministering to black and Latino communities, already confronted with many unmarried families, are choosing to emphasize a Golden Rule theology, connected to generic norms of good behavior, rather than insisting on the primacy of marriage. Whites, in contrast, are more likely to attend congregations where ministries offer explicit support for marriage preparation and ongoing support for marriage as an inviolable union.

The story is different when we look at marital stability rather than marital quality. Regular church attendance substantially reduces divorce rates, but only for whites. African Americans and Latinos who attend regularly have divorce rates no higher or lower than those of their unchurched peers. One possibility here concerns the low emphasis placed on marriage by pastors and lay religious leaders serving black and Latino churches. Another explanation concerns sample selection: whites already inclined to reject divorce are likely to attend churches that reaffirm their beliefs. This understanding is rooted in the differing motivations of whites, blacks, and Latinos for attending religious services. Many nonwhites, especially blacks, participate in organized religion because such attendance is more conventional among their friends, family members, and communities.[40] In other words, they attend church in part because it is the expected thing to do. For whites, churchgoing has become less conventional. Overall, they attend less than do blacks and

Latinos. This means that the whites who do go to church are more likely to do so because of their personal inclination, not because they have been socialized to do so. This inclination perhaps translates into a more deeply held rejection of divorce, a belief system that is only reinforced by their religious participation. This might explain why regular attendance reduces divorce only for whites.

Shared religious attendance is clearly related to the quality of black and Latino relationships. Part of the story here too may be due to selection (couples who are happier together may also be inclined to do many things together, including attending church). But selection probably is not the whole story. Our evidence for this contention is our identification of two of the mechanisms through which religious participation improves relationship quality: religious friends and shared prayer. Latino and black couples who attend church together enjoy significantly happier relationships, in large part because they socialize with friends who share their faith and especially because they pray with one another.

Chapter 6

Conclusion

This book paints a largely positive portrait of African American and Latino family life in the United States, especially compared to some contemporary accounts.[1] We find that most African Americans and Latinos will marry at some point in their lives, most of them are married or in a live-in relationship when they have children, and most black and Latino couples are happy and faithful. When it comes to "family values," a clear majority of blacks and Latinos value marriage above single living, and they are also more likely than whites to oppose premarital sex. Moreover, the vast majority abides by a code of decency that encompasses employment, steering clear of drug use, and avoiding incarceration; this code furnishes a social and economic context that fosters a strong family life. Taken together, these findings suggest that black and Latino family life is in better shape than some critics have suggested.

In many ways the broad contours of white and Latino family life are similar. This raises the question of what scholars have called the Hispanic paradox: the fact that Latinos are healthier than one might expect, given their economic status in American society. Our book suggests that this paradox extends to family life. Latinos are about as likely to marry, stay married, and enjoy a happy relationship as are whites in the United States. The median age at first marriage is 25 for Latinas and white women, but 31 for African American women. Likewise, only 35 percent of Latinos divorce within the first ten years of marriage, compared to 39 percent of whites and 52 percent of African Americans. The paradox resides in the fact that Latinos generally have less education and income than do whites. And they have about the same levels of education and income as do African Americans, who marry less often and later, and divorce more often. We are not entirely sure if personal factors such as individual ambition associated with migration, or cultural factors like Latino familism—things our data analysis does not completely capture—account for this Hispanic paradox.[2] But it is worth noting that foreign-born Latinos are especially likely to get married and stay married, which suggests that either they bring a strong family orientation from the land of their birth, or they enjoy distinctive personal qualities as immigrants that somehow strengthen their family lives (or some combination of both).

FAMILY FRAGILITY

This book has also explored some of the structural and cultural sources of family fragility among African Americans. Their non-marital childbearing, single parenthood, and divorce rates are comparatively high, and their marriage quality and rates are comparatively low. Today 52 percent of African American children live with a single parent, compared to 27 percent of Latino children and 19 percent of white children.[3] As we have observed throughout this book, black family fragility is in some ways surprising. Religion is generally a force for family harmony, and African Americans attend church more often than anyone. This led us to wonder if religion plays a different role for

African American families than it does for Americans more generally. Evidence does not suggest that religion works against black family strength. Indeed, for African Americans, as for other Americans, it appears to be a largely positive force in family life.

So what does account for the relative fragility of African American families? When it comes to nonmarital childbearing and divorce, we are able to identify some structural factors, such as income and education, and some cultural factors, such as attitudes and sexual behavior, that account for a substantial share of the racial divide. For other outcomes, such as marriage rates and relationship quality, we are not able to explain the divide with the data available to us. Like other scholars, we do not fully know what makes black family life distinctive in these way.

Still, our findings and our reading of the literature point to four key factors that contribute to racial differences in American family life. First, the nation's poisonous legacy of slavery, segregation, and discrimination continues to play an important role in accounting for the racial fissures in family life. Second, the unraveling of America's strong industrial economy, which used to furnish stable, decent-paying jobs to blue-collar men, has since the 1970s resulted in fewer employment opportunities for low-skilled workers. This has undercut the economic foundations of black family life. Third, cultural factors, such as greater acceptance of single motherhood, play a role. Finally, ill-conceived public policies—such as drug laws that have had a disparate impact upon blacks, or means-tested programs that penalize marriage among lower-income couples—have tragically injured black family life.

The consequences have been especially grievous for black men, as evidenced by low employment and high rates of incarceration and infidelity. Between 2000 and 2012, 38 percent of black men aged 18–60 were not employed full-time, compared to 24 percent of Latino men and 26 percent of white men.[4] This trend has left black men less marriageable, a key development in the relatively high level of family fragility among African Americans.

All of these dynamics have operated in concert to take a serious toll on black families. Although academia continues to debate the relative importance that discrimination, poverty, public policy, and culture play in accounting for black family fragility, no one can dispute the fact that single parenthood and family instability coupled with lower relationship quality pose challenges to African American men, women, and children. Given the strong relationship between marriage and overall well-being, African Americans' retreat from marriage has tragically undermined equality in the United States.

For Latinos, family life is comparatively strong in many respects. But when it comes to nonmarital childbearing, Latinos are vulnerable. Today more than 50 percent of Latino children are born out of wedlock, well above the 29 percent figure for whites.[5] We attribute this disparity in part to Latino economic disadvantage, which tends to make young women of any racial/ethnic group more likely to welcome the birth of a child and less likely to marry in the wake of a nonmarital pregnancy. Our data analysis indeed shows that socioeconomic factors account for a substantial portion of the Latino–white divide in nonmarital childbearing.

Cultural factors also appear to play a role. Nonmarital cohabitation, which in itself increases the risk of a nonmarital birth, is more common among Latinos than among whites, perhaps because of the long-standing Latin American tradition of "consensual unions." Latinos are less likely than whites to use contraception consistently, and they more often embrace a pronatalist mindset; 43 percent of unmarried Latinas say that they would be happy if they got pregnant, compared to 35 percent of black women and 27 percent of white women. Latinas are also less likely to have had an abortion than are their black or white peers. These distinctive beliefs and behaviors increase the odds of nonmarital childbearing among Latinos; indeed, cultural factors measured in this book account for a large proportion of the Latino–white divide in nonmarital childbearing. Another way to put it is this: Latinos are more likely to welcome children both inside and outside of marriage.

THEY CAME AWAY STRONGER

Despite facing severe economic headwinds, an enduring legacy of discrimination and xenophobia, and perhaps the challenges of adapting to a new nation, most African Americans and Latinos marry, enjoy happy relationships, and abide by a code of decency that increases the odds of enjoying a good family life. These triumphs are often facilitated by religious faith, which serves as an important source of personal, familial, and communal strength for many Latinos and, especially, many African Americans.

Latinos and African Americans are more likely to regularly attend church than are whites, and faith is more salient for blacks than it is for whites or Latinos. Seventy percent of African Americans aged 18 to 55 consider themselves moderately or very religious, compared to 61 percent of Latinos and 52 percent of whites.[6] When it comes to attending church, 36 percent of African Americans aged 18 to 55 go regularly (several times a month or more), compared to 29 percent of Latinos and 24 percent of whites.[7] As we have seen, churchgoing is associated with numerous benefits for both blacks and Latinos. Sociologist Elijah Anderson has argued that a code of decency, characterized by regular work, law-abiding behavior, and kindness toward romantic partners, has been sustained in part by the black Church.[8] Consistent with Anderson, we find that regular churchgoing is associated with employment, sexual fidelity, temperance, and law-abiding behavior among African Americans, as well as among Latinos and whites. After controlling for a range of socio-demographic factors, church attendance produces an 8-percentage-point reduction in idleness (being out of work and school) for black men, a 9-point reduction for Latino men, and a 6-point reduction for white men. Statistics like these underscore our contention that religion is a force for decent behavior among all kinds of Americans.

And we know that this decent behavior sets the stage for happier and more stable families. As sociologists Kathryn Edin and Maria Kefalas have noted, it is not just financial challenges that can pose a threat to relationships: "It is usually the young father's criminal behavior, spells of incarceration that so often follow, a pattern of intimate violence, his chronic infidelity, and an inability to leave drugs and alcohol alone that cause relationships to falter and die."[9] Insofar as religion protects Latinos and blacks, especially men, from the code of the street, it lays the groundwork for better relationships.

Religion also shapes the beliefs and behaviors associated with sex and nonmarital childbearing among blacks and Latinos, but it does so in ways that sometimes appear less powerful than for whites. As we might expect, religion is associated with more traditional beliefs across the board. Blacks, Latinos, and whites who regularly attend church are about 20 percentage points more likely to believe that premarital sex is always wrong. As for behavior, there is a 16-percentage-point difference between churchgoing and unchurched black women in rates of premarital sex in the last year, a 12-point difference for Latinas, and a 28-point difference for white women. Likewise, the negative association between church attendance and nonmarital childbearing is strongest for white women. We suspect that the abundance of nontraditional families in black and Latino congregations has often left their clergy and lay leaders disinclined to address questions of sex and out-of-wedlock childbearing. This may help explain why religion is less likely to guide the sexual and reproductive behavior of blacks and Latinos. Even if they agree with doctrines that discourage nonmarital sex, if they are not hearing the message regularly, it is not shaping behavior.

Chapter 4 indicates that church attendance is strongly related to higher rates of marriage. And the effect is large: regular church attendance increases the odds of marriage by between 30 and 60 percent. Religiosity is correlated with marriage-friendly attitudes, a social context where dating couples are likely to encounter happily married peers, and a proclivity for decent behavior, especially on the part of men.

Latinas are the one exception to the attendance–marriage connection: religiosity is not strongly associated with higher marriage rates for these women. This may be because they already happen to be some of the most marriage-minded women in America. A clear majority of unmarried Latinas believe that it is "better to get married than to stay single." This is not the case for black or white women. Perhaps as a result, Latinas marry at about the same age as do white women, even though they and their male peers have fewer economic resources.

When it comes to the quality and stability of relationships, this book paints a mixed picture vis-à-vis religion. For blacks, Latinos, and whites alike, we find that regular religious attendance on the part of both partners is associated with about a 10-percentage-point increase in the odds that partners report being very happy in their relationships. Our analyses suggest that these religious effects are explained by strong religious friendship networks and shared prayer. Couples who socialize with their fellow parishioners and pray together are more likely to have good relationships. But to our surprise, we do not find that religious attendance reduces the chances of divorce for blacks and Latinos (churchgoing is associated with less divorce for whites). Judging by our conversations with black and Latino parishioners, as well as with their clergy, we suspect that those ministering to black and Latino communities—congregations with large numbers of divorcées, single parents, and people living out of wedlock with their partners—are not eager to preach the advantages of lifelong marriage (much like their treatment of nonmarital sex and single parenting).

Overall, *Soul Mates* shows that religion is a force for good in African American and Latino family life. Blacks and Latinos who attend church regularly are more likely to abide by the code of decency, to have their children in wedlock, to get married, and to enjoy high-quality relationships. The family-friendly attitudes, social networks, and religious rituals associated with regular church attendance appear to help explain our findings. It is also possible that some of the ostensible effects of religion are actually what social scientists call *selection effects*: family-oriented people such as Michael and Latisha Brown, whom we first encountered in chapter 1, seek out religious institutions to reinforce their existing orientation toward marriage and family life. That said, we are confident that many of the benefits of religion cannot be attributed to selection. We discuss this contention at greater length in the appendix. For now, we invoke the work of economist Daniel Hungerman, which tested the selection hypothesis using sophisticated statistical models that exploit regional variation in conditions relevant to religious people, such as blue laws.[10] The results of this study, the most rigorous test to date of the selectivity hypothesis, indicate that the effects of religion are indeed largely causal, and not representative of selection alone.

In any event, it is clear that religion is no panacea. Sometimes the benefits of religion are modest, and in some categories—most notably, marital stability—religion has no impact at all for blacks and Latinos. It is also the case that religious couples who experience disharmony—especially where she is religious and he is not—fare worse on some outcomes, such as relationship quality. This is one of the reasons why we are convinced that religion is not the answer to all the challenges facing black and Latino families, or American families as a whole.

The religion–family associations documented in *Soul Mates* may have some applicability outside the heterosexual churchgoers we have examined. Our data did not allow us to study same-sex couples. However, it is entirely possible that the benefits of religion extend to this population. Some faiths proscribe homosexual practice, while others, such as the Episcopal Church and the United Churches of Christ, affirm gay and lesbian couples. Gay and lesbian partners may benefit from regular attendance in much the same way our study population often does, especially in congregations that actively welcome them.

Although organized religion is the primary civic institution in America that promotes good behavior for its members, it is not the only one. Quasi-religious or secular organizations may provide similar benefits.[11] One example is Alcoholics Anonymous, which in addition to sobriety seeks to instill decent behavior in its membership.[12] Otherwise few secular alternatives to organized religion have really gained much traction, although anthropologist T. M. Luhrmann has speculated that this may be changing.[13] Future research should endeavor to explore how such organizations can promote happy and stable relationships. The existence of these organizations also underscores a point we have made repeatedly in this book: although religion benefits many Latino and African American families, it is neither a panacea nor a one-size-fits-all solution. Some people may benefit more from secular support. Others are doing fine without any institutional involvement. Still others need more help than church membership can provide.

PUBLIC POLICIES FOR STRONGER FAMILIES

This book has highlighted many of the challenges facing disadvantaged American families, many of whom are African American or Latino. With this in mind, we believe that America should do more to strengthen the economic foundations of poor and working-class families, to improve the marriageability of less educated men, and to reform policies that currently penalize marriage among lower-income couples. We offer several suggestions that have received bipartisan support in our polarized nation.

The earned income tax credit should be expanded, both to increase the incomes of poor and working-class families and to create new incentives to draw under- or unemployed adults into the labor force.[14] Expanding the child tax credit from $1,000 per child to $3,000 per child and making it fully refundable would give lower-income families more resources to cover transportation, educational expenses, and childcare costs.[15] These changes would be particularly beneficial to black and Latino families, given their concentration in low-wage jobs.

Two government interventions would improve the marriageability of lower-income men. First, state and federal laws should be reformed to eliminate jail time for nonviolent drug offenders (instead, they should receive treatment).[16] This is important, because minorities are especially likely to be imprisoned for drug offenses. Such a reformation would reduce the odds that lower-income men end up incarcerated, an upheaval that can have devastating consequences for families and their economic future.[17] Second, funding should be increased for proven vocational education and apprenticeship programs, such as Career Academies, which improve job opportunities for young adults, especially men, who do not pursue four-year college degrees.[18]

Many means-tested federal programs, most notably Medicaid, unintentionally penalize marriage. They do so because adding a second earner, typically a husband, to a household roster will often cause a family's income to rise above the income thresholds for benefit receipt. Consequently, low-income couples or mothers can see their benefits reduced or cut off when they marry.[19] We believe that the penalties associated with the nation's means-tested aid programs should be eliminated or minimized so as to reduce the financial barriers to marriage facing low-income couples, many of whom are black or Latino.

Finally, we recommend permanent legal residency for legal and undocumented immigrants who have been living and working in the United States. Immigration reform along these lines would boost the social and economic fortunes of Latinos in the United States and accelerate their incorporation into the social and civic fabric of the country. It would also make it easier for undocumented Latinos to marry their partners.

Individually, none of these steps forward are likely to eliminate racial gaps in marriage rates or dramatically reduce the share of children born to unmarried Latinos or African Americans. But by shoring up the sometimes shaky economic foundations of minority families, we might be able to strengthen them—and thereby strengthen black and Latino communities. These are the families who need the most help due to enduring American inequality.

CIVIC AND RELIGIOUS STRATEGIES FOR STRONGER FAMILIES

Especially in a nation as diverse as the United States, new secular and religious civic initiatives could do much to strengthen family life. On the secular front, a social marketing campaign and nonprofit initiatives to provide relationship education to couples seem particularly promising. Successful campaigns against smoking, drunk driving, and teenage pregnancy have proven to us that culture matters in shaping behavior and that top-down efforts to change popular actions can actually succeed. Take the National Campaign to Prevent Teenage and Unplanned Pregnancy. It has worked with state and local organizations, advertising agencies, Hollywood producers, and religious institutions in its successful efforts to change norms and behaviors related to teen pregnancy.[20] A similar campaign organized around what Brookings Institution scholars Ron Haskins and Isabel Sawhill have called the "success sequence"—young adults putting education, work, marriage, and parenthood in that order—could also play a valuable role in delaying parenthood, strengthening marriage, and stabilizing family life.[21]

There are also promising local initiatives designed to strengthen family life, such as First Things First in Chattanooga, Tennessee.[22] Serving primarily African American and white families in southeast Tennessee, it provides education on marriage, fatherhood, and parenting and sponsors a range of public events, such as Chattanooga's Ultimate Date Night, to help couples forge strong and happy relationships. Good programs like this need to be replicated across the country.

Religious efforts—congregational, regional, or ecumenical—to strengthen family life among African Americans and Latinos (among others) should focus, frankly, on men. The message should be one of relationship formation and sustenance; in everyday language, finding a partner, getting married, and sticking together. Why single out men? The answer is simple: they are more at risk. Churches and other religious groups should target men with messages and ministries that stress the importance of fidelity, emotional engagement in marriage and family life, and sacrificing generously for one's family. Both this book and previous research suggest that these ideas pay real dividends for men, their mates, and their children.[23] Churches should also be strategic about how they deliver these messages. One black Baptist pastor in Seattle scheduled a men's ministry in conjunction with Monday Night Football and delivered his message at half time. The point is that such messages are probably most likely to be heard and internalized in contexts where most men feel comfortable.

Finally, messages and ministries targeting men could help black and Latino churches close the large gender gap in religious participation. As figure 6.1 indicates, women beat men in regular church attendance by 13 percentage points among African Americans, and by 10 points among Latinos.

Given the challenges that Latinos and especially African Americans face in today's job market, churches should take an active role in launching employment ministries, either as congregations or on a regional or ecumenical basis. These ministries could provide instruction on finding and keeping jobs, cultivate job skills (such as basic computer experience, office etiquette, and customer-service techniques), and provide an emotional outlet for parishioners who are un- or underemployed. Given the importance of employment, especially on the part of men, for

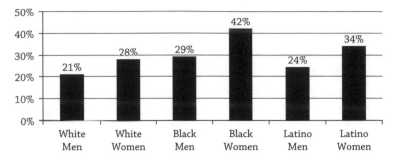

Figure 6.1 Frequent Church Attendance, by Race/Ethnicity and Sex.
Source: General Social Survey, 2000–2012. N = 14,449.

the quality and stability of family life, such ministries could play just as useful a role in strengthening black and Latino families as would preaching about them from the pulpit.[24]

Given the complexity, confusion, and ambiguities associated with contemporary dating, marriage, and family life, we believe that churches, or local groups of congregations, should address dating and family life early and often, but in a manner that is pastorally sensitive to the lived experience of the audience to whom the messages are directed. Clergy cannot ignore the feelings of the large numbers of single parents and other unmarried adults in their congregations, of course. And the precise message will vary by religious tradition, race, ethnicity, and economic situation, but the following themes are worth highlighting. First, when it comes to dating and mating, adolescents and young adults should be encouraged to take things slowly and to save childbearing for marriage. Couples should also be required to take a premarital preparation course before they marry in a church, because young adults who do these things are more likely to enjoy strong marriages.[25]

Second, churches and other ministries should do more to speak honestly, both with children and adults, about the good parts and the challenges of married life. Such discourse would include messages about forgiveness, fidelity, and mutual generosity, as well as the value of building a spiritual life together. The message of this book and of social science more generally is clear: pursuing these virtues fosters strong and stable families, especially when rooted in a shared faith.[26] (As our book makes clear, the benefits are weaker for families marked by serious religious differences.) Moreover, religious institutions must be adamant that domestic violence is not to be tolerated and that afflicted couples should consider separating. Chemical dependency also needs to be taken seriously by clergy, with appropriate referrals to rehabilitation programs or support groups. Honesty is key in all of this: clergy and lay leaders need to be candid about the joys and struggles that they and other lay members have faced, both for sincerity's sake and to give succor to spouses and parents who are similarly struggling. Indeed, research suggests that couples are more likely to have hope for their relationship when they realize that other couples struggle with similar challenges.[27]

For black Protestants, the message and ministry around family life might be framed in the context of two themes that have had an enduring place in the black church. One is racial uplift, as articulated by figures as varied as Booker T. Washington, Malcolm X, and Martin Luther King, Jr. One study of African American churches found that most black religious leaders think that part of their mission is to convey to their congregations a sense of black pride.[28] This sense of racial uplift could be linked to efforts to strengthen and stabilize black family life so as to give those efforts greater salience among churchgoing African Americans.

As religion scholars C. Eric Lincoln and Lawrence H. Mamiya have noted, a liberationist theme, stressing the power of faith to free black people from the bonds of slavery, Jim Crow, and racism, has played a central role in the African American religious experience; this theme could also be incorporated into discussions of family matters.[29] How might a liberationist theme relate to black family life? Harvard sociologist Orlando Patterson argues that the relative fragility of black families is rooted in the legacy of "slavery and the system of racial oppression," making it difficult for blacks to marry and to form stable unions.[30] Efforts to strengthen black family life could be framed as an attempt to come to terms with this legacy and to free African American families from the repugnant vestiges of American racism.

Latino religious leaders, both clerical and lay, should build upon a long-standing Latino familism that has traditionally valorized strong ties within extended families and exuberantly celebrated the arrival of children. This familism has been an important source of solidarity among Latinos over the years, and even today it seems to foster marital stability. At the same time, the pronatalism associated with Latino familism appears to be a force driving higher rates of nonmarital childbearing. Catholic and Protestant leaders serving the Latino community should emphasize that marriage provides a particularly strong foundation for the future well-being of children.

The Catholic Church could more clearly connect its own family teachings to its deep tradition of rituals associated with domestic life and the life cycle, such as the *quinceañera* Mass (the Catholic celebration of a young woman's fifteenth birthday), to provide guidance and inspiration to younger Latinos.[31] Public processions, a long-standing staple of Latino Catholic life, might also be valuable in strengthening Catholic identity among younger Latinos. Such processions, along with a renewed focus on domestic and life-cycle rituals, could help to both strengthen religious identity and to protect Latino teens and young adults from being drawn into the negative features of American life. Finally, the Catholic Church could do more to bring Latino men into the fold: our analyses of 18- to 60-year-olds in the General Social Survey indicate that Catholic women are 41 percent more likely to regularly attend church than are Catholic men. Among Latino Protestants, most of whom are evangelical or Pentecostal, women are only 17 percent more likely than men to regularly attend church.[32]

Latino Protestants attend more regularly, their churches are more successful at pulling in men, and their clergy are more likely to address sex and nonmarital childbearing directly.[33] Still, based on our interviews with clergy and especially laity, Protestant churches and ministries serving younger Latinos need to move beyond their traditional legalism in their messages.[34] In speaking about sex and childbearing authentically and honestly, churches and ministries can articulate a positive theology of family life to engage an audience that is better educated and more assimilated than their first-generation forebears. In other words, religious and lay leaders serving Latino Protestants need to thread the needle between accommodating and resisting the family trends characteristic of twenty-first-century America.

CONCLUSION

Soul Mates paints a nuanced picture. On the one hand, most African Americans and Latinos enjoy high-quality relationships, have their children while married or living together, marry at some point in their lives, aspire to a strong marriage and family life, and abide by a code of decency that serves them and their families well.[35] Religious practice—be it church attendance, shared prayer, or engagement in religious friendship networks—improves marriage and family life among blacks and Latinos. Indeed, faith is a family-friendly force in many ways. On the other hand, for some African Americans and Latinos, especially those with the least education and income, there is a gap between the aspiration to enjoy a strong and stable family life and the ability to realize that dream. Clearly religion is no panacea to the challenges facing black and Latino families or, for that matter, families of any race or ethnicity. By our reckoning, it will take a range of economic, cultural, and religious developments to bridge the racial and ethnic divides in American family life. Given the importance of a happy, stable family to the welfare of our children, the cause of equal opportunity in America, and the lived experiences of African Americans and Latinos themselves, we can think of few worthier causes.

APPENDIX

Data and Analysis

As noted in chapter 1, this book is primarily based on the analysis of six national data sets: the 1979 and 1997 cohorts of the National Longitudinal Surveys of Youth (respectively referred to as NLSY79 and NLSY97), the National Longitudinal Study of Adolescent Health (now known as the National Longitudinal Study of Adolescent to Adult Health, but referred to here by its usual name, Add Health), the 1972–2012 General Social Surveys (GSS), the 2006 National Survey of Religion and Family Life (NSRFL), and the 2006–2010 National Survey of Family Growth (NSFG). The working sample size for each data set varies depending upon the variables being analyzed, so it is noted throughout the manuscript. Missing data are deleted listwise, except when large numbers of missing cases may represent substantively meaningful differences between respondents. For these items we code additional dummy variables for missing data or, for continuous variables, mean imputation with a missing-data dummy. More sophisticated means of handling missing data, such as multiple imputation, do not produce appreciably better estimates of regression coefficients or standard errors.[1]

All six data sets are the product of multistage cluster samples, so standard errors are computed using the Huber-White algorithm. All results in this book based on multivariate analysis are statistically significant at the .05 level unless otherwise indicated.

To the extent possible we use the same variable definitions through-out the book. In particular, we rely on one measure of religious partici-pation: frequent church attendance determined by going several times a month or more ("almost weekly" in one case).[2] We also employ one coding scheme for denomination, the method proposed by Brian Steensland, W. Bradford Wilcox, and their colleagues.[3]

Chapter 2

Figures 2.9–2.16 are based on regression standardization. All indepen-dent variables are set at their means, except for race/ethnicity, religious participation, and sex (where applicable). Predicted probabilities are then computed via logistic regression models. For each analysis we test for inter-actions between race/ethnicity, religious participation, and, if applicable, sex. Significant interactions are retained when predicted probabilities are computed.

Chapter 3

The timing of a first premarital birth is explored using event history anal-ysis of data from both NLSY97 and Add Health. The former offers mul-tiple waves of data and comparably accurate measurement of time-related variables, so continuous time methods are appropriate. Since the analysis employs time-varying independent variables, parametric models are not suitable. Accordingly we estimate Cox proportional hazards models. The models include a variable intended to account for panel attrition. Here and elsewhere, we experimented with lagging values on independent variables six months or a year so as to better determine causality. This had no appre-ciable effect on the results.

A drawback of NLSY97 is its limited measures of culture. With fewer, more widely spaced waves of data collection, the Add Health design is not as strong. However, it offers extensive measures of culture. Using Add Health we analyze measures of culture and socioeconomic status at Wave I (1994–1995) and reports of a nonmarital birth by Wave IV (2008–2009). Analysis of Add Health is conducted using discrete-time event history models, estimated via complementary log-log regression. This provides better estimates than logistic regression when the discrete data approxi-mate a continuous phenomenon.[4] Duration dependence is modeled with a vector of dummy variables.

Finally, we note that we were able to obtain analogous results using both NLSY97 and Add Health.

Chapter 4

Our analysis of entry into first marriage is primarily based on NLSY97 data. We estimate Cox proportional hazards models similar to those used in chapter 3. We also analyze the Add Health data when examining how culture matters.

Chapter 5

Analyses of relationship quality use NSRFL data. Similar to the chapter 2 analyses, results are based on regression standardization.

We explore divorce using data from NLSY79. Add Health and NLSY97 are fairly recent data sets. Consequently, the respondents are young, and most have not had enough time to get married and, possibly, get divorced. In contrast, NLSY79 respondents are now mostly in their fifties, old enough for us to know how they fared in their marriages. Like premarital fertility and entry into marriage, divorce is studied using Cox proportional hazards models.

Sample Selection

A common question about our findings is sample selection. Does religious participation in and of itself actually produce the benefits described in this book, or is it simply the case that the same kinds of people likely to attend church are also likely to avoid premarital pregnancy, get married, and enjoy a stable relationship? This is a common critique of social science research. In fact, it is a generic criticism that can be applied to virtually any finding. It is often invoked to account for ideologically troublesome results.

We have attempted to address this issue in several ways. First, we have shown that the effects of religion persist after controlling for numerous social, demographic, and psychological differences between survey respondents. Second, whenever possible we employ longitudinal data, in which religious participation occurred at an earlier point in time than did the outcomes we sought to study.[5] Third, we conducted exploratory analyses to ascertain whether some of the relationship outcomes we examine could themselves predict religious attendance (that is, we sought to reverse the order of causality). Doing so revealed no consistent pattern of association.

Although all of these techniques are usual social science practices, none is an ironclad way of measuring or accounting for sample selection. In recent years economists have pioneered an approach that involves exploiting naturally occurring experiments. Unfortunately, no good instrumental variables have emerged for studying the effects of religion.[6] As an alternative, economist Daniel Hungerman recently proposed an approach that capitalizes on area-level differences in laws and conditions that should have particular relevance to the pious.[7] He concludes that the effects of religion are essentially causal, a finding we are naturally pleased to report.

Our final point is broader. It is easy to allege sample selection bias as an explanation for any social science finding not produced by an experimental study. To do so invites speculation about the mechanisms that might be driving the sample selection. We therefore welcome future research in this area. It will enhance our understanding of how religious participation influences individual well-being.

NOTES

Chapter 1

1. We have changed the names and some of the identifying details of the respondents included in this book.
2. For noteworthy academic accounts of the challenges facing poor and/or minority couples and families, see Elijah Anderson, *Code of the Street: Decency, Violence, and the Moral Life of the Inner City* (New York: Norton, 1999); Kathryn Edin and Maria Kefalas, *Promises I Can Keep: Why Poor Women Put Motherhood before Marriage* (Berkeley: University of California Press, 2005); and M. Belinda Tucker and Claudia Mitchell-Kernan, *The Decline in Marriage among African Americans: Causes, Consequences, and Policy Implications* (New York: Russell Sage, 1995). For recent journalistic accounts, see Adrian Nicole LeBlanc, *Random Family: Love, Drugs, Trouble, and Coming of Age in the Bronx* (New York: Scribner, 2003); and Nicholas Lemann, *The Promised Land: The Great Black Migration and How It Changed America* (New York: Vintage, 1992). For an exception, a work that does discuss religion, see Mary Pattillo-McCoy, *Black Picket Fences: Privilege and Peril among the Black Middle Class* (Chicago: University of Chicago Press, 1999).
3. Andrew J. Cherlin, "The Deinstitutionalization of American Marriage," *Journal of Marriage and Family* 66 (2004): 848–861.
4. Arland Thornton and Linda Young-DeMarco, "Four Decades of Trends in Attitudes toward Family Issues in the United States: The 1960s through the 1990s," *Journal of Marriage and Family* 63 (2001): 1009–1037.

5. Andrew J. Cherlin, *Marriage, Divorce, Remarriage*, rev. ed. (Cambridge, MA: Harvard University Press, 1992); and Sara McLanahan, "Diverging Destinies: How Children Fare under the Second Demographic Transition," *Demography* 41 (2004): 607–627.

6. Paul R. Amato et al., *Alone Together: How Marriage in America Is Changing* (Cambridge, MA: Harvard University Press, 2007); Barbara Dafoe Whitehead and David Popenoe, *The State of Our Unions 2006: The Social Health of Marriage in America* (New Brunswick, NJ: National Marriage Project, 2006); and Betsey Stevenson and Justin Wolfers, "Marriage and Divorce: Changes and Their Driving Forces," *Journal of Economic Perspectives* 21 (2007): 27–52. There are some countervailing trends. See, for instance, Suzanne Bianchi, John P. Robinson, and Melissa A. Milkie, *Changing Rhythms of American Family Life* (New York: Russell Sage, 2006), which shows that parents are now spending more one-on-one time with their children than they did in the 1960s.

7. David T. Ellwood and Christopher Jencks, "The Spread of Single-Parent Families in the United States since 1960," in *The Future of the Family*, ed. Daniel P. Moynihan, Timothy M. Smeeding, and Lee Rainwater (New York: Russell Sage, 2004), 25–65; and McLanahan, "Diverging Destinies."

8. R. S. Oropesa and Nancy S. Landale, "The Future of Marriage and Hispanics," *Journal of Marriage and Family* 66 (2004): 901–920.

9. Elizabeth Marquardt et al., "The President's Marriage Agenda for the Forgotten Sixty Percent," in *The State of Our Unions 2012* (Charlottesville, VA: National Marriage Project and Institute for American Values, 2012).

10. Esther Lamidi, "Single, Cohabiting, and Married Households, 1995–2012" (FP-14-1), National Center for Family & Marriage Research, 2014, http://ncfmr.bgsu.edu/pdf/family_profiles/file141218.pdf. Cohabitation rates appear low because they reflect individuals cohabiting at the time of the survey. Data on whether respondents had ever cohabited would yield much larger numbers. For instance, sociologists Larry Bumpass and Hsien-Hen Lu show that half of young people will live out of wedlock with partners prior to marriage. See Larry L. Bumpass and Hsien-Hen Lu, "Trends in Cohabitation and Implications for Children's Family Contexts in the United States," *Population Studies* 54 (2000): 29–41.

11. Cherlin, *Marriage, Divorce, Remarriage*; and Joshua R. Goldstein, "The Leveling of Divorce in the United States," *Demography* 36 (1999): 409–414.

12. Roberto Suro, "The Hispanic Family in Flux," CCF Working Paper (Washington, DC: Center on Children & Families, Brookings Institution,

2007), http://www.brookings.edu/~/media/research/files/papers/ 2007/11/hispanicfamily-suro/11_hispanicfamily_suro.pdf. See also Rose Kreider and Jason M. Fields, "Number, Timing, and Duration of Marriages and Divorces: Fall 1996," Current Population Reports, P70–80 (Washington, DC: US Census Bureau, 2001). For evidence that divorce is more common among native-born Latinos, see Julie A. Phillips and Megan M. Sweeney, "Premarital Cohabitation and Marital Disruption among White, Black and Mexican American Women," *Journal of Marriage and Family* 67 (2005): 296–314.

13. See Casey E. Copen, Kimberly Daniels, and William D. Mosher, "First Premarital Cohabitation in the United States: 2006–2010 National Survey of Family Growth," National Health Statistics Reports 64 (Hyattsville, MD: National Center for Health Statistics, 2013), table 3.

14. Oropesa and Landale, "The Future of Marriage and Hispanics."

15. US Census Bureau, Current Population Survey, March Demographic Supplement, 1970–2013. Figures refer to children living with two married parents, and they exclude multi-racial/multi-ethnic children.

16. Ibid.

17. William Julius Wilson, *The Truly Disadvantaged: The Inner City, the Underclass, and Public Policy* (Chicago: University of Chicago Press, 1987).

18. Maggie Gallagher, *The Abolition of Marriage: How We Destroy Lasting Love* (Washington, DC: Regnery Publishing, 1996); Charles Murray, *Losing Ground: American Social Policy, 1950–1980* (New York: Basic Books, 1984); and Lawrence Mead, *The New Politics of Poverty: The Nonworking Poor in America* (New York: Basic Books, 1993).

19. Charles M. Blow, "For Some Folks, Life Is a Hill," *New York Times*, November 29, 2013.

20. See US Census Bureau, Current Population Survey, Annual Social and Economic Supplement, 2013, table 1: "Educational Attainment." http:// www.census.gov/hhes/socdemo/education/data/cps/2013/tables.html

21. Paul Krugman, *The Conscience of a Liberal* (New York: W. W. Norton and Company, 2007); and Timothy Noah, *The Great Divergence: America's Growing Inequality Crisis and What We Can Do about It* (New York: Bloomsbury, 2012).

22. Daphne Spain and Suzanne Bianchi, *Balancing Act: Motherhood, Marriage, and Employment among American Women* (New York: Russell Sage, 1996), 77.

23. Wilson, *The Truly Disadvantaged*.

24. Spain and Bianchi, *Balancing Act*, 81.

25. Thomas J. Espenshade, "Marriage Trends in America: Estimates, Implications, and Underlying Causes," *Population and Development Review* 11 (1985): 193–245.

26. Arlie Hochschild, with Anne Machung, *The Second Shift* (New York: Avon Books, 1989); Julie E. Press and Eleanor Townsley, "Wives' and Husbands' Housework Reporting: Gender, Class, and Social Desirability," *Gender and Society* 12 (1998): 188–218; and Scott J. South and Glenna Spitze, "Housework in Marital and Nonmarital Households," *American Sociological Review* 59 (1994): 327–347.

27. On the relationship between women's employment and divorce, see Marianne Bertrand, Jessica Pan, and Emir Kamenica, "Gender Identity and Relative Income within Households," Working Paper 19023 (Cambridge, MA: National Bureau of Economic Research, 2013); and Hiromi Ono, "Husbands' and Wives' Resources and Marital Dissolution in the United States," *Journal of Marriage and Family* 60 (1998): 674–689.

28. On women's economic gains relative to men's, see Annette Bernhardt, Martina Morris, and Mark S. Handcock, "Women's Gains or Men's Losses? A Closer Look at the Shrinking Gender Gap in Earnings," *American Journal of Sociology* 101 (1995): 302–328.

29. Murray, *Losing Ground*, 163–164; and Stevenson and Wolfers, "Marriage and Divorce."

30. Adam Carasso and C. Eugene Steuerle, "The Hefty Marriage Penalty on Marriage Facing Many Households with Children," *The Future of Children* 15 (2005): 157–175.

31. For reviews of the research on public policy, family law, and the family revolution, see Ellwood and Jencks, "The Spread of Single-Parent Families"; Robert Moffitt, "The Effect of Welfare on Marriage and Fertility," in *Welfare, the Family, and Reproductive Behavior*, ed. Robert Moffitt (Washington, DC: National Academy Press, 1998), 50–97; and Stevenson and Wolfers, "Marriage and Divorce."

32. Peter Clecak, *America's Quest for the Ideal Self: Dissent and Fulfillment in the 60s and 70s* (New York: Oxford University Press, 1983); and Steven Pinker, *The Better Angels of Our Nature: The Decline of Violence in History and Its Causes* (London: Allen Lane, 2011).

33. Robert Putnam, *Bowling Alone: The Collapse and Revival of American Community* (New York: Simon & Schuster, 2000), 71.

34. Wade Clark Roof, *A Generation of Seekers: The Spiritual Journeys of the Baby Boom Generation* (New York: Harper Collins, 1993).

35. Daniel Bell, *The Cultural Contradictions of Capitalism* (New York: Basic Books, 1978), xvii.

36. George A. Akerlof, Janet L. Yellen, and Michael L. Katz, "An Analysis of Out-of-Wedlock Childbearing in the United States," *Quarterly Journal of Economics* 111 (1996): 277–317.

37. George A. Akerlof, "Men Without Children," *Economic Journal* 108 (1998): 287–309.

38. W. Bradford Wilcox, "Suffer the Little Children: Marriage, the Poor, and the Commonweal," in *The Meaning of Marriage: Family, State, Market, and Morals*, ed. Robert George and Jean Bethke Elshtain (Dallas, TX: Spence, 2006), 242–253.

39. Akerlof, Yellen, and Katz, "An Analysis of Out-of-Wedlock Childbearing," 313.

40. On the labor force argument, see Wilson, *The Truly Disadvantaged*. On the effects of racial disparities in imprisonment, see Bruce Western, *Punishment and Inequality in America* (New York: Russell Sage, 2006).

41. Robert D. Mare and Christopher Winship, "Socioeconomic Change and the Decline of Marriage for Blacks and Whites," in *The Urban Underclass*, ed. Christopher Jencks and Paul E. Peterson (Washington, DC: Brookings, 1991), 175–196.

42. US Census Bureau, *Statistical Abstract of the United States: 1970*, 90th ed.

43. Carmen DeNavas-Walt, Bernadette D. Proctor, and Jessica Smith, "Income, Poverty, and Health Insurance Coverage in the United States: 2006," Current Population Reports, P60-233 (Washington, DC: US Census Bureau, 2007).

44. Edin and Kefalas, *Promises I Can Keep*, 6.

45. Ibid., 9; and Andrew J. Cherlin, *The Marriage-Go-Round: The State of Marriage and the Family in America Today* (New York: Vintage, 2009).

46. See Mare and Winship, "Socioeconomic Change"; and Daniel T. Lichter et al., "Race and the Retreat from Marriage: A Shortage of Marriageable Men?" *American Sociological Review* 57 (1992): 781–799.

47. Orlando Patterson, *Rituals of Blood: Consequences of Slavery in Two American Centuries* (New York: Basic, 1998), 166.

48. Ibid., 158–160.

49. Ibid., 158.

50. David Brooks, "Immigrants to Be Proud Of," *New York Times*, March 30, 2006.

51. Oropesa and Landale, "The Future of Marriage and Hispanics."

52. Ibid. See also Nancy S. Landale and R. S. Oropesa, "Hispanic Families: Stability and Change," *Annual Review of Sociology* 33 (2007): 381–405.

53. US Census Bureau, *Statistical Abstract of the United States: 1995*, 115th ed.

54. DeNavas-Walt, Proctor, and Smith, "Income, Poverty, and Health Insurance Coverage."

55. Oropesa and Landale, "The Future of Marriage and Hispanics."

56. Pierette Hondagneu-Sotelo, *Domestica: Immigrant Workers Cleaning and Caring in the Shadows of Affluence* (Berkeley: University of California Press, 2001).

57. Oropesa and Landale, "The Future of Marriage and Hispanics," 910.

58. Alejandro A. Portes and Ruben G. Rumbaut, *Legacies: The Story of the Immigrant Second Generation* (Berkeley: University of California Press, 2000).

59. Tony Brown et al., "'Being Black and Feeling Blue': The Mental Health Consequences of Racial Discrimination," *Race and Society* 2 (2000): 117–131; and Brian Karl Finch et al., "Perceived Discrimination and Depression among Mexican-Origin Adults in California," *Journal of Health and Social Behavior* 41 (2000): 295–313.

60. Oropesa and Landale, "The Future of Marriage and Hispanics."

61. See, for instance, Elizabeth E. Brusco, *The Reformation of Machismo: Evangelical Conversion and Gender in Colombia* (Austin: University of Texas Press, 1995).

62. Maxine Baca Zinn and Angela Y. H. Pok, "Tradition and Transition in Mexican-Origin Families," in *Minority Families in the United States: A Multicultural Perspective*, ed. Ronald L. Taylor (Upper Saddle River, NJ: Pearson, 2002), 79–100; Vonnie C. McLoyd et al., "Marital Processes and Parental Socialization in Families of Color: A Decade Review and Research," *Journal of Marriage and Family* 62 (2000): 1070–1093; and Jenna Mahay and Edward O. Laumann, "Neighborhoods as Sex Markets," in *The Sexual Organization of the City*, ed. Edward O. Laumann et al. (Chicago: University of Chicago Press, 2004), 69–92. Our data in chapter 5 tell a similar story.

63. Oropesa and Landale, "The Future of Marriage and Hispanics."

64. Laura Lippman and W. Bradford Wilcox, *World Family Map* (Washington, DC: Child Trends, 2014).

65. Donald F. Roberts et al., "Kids and Media @ the New Millennium" (Menlo Park, CA: Kaiser Family Foundation, 1999); and Victoria J. Rideout, Ulla G. Foehr, and Donald F. Roberts, "Generation M[2]: Media in the Lives of 8- to 18-Year-Olds" (Menlo Park, CA: Kaiser Family Foundation, 2010).

66. Portes and Rumbaut, *Legacies*, 65.

67. Suro, "The Hispanic Family in Flux," 3.

68. Portes and Rumbaut, *Legacies*.

69. Oropesa and Landale, "The Future of Marriage and Hispanics."

70. Carol B. Stack, *All Our Kin: Strategies for Survival in a Black Community* (New York: Harper & Row, 1974).

71. Baca Zinn and Pok, "Tradition and Transition in Mexican-Origin Families"; and Landale and Oropesa, "Hispanic Families."

72. For a discussion of the historic contributions of the black church to family life, see E. Franklin Frazier, *The Negro Church in America* (New York: Schocken Books, 1974); and C. Eric Lincoln and

Lawrence H. Mamiya, *The Black Church in the African American Experience* (Durham, NC: Duke University Press, 1990). For a discussion of the historic contributions of the Catholic Church to Latino family life, see Allen Figueroa Deck, *The Second Wave: Hispanic Ministry and the Evangelization of Cultures* (New York: Paulist Press, 1989).

73. Anderson, *Code of the Street*, 38.

74. For a similar argument, see Edin and Kefalas, *Promises I Can Keep*.

75. See Sara McLanahan and Gary Sandefur, *Growing Up with a Single Parent* (Cambridge, MA: Harvard University Press, 1994); and W. Bradford Wilcox et al., *Why Marriage Matters, Third Edition: Thirty Conclusions from the Social Sciences* (New York: Institute for American Values, 2011).

76. David Popenoe, Jean Bethke Elshtain, and David Blankenhorn, *Promises to Keep: Decline and Renewal of Marriage in America* (Lanham, MD: Rowman & Littlefield, 1996).

77. Stevenson and Wolfers, "Marriage and Divorce."

78. Nicholas H. Wolfinger, *Understanding the Divorce Cycle: The Children of Divorce in Their Own Marriages* (New York: Cambridge University Press, 2005).

79. Daniel T. Lichter, Zhenchao Qian, and Leanna M. Mellott, "Marriage or Dissolution? Union Transitions among Poor Cohabiting Women," *Demography* 43 (2006): 223–240.

80. See W. Bradford Wilcox and John P. Bartkowski, "Devoted Dads: Religion, Class, and Fatherhood," in *Situated Fathering: A Focus on Physical and Social Spaces*, ed. William Marsiglio and Greer Fox (Lanham, MD: Rowman & Littlefield, 2005), 299–320; Jonathan Gruber, "Is Making Divorce Easier Bad for Children? The Long-Run Implications of Unilateral Divorce," *Journal of Labor Economics* 22 (2004): 799–833; and Raj Chetty et al., "The Economic Impacts of Tax Expenditures: Evidence from Spatial Variation across the U.S." (Cambridge, MA: Equality of Opportunity Project, 2013).

81. James A. Davis, Tom W. Smith, and Peter V. Marsden, *GSS 1972–2006 Cumulative Codebook on CD-ROM* (University of Connecticut: The Roper Center, 2006).

82. Robert M. Groves et al., "Plan and Operation of Cycle 6 of the National Survey of Family Growth," Vital and Health Statistics series 1, no. 42 (Hyattsville, MD: US Department of Health and Human Services, 2005).

83. Although American higher-education faculty are far more secular than Americans in general, the majority still believe in God. See Neil Gross and Solon Simmons, "The Religiosity of American College and University Professors," *Sociology of Religion* 70 (2009): 101–129.

84. The first two sets of figures are for adults aged 18 through 55 in the 2000–2012 General Social Survey (GSS). N = 2,096 (black), 1,396 (Latino). The congregations estimate is based on figures found in Mark Chaves, *Congregations in America* (Cambridge, MA: Harvard University Press, 2004), 24–25.

85. Jeffrey S. Passel and D'Vera Cohn, "U.S. Population Projections: 2005–2050" (Washington, DC: Pew Research Center, 2008).

Chapter 2

1. Anthony Paik, Edward O. Laumann, and Martha Van Haitsma, "Commitment, Jealousy, and the Quality of Life," in *The Sexual Organization of the City*, ed. Edward O. Laumann et al. (Chicago: University of Chicago Press, 2004), 194–225; Orlando Patterson, *Rituals of Blood: Consequences of Slavery in Two American Centuries* (New York: Basic Books, 1998); and Yoosik Youm and Anthony Paik, "The Sex Market and Its Implications for Family Formation," in *The Sexual Organization of the City*, ed. Edward O. Laumann et al. (Chicago: University of Chicago Press, 2004), 165–193. See also chapter 5 of this book.

2. Ten percent of blacks had used illegal drugs in the prior month, compared to 8 percent of whites and 6 percent of Hispanics. Twenty-six percent of Hispanics reported binge drinking, compared to 24 percent of whites and 20 percent of blacks. Substance Abuse and Mental Health Services Administration, *Results from the 2008 National Survey on Drug Use and Health: National Findings*, NSDUH Series H-36, HHS Publication No. SMA 09-4434 (Rockville, MD: Office of Applied Studies, US Department of Health and Human Services, 2009).

3. Ronald C. Kessley and Harold W. Neighbors, "A New Perspective on the Relationships among Race, Social Class, and Psychological Distress," *Journal of Health and Social Behavior* 27 (1986): 107–115; and James Alan Neff and Sue Keir Hoppe, "Race/Ethnicity, Acculturation, and Psychological Distress: Fatalism and Religiosity as Cultural Resources," *Journal of Community Psychology* 21 (1993): 3–20. For a contrary finding, see Stephanie A. Riolo et al., "Prevalence of Depression by Race/Ethnicity: Findings from the National Health and Nutrition Examination Survey III," *American Journal of Public Health* 95 (2005): 998–1000.

4. Bruce Western, Leonard M. Lopoo, and Sara McLanahan, "Incarceration and the Bonds between Parents in Fragile Families," in *Imprisoning America*, ed. Mary Patillo, David Weiman, and Bruce Western (New York: Russell Sage, 2004), 21–45.

5. William Julius Wilson, *When Work Disappears: The World of the New Urban Poor* (New York: Knopf, 1997); and Bureau of Labor Statistics, "Labor Force Statistics from the Current Population Survey" (Washington, DC: United States Department of Labor, 2015), http://www.bls.gov/cps/tables.htm.

6. Elijah Anderson, *Code of the Street: Decency, Violence, and the Moral Life of the Inner City* (New York: Norton, 1999).

7. Mary Pattillo-McCoy, *Black Picket Fences: Privilege and Peril among the Black Middle Class* (Chicago: University of Chicago Press, 1999).

8. See, for instance, Western, Lopoo, and McLanahan, "Incarceration and the Bonds between Parents in Fragile Families."

9. Anderson, *Code of the Street.* See also Omar M. McRoberts, *Streets of Glory: Church and Community in a Black Urban Neighborhood* (Chicago: University of Chicago Press, 2003), 97–99.

10. Émile Durkheim, *The Elementary Forms of Religious Life*, trans. Karen E. Fields (New York: Free Press, 1995), 419.

11. Western, Lopoo, and McLanahan, "Incarceration and the Bonds between Parents in Fragile Families"; and Liana C. Sayer et al., "She Left, He Left: How Employment and Satisfaction Affect Men's and Women's Decisions to Leave Marriages," *American Journal of Sociology* 116 (2011): 1982–2018.

12. Paul R. Amato and Stacy J. Rogers, "A Longitudinal Study of Marital Problems and Subsequent Divorce," *Journal of Marriage and Family* 59 (1997): 612–624.

13. Ibid.

14. Tavis Smiley and Cornel West, *The Rich and the Rest of Us: A Poverty Manifesto* (Carlsbad, CA: Hay House, 2012).

15. See, e.g., Larry L. Bumpass, Teresa Castro Martin, and James A. Sweet, "The Impact of Family Background and Early Marital Factors on Marital Disruption," *Journal of Family Issues* 12 (1991): 22–42.

16. On marriage and employment, Megan M. Sweeney, "Two Decades of Family Change: The Shifting Economic Foundations of Marriage," *American Sociological Review* 67 (2002): 132–147; Sayer et al., "She Left, He Left"; Alfred DeMaris et al., "Distal and Proximal Factors in Domestic Violence: A Test of an Integrated Model," *Journal of Marriage and Family* 65 (2003): 652–667; and Ann L. Coker et al., "Frequency and Correlates of Intimate Partner Violence by Type: Physical, Sexual, and Psychological Battering," *American Journal of Public Health* 90 (2000): 553–559.

17. Carmen DeNavas-Walt, Bernadette D. Proctor, and Jessica Smith, "Income, Poverty, and Health Insurance Coverage in the United States: 2012," *Current Population Reports* P60-245 (Washington, DC: US Census Bureau, 2013), fig. 1.

18. William Julius Wilson, *The Truly Disadvantaged: The Inner City, the Underclass, and Public Policy* (Chicago: University of Chicago Press, 1987).

19. See Bumpass et al., "The Impact of Family Background"; and Sweeney, "Two Decades of Family Change."

20. On the relative contributions of white and black wives to family income, Richard Fry and D'Vera Cohn, "Women, Men and the New Economics of Marriage" (Washington, DC: Pew Research Center, 2010).

21. Raul Hernandez-Coss, *Lessons from the U.S.–Mexico Remittances Corridor on Shifting from Informal to Formal Transfer Systems* (New York: World Bank, 2005).

22. Jeffrey Dew, "Has the Marital Time Cost of Parenting Changed over Time?" *Social Forces* 88 (2009): 519–541.

23. Jeffrey Dew, "The Gendered Meaning of Assets for Divorce," *Journal of Family and Economic Issues* 30 (2009): 20–31; and Sweeney, "Two Decades of Family Change."

24. Devah Pager, *Marked: Race, Crime, and Finding Work in an Era of Mass Incarceration* (Chicago: University of Chicago Press, 2007).

25. For a discussion of the impact of crime and incarceration on family life, Western, Lopoo, and McLanahan, "Incarceration and the Bonds between Parents in Fragile Families."

26. Michelle Alexander, *The New Jim Crow: Mass Incarceration in the Age of Colorblindness* (New York: New Press, 2012).

27. Travis Hirschi and Michael Gottfredson, "Age and the Explanation of Crime," *American Journal of Sociology* 89 (1983): 552–584.

28. Substance Abuse and Mental Health Services Administration 2009; and National Institute on Drug Abuse, "Epidemiologic Trends in Drug Abuse." Proceedings of the Community Epidemiology Work Group (Washington, DC: US Department of Health and Human Services, National Institutes of Health, 2008).

29. DeMaris et al., "Distal and Proximal Factors in Domestic Violence"; Coker et al., "Frequency and Correlates of Intimate Partner Violence by Type"; and Douglas A. Parker, Thomas C. Harford, and Irwin M. Rosenstock, "Alcohol, Other Drugs, and Sexual Risk-Taking among Young Adults," *Journal of Substance Abuse* 6 (1994): 87–93.

30. On husbands' employment and divorce, see Marianne Bertrand, Jessica Pan, and Emir Kamenica, "Gender Identity and Relative Income within Households," Working Paper 19023 (Cambridge, MA: National Bureau of Economic Research, 2013); and Hiromi Ono, "Husbands' and Wives' Resources and Marital Dissolution in the United States," *Journal of Marriage and Family* 60 (1998): 674–689.

31. GSS 2008, N = 1,358.

32. Amato and Rogers, "A Longitudinal Study of Marital Problems"; Kathryn Edin and Maria Kefalas, *Promises I Can Keep: Why Poor Women Put Motherhood before Marriage* (Berkeley: University of California Press, 2005); and Denise Previti and Paul R. Amato, "Is Infidelity a Cause or a Consequence of Poor Marital Quality?" *Journal of Social and Personal Relationships* 21 (2004): 217–230.

33. Youm and Paik, "The Sex Market and Its Implications for Family Formation."

34. Marcia J. Carlson and Frank F. Furstenberg, Jr., "The Prevalence and Correlates of Multipartnered Fertility among Urban U.S. Parents," *Journal of Marriage and Family* 68 (2006): 718–732.

35. Patterson, *Rituals of Blood*; and Stephen Ellingson, "Constructing Causal Stories and Moral Boundaries: Institutional Approaches to Sexual Problems," in *The Sexual Organization of the City*, ed. Edward O. Laumann, Stephen Ellingson, Jenna Mahay, Anthony Paik, and Yoosik Youm (Chicago: University of Chicago Press, 2004), 283–308.

36. Bureau of Labor Statistics, "Employment Projections" (Washington, DC: US Department of Labor, 2013). http://www.bls.gov/emp/ep_ chart_001.htm.

37. Lawrence Mishel and Jared Bernstein, "Declining Wages for High School and College Graduates: Pay and Benefits Trends by Education, Gender, Occupation, and State, 1979–1991" (Washington, DC: Economic Policy Institute, 1992).

38. Sarah Crissey, "Educational Attainment in the United States: 2007," Current Population Reports P20-560 (Washington, DC: US Census Bureau, 2009).

39. Devah Pager and Hana Shepherd, "The Sociology of Discrimination: Racial Discrimination in Employment, Housing, Credit, and Consumer Markets," *Annual Review of Sociology* 34 (2008): 181–209.

40. Francisco L. Rivera-Batiz, "Undocumented Workers in the Labor Market: An Analysis of the Earnings of Legal and Illegal Mexican Immigrants in the United States," *Journal of Population Economics* 12 (1999): 91–116.

41. Recent research provides evidence that media consumption can indeed affect sexual behavior. Economists Melissa Kearney and Phillip Levine attribute a substantial portion of the recent decline in the teen birth rate to the popular MTV reality television franchise *16 and Pregnant*. See Melissa S. Kearney and Phillip B. Levine, "Media Influences on Social Outcomes: The Impact of MTV's *16 and Pregnant* on Teen Childbearing," Working Paper 19795 (Cambridge, MA: National Bureau of Economic Research, 2014). This research came to our attention via

Nicholas Kristof, "TV Lowers Birthrate (Seriously)," *New York Times*, March 19, 2014.

42. Victoria J. Rideout, Ulla G. Foehr, and Donald F. Roberts, "Generation M^2: Media in the Lives of 8- to 18-Year-Olds" (Menlo Park, CA: Kaiser Family Foundation, 2010), 5.

43. Patterson, *Rituals of Blood*, 251.

44. Ibid., 277.

45. Travis L. Dixon and Daniel Linz, "Overrepresentation and Underrepresentation of African Americans and Latinos as Lawbreakers on Television News," *Journal of Communication* 50 (2000): 131–154; and Dana E. Mastro and Amanda L. Robinson, "Cops and Crooks: Images of Minorities on Primetime Television," *Journal of Criminal Justice* 28 (2000): 385–396.

46. John Yinger, "Evidence on Discrimination in Consumer Markets," *Journal of Economic Perspectives* 12 (1998): 23–40; and Pager and Shepherd, "The Sociology of Discrimination."

47. Nancy Krieger et al., "Experiences of Discrimination: Validity and Reliability of a Self-Report Measure for Population Health Research on Racism and Health," *Social Science and Medicine* 61 (2005): 1576–1596; Brenda Major and Laurie T. O'Brien, "The Social Psychology of Stigma," *Annual Review of Psychology* 56 (2005): 393–421; and Vickie M. Mays, Susan D. Cochran, and Namdi W. Barnes, "Race, Race-Based Discrimination, and Health Outcomes among African Americans," *Annual Review of Psychology* 58 (2007): 201–225.

48. David R. Williams and Selina A. Mohammed, "Discrimination and Racial Disparities in Health: Evidence and Needed Research," *Journal of Behavioral Medicine* 32 (2008): 20–47.

49. Peter M. Blau and Otis Dudley Duncan, *The American Occupational Structure* (New York: Wiley, 1967).

50. Sara S. McLanahan and Gary Sandefur, *Growing up with a Single Parent: What Helps, What Hurts* (Cambridge, MA: Harvard University Press, 1994).

51. Nicholas H. Wolfinger, *Understanding the Divorce Cycle: The Children of Divorce in Their Own Marriages* (New York: Cambridge University Press, 2005).

52. Wilson, *The Truly Disadvantaged*; and Anderson, *Code of the Street*.

53. Patterson, *Rituals of Blood*.

54. Mary Pattillo-McCoy, *Black Picket Fences: Privilege and Peril among the Black Middle Class* (Chicago: University of Chicago Press, 1999).

55. Elizabeth E. Brusco, *The Reformation of Machismo: Evangelical Conversion and Gender in Colombia* (Austin: University of Texas Press, 1995); Jenny Rivera, "Domestic Violence against Latinas by Latino Males: An

Analysis of Race, National Origin, and Gender Differentials," *Boston College Third World Law Journal* 14 (1994): 231–257; and Glenda Kaufman Kantor, "Alcohol and Spouse Abuse: Ethnic Differences," in *Alcohol and Violence*, vol. 13 of *Recent Developments in Alcoholism*, ed. Marc Galanter (New York: Plenum, 1983), 57–79.

56. Raul Caetano, "Alcohol Use and Depression among U.S. Hispanics," *British Journal of Addiction* 82 (1987): 1245–1251; Jessica N. Cleck and Julie A. Blendy, "Making a Bad Thing Worse: Adverse Effects of Stress on Drug Addiction," *Journal of Clinical Investigation* 118 (2008): 454–461; and Sonja E. Siennick, "The Timing and Mechanisms of the Offending-Depression Link," *Criminology* 45 (2007): 583–615.

57. Guy Bodenmann, "The Influence of Stress and Coping on Close Relationships: A Two-Year Longitudinal Study," *Swiss Journal of Psychology* 56 (1997): 156–164; Linda B. Story and Thomas N. Bradbury, "Understanding Marriage and Stress: Essential Questions and Challenges," *Clinical Psychology Review* 23 (2004): 1139–1162; and Carol B. Cunradi et al., "Problem Drinking, Unemployment, and Intimate Partner Violence among a Sample of Construction Industry Workers and Their Partners," *Journal of Family Violence* 24 (2009): 63–74.

58. See, for instance, Christopher G. Ellison and Robert Joseph Taylor, "Turning to Prayer: Social and Situational Antecedents of Religious Coping among African Americans," *Review of Religious Research* 38 (1996): 111–131.

59. For a discussion of the link between stress and substance abuse, Jean E. Rhodes and Leonard A. Jason, "A Social Stress Model of Substance Abuse," *Journal of Consulting and Clinical Psychology* 58 (1990): 395–401. For a discussion of the link between stress and risky behavior, Kathryn E. Mazzaferro et al., "Depression, Stress, and Social Support as Predictors of High-Risk Sexual Behaviors and STIs in Young Women," *Journal of Adolescent Health* 39 (2006): 601–603.

60. Robert A. Hummer et al., "Religious Involvement and U.S. Adult Mortality," *Demography* 36 (1999): 273–285. See also Loren Marks et al., "Religion and Health among African Americans: A Qualitative Examination," *Research on Aging* 27 (2005): 447–474.

61. We are not the first to observe this. See, for instance, Vaughn R. A. Call and Tim B. Heaton, "Religious Influence on Marital Stability," *Journal for the Scientific Study of Religion* 36 (1997): 382–392.

62. Sociologists Paul Amato and Stacy Rogers also found that church attendance reduced substance abuse. Amato and Rogers, "A Longitudinal Study of Marital Problems."

63. Others have reported this finding. See, for instance, David C. Atkins and Deborah E. Kessel, "Religiousness and Infidelity: Attendance, but

not Faith and Prayer, Predict Marital Fidelity," *Journal of Marriage and Family* 70 (2008): 407–418.

64. Adultery is both a cause and a consequence of a bad marriage. Previti and Amato, "Is Infidelity a Cause or a Consequence of Poor Marital Quality?"

65. Amy M. Burdette et al., "Are There Religious Variations in Marital Infidelity?" *Journal of Family Issues* 28 (2007): 1553–1581.

66. Kathleen T. Brady and Susan C. Sonne, "The Role of Stress in Alcohol Use, Alcoholism Treatment, and Relapse," *Alcohol Research and Health* 23 (1999): 263–271; Elizabeth S. Allen et al., "Premarital Precursors of Marital Infidelity," *Family Process* 47 (2008): 243–259; and Lisa Gorman and Adrian Blow, "Concurrent Depression and Infidelity: Background, Strategies for Treatment, and Future Research," *Journal of Couple and Relationship Therapy* 7 (2008): 39–58.

67. Christopher G. Ellison and Jeffrey S. Levin, "The Religion–Health Connection: Evidence, Theory, and Future Directions," *Heath Education and Behavior* 25 (1998): 700–720.

68. See, for instance, David G. Myers, "Religion and Human Flourishing," in *The Science of Subjective Well-Being*, ed. Michael Eid and Randy J. Larsen (New York: Guilford, 2008), 323–375; and Ellison and Levin, "The Religion–Health Connection."

Chapter 3

1. Divorce runs in families. Nicholas H. Wolfinger, *Understanding the Divorce Cycle: The Children of Divorce in Their Own Marriages* (New York: Cambridge University Press, 2005).

2. Sheela Kennedy and Larry Bumpass, "Cohabitation and Trends in the Structure and Stability of Children's Family Lives," Paper presented at the annual meeting of the Population Association of America, Washington, DC, 2011; and W. Bradford Wilcox et al., *Why Marriage Matters, Third Edition* (New York: Institute for American Values, 2011).

3. Paul R. Amato, "The Impact of Family Formation Change on the Cognitive, Social, and Emotional Well-Being of the Next Generation," *The Future of Children* 15 (2005): 75–96; Sara McLanahan and Gary Sandefur, *Growing Up with a Single Parent: What Helps, What Hurts* (Cambridge, MA: Harvard University Press, 1994); Cynthia Osborn and Sara McLanahan, "Partnership Instability and Child Well-Being," *Journal of Marriage and Family* 69 (2010): 1065–1083; and Jane Waldfogel, Terry-Ann Craigie, and Jeanne Brooks-Gunn, "Fragile Families and Child Wellbeing," *The Future of Children* 20 (2010): 87–112.

4. Daniel T. Lichter, Deborah Roempke Graefe, and J. Brian Brown, "Is Marriage a Panacea? Union Formation among Economically Disadvantaged Unwed Mothers," *Social Problems* 50 (2003): 60–86; and Dawn M. Upchurch, Lee A. Lillard, and Constantijn W. A. Panis, "The Impact of Nonmarital Childbearing on Subsequent Marital Formation and Dissolution," in *Out of Wedlock: Causes and Consequences of Nonmarital Fertility*, ed. L. L. Wu and B. Wolfe (New York: Russell Sage, 2001), 344–380.

5. These results are calculated from life tables based on weighted NSFG 2006–2010 data. Time-to-marriage N = 6,156 (whites), 2,412 (blacks), 2,722 (Latinos). Time-to-premarital birth N = 6,128 (whites), 2,411 (blacks), 2,715 (Latinos). For more on this trend, Julia Arroyo, Krista K. Payne, Susan L. Brown, and Wendy D. Manning, "Crossover in Median Age at First Marriage and First Birth: Thirty Years of Change," *National Center for Family & Marriage Research*, FP-13-06 (2013).

6. On changing motivations for marriage, Andrew J. Cherlin, *The Marriage-Go-Round: The State of Marriage and the Family in America Today* (New York: Vintage, 2009); Stephanie Coontz, *Marriage, a History: From Obedience to Intimacy, or How Love Conquered Marriage* (New York: Viking, 2005); and Steven Mintz and Susan Kellogg, *Domestic Revolutions: A Social History of American Family Life* (New York: Free Press, 1988).

7. Daniel Schneider, "Wealth and the Marital Divide," *American Journal of Sociology* 117 (2011): 627–667.

8. William Julius Wilson, *When Work Disappears: The World of the New Urban Poor* (New York: Knopf, 1997).

9. Lawrence L. Wu, "Effects of Family Instability, Income, and Income Instability on the Risk of a Premarital Birth," *American Sociological Review* 61 (1996): 386–406.

10. Kathryn Edin and Maria Kefalas, *Promises I Can Keep: Why Poor Women Put Motherhood before Marriage* (Berkeley: University of California Press, 2005); and Arline T. Geronimus, "Teenage Childbearing and Social and Reproductive Disadvantage: The Evolution of Complex Questions and the Demise of Simple Answers," *Family Relations* 40 (1991): 463–471.

11. Heather Mac Donald, "Hispanic Family Values?" *City Journal* (Autumn 2006).

12. Edin and Kefalas, *Promises I Can Keep*, 32.

13. National Longitudinal Study of Adolescent to Adult Health (Add Health), Wave II. N = 3,089 (white women), 1,263 (black women), 919 (Latina women); weighted.

14. Previous research demonstrates a strong correlation between nonintact parenting and the likelihood of a nonmarital birth. Lawrence L. Wu,

"Effects of Family Instability, Income, and Income Instability on the Risk of a Premarital Birth," *American Sociological Review* 61 (1996): 386–406; and Lawrence L. Wu and Brian C. Martinson, "Family Structure and the Risk of a Premarital Birth," *American Sociological Review* 58 (1993): 210–232. Moreover, growing up in a nonintact family affects one's own attitudes toward family formation. William G. Axinn and Arland Thornton, "The Influence of Parents' Marital Dissolutions on Children's Attitudes Toward Family Formation," *Demography* 33 (1996): 66–81.

15. Add Health, Wave 1. N = 10,450 (white), 4,453 (African American), 3,516 (Latino). Results are weighted and refer to adults aged 24 through 32 in 2008.

16. Noreen Goldman and Anne Pebley, "Legalization of Consensual Unions in Latin America," *Biodemography and Social Biology* 28 (1981): 49–61.

17. Traditionalism in Latino family behavior appears to weaken with acculturation into American society. Frank D. Bean, Ruth R. Berg, and Jennifer V. W. Van Hook, "Socioeconomic and Cultural Incorporation and Marital Disruption among Mexican Americans," *Social Forces* 75 (1996): 593–617; and Nancy S. Landale and Nimfa B. Ogena, "Migration and Union Dissolution among Puerto Rican Women," *International Migration Review* 29 (1995): 671–692.

18. Lawrence B. Finer and Stanley K. Henshaw, "Disparities in Rates of Unintended Pregnancy in the United States, 1994 and 2001," *Perspectives on Sexual and Reproductive Health* 38 (2006): 90–96.

19. This analysis is based on the first four waves of the Add Health survey. Add Health has a variety of measures of culture, including guilt about premarital sex, whether respondent would be happy to have a baby, whether respondent would be embarrassed by a pregnancy, whether respondent thinks it is OK to have a child out of wedlock, whether respondent consumed thirty or more hours of media per week, whether s/he used birth control the last time s/he had sex, the number of sex partners s/he has had, and family structure of origin. N = 8,552 (men), 9,258 (women). Standard errors are adjusted for survey-design effects. See the appendix for more information about this analysis, as well as a comparison of the relative strengths of NLSY97 and Add Health for studying nonmarital fertility. Finally, we estimated models that accounted for both structural and cultural factors. Each, it seems, has a unique effect on the chances of a premarital birth.

20. We conducted a similar analysis using NLSY97 (N = 4,310 for men and 4,040 for women). Although the structure of the data is arguably stronger than it is for Add Health—thirteen annual waves of data for NLSY97, four waves of data spread over approximately thirteen

years for Add Health—NLSY measures of culture are limited to family structure of origin, premarital cohabitation, use of birth control, and number of sexual partners (except for family structure, these are all time-varying independent variables). The results are roughly similar across data sets. Using NLSY97, adjusting for cultural differences has a noteworthy effect—albeit slightly smaller than for Add Health—on African American rates of nonmarital birth. Consistent with Add Health, NLSY97 shows that the effects of cultural differences are modest for Latinos. Finally, we ran models that included both the culture and the structural measures. These indicated that each set of variables has a unique effect on premarital fertility. The data are ambiguous as to which is most important overall.

21. Among Latinos, evangelicals and Pentecostals have substantially more conservative attitudes regarding the family than do Catholics. Christopher G. Ellison, Nicholas H. Wolfinger, and Aida I. Ramos-Wada, "Attitudes toward Marriage, Divorce, Cohabitation, and Casual Sex among Working-Age Latinos: Does Religion Matter?" *Journal of Family Issues* 34 (2013): 295–322.

22. On Latino familism, William A. Vega, "Hispanic Families in the 1980s: A Decade of Research," *Journal of Marriage and Family* 52 (1990): 1015–1024; and Norma Williams, *The Mexican American Family: Tradition and Change* (New York: General Hall, 1990).

23. W. Bradford Wilcox and Nicholas H. Wolfinger, "Living and Loving 'Decent': Religion and Relationship Quality among Urban Parents," *Social Science Research* 37 (2008): 828–843.

Chapter 4

1. Previous research notes a connection between parental divorce and attitudes toward marriage. William G. Axinn and Arland Thornton, "The Influence of Parents' Marital Dissolutions on Children's Attitudes toward Family Formation," *Demography* 33 (1996): 66–81.

2. According to a 2010 report by the Pew Research Center, fully 88 percent of black respondents (compared with 62 percent of whites and 77 percent of Hispanics) say that in order to be ready for marriage, a man must be able to support a family financially. Likewise, 50 percent of black respondents (compared with 47 percent of Hispanics and 28 percent of whites) say that a woman must be able to support a family financially in order to be ready for marriage. Pew Research Center, "The Decline of Marriage and Rise of New Families" (Washington, DC: Pew Research Center, 2010).

3. W. Bradford Wilcox and Nicholas H. Wolfinger, "Then Comes Marriage? Religion and Marriage in Urban America," *Social Science Research* 36 (2007): 569–589; and W. Bradford Wilcox and Nicholas H. Wolfinger, "Living and Loving 'Decent': Religion and Relationship Quality among Urban Parents," *Social Science Research* 37 (2008): 828–843.

4. Linda Waite and Maggie Gallagher, *The Case for Marriage* (New York: Doubleday, 2000); and W. Bradford Wilcox et al., *Why Marriage Matters, Third Edition: Thirty Conclusions from the Social Sciences* (New York: Institute for American Values, 2011).

5. For blacks, Lorraine Blackman et al., *The Consequences of Marriage for African Americans: A Comprehensive Literature Review* (New York: Institute for American Values, 2005). For Latinos, Wilcox et al., *Why Marriage Matters*, 32. For both blacks and Latinos, Robert I. Lerman and W. Bradford Wilcox, *For Richer, for Poorer: How Family Structures Economic Success in America* (Washington, DC: AEI and Institute for Family Studies, 2014).

6. Waite and Gallagher, *The Case for Marriage*.

7. On intentions to marry, our analysis of the National Survey of Family Growth (NSFG). Fifty-six percent of African Americans (N = 4,157) and 68 percent of Latinos (N = 5,124) agree that it is better to get married than to stay single. See also Arland Thornton and Linda Young-DeMarco, "Four Decades of Trends in Attitudes toward Family Issues in the United States: The 1960s through the 1990s," *Journal of Marriage and Family* 63 (2001): 1009–1037.

8. Blackman et al., *Consequences of Marriage*; and Wilcox et al., *Why Marriage Matters*.

9. D'Vera Cohn, Jeffrey S. Passel, Wendy Wang, and Gretchen Livingston, "Barely Half of U.S. Adults Are Married—A Record Low" (Washington, DC: Pew Research Center, 2011); and Elizabeth Marquardt et al., "The President's Marriage Agenda for the Forgotten Sixty Percent," in *The State of Our Unions 2012* (Charlottesville, VA: National Marriage Project and Institute for American Values, 2012), fig. 2.

10. W. Bradford Wilcox, Elizabeth Marquardt, David Popenoe, and Barbara Dafoe Whitehead, *The State of Our Unions 2011* (Charlottesville, VA: Institute for American Values and the National Marriage Project, 2011), fig. 3.

11. Joyce A. Martin et al., "Births: Final Data for 2009," National Vital Statistics Reports 60(1) (Hyattsville, MD: National Center for Health Statistics, 2011), table C.

12. On nonmarital fertility among blacks and Latinos, see Martin et al., "Births: Final Data for 2009," table 15. On nonmarital fertility and poverty, see Matthew McKeever and Nicholas H. Wolfinger, "Thanks

for Nothing: Income and Labor Force Participation for Never-Married Mothers since 1982," *Social Science Research* 40 (2011): 63–76; and Matthew McKeever and Nicholas H. Wolfinger, "Over the Long Haul: The Persistent Economic Consequences of Single Motherhood," in *Economic Stress and the Family*, ed. S. L. Blair (Bingley, UK: Emerald, 2012), 1–39. On nonmarital fertility and subsequent marriage rates, see Daniel T. Lichter and Deborah Roempke Graefe, "Finding a Mate? The Marital and Cohabitation Histories of Unwed Mothers," in *Out of Wedlock: Causes and Consequences of Nonmarital Fertility*, ed. Lawrence L. Wu and Barbara Wolfe (New York: Russell Sage, 2001), 317–343; Daniel T. Lichter, Deborah Roempke Graefe, and J. Brian Brown, "Is Marriage a Panacea? Union Formation among Economically Disadvantaged Unwed Mothers," *Social Problems* 50 (2003): 60–86; and Dawn M. Upchurch, Lee A. Lillard, and Constantijn W. A. Panis, "The Impact of Nonmarital Childbearing on Subsequent Marital Formation and Dissolution," in *Out of Wedlock: Causes and Consequences of Nonmarital Fertility*, ed. Lawrence L. Wu and Barbara Wolfe (New York: Russell Sage, 2001), 344–380.

13. Diana B. Elliott et al., "Historical Marriage Trends from 1890–2010: A Focus on Race Differences," Paper presented at the annual meeting of the Population Association of America, San Francisco, CA, SEHSD Working Paper 2012-12 (2012). http://www.Census.gov. See also Heather Koball, "Have African American Men Become Less Committed to Marriage? Explaining the Twentieth Century Racial Cross-over in Men's Marriage Timing," *Demography* 35 (1998): 251–258.

14. Institute for American Values and the National Marriage Project, "Social Indicators of Marital Health and Well-Being," in *The State of our Unions 2012* (Charlottesville, VA: National Marriage Project and Institute for American Values, 2012), 70, fig. 5.

15. Source: NSFG 2006–2010. N = 1,753 (whites), 597 (blacks), 543 (Latinos). Results are weighted.

16. Cohn et al., "Barely Half of U.S. Adults Are Married"; and Institute for American Values and the National Marriage Project, "Social Indicators of Marital Health and Well-Being," 65, fig. 2.

17. Joshua R. Goldstein and Catherine T. Kenney, "Marriage Delayed or Marriage Forgone? New Cohort Forecasts of First Marriage for U.S. Women," *American Sociological Review* 66 (2001): 506–519. Estimates for Latinos are not available.

18. Calculations based on the NSFG 2006–2010.

19. Sara S. McLanahan and Gary Sandefur, *Growing Up with a Single Parent: What Helps, What Hurts* (Cambridge, MA: Harvard University Press, 1994). On the adverse consequences of a high-conflict marriage

for children, Paul R. Amato, Laura Spencer Loomis, and Alan Booth, "Parental Divorce, Marital Conflict, and Offspring Well-Being during Early Adulthood," *Social Forces* 73 (1995): 895–915.

20. Liberals: perhaps the most notable example is William Julius Wilson, *The Truly Disadvantaged: The Inner City, the Underclass, and Public Policy* (Chicago: University of Chicago Press, 1987). Conservatives: Maggie Gallagher, *The Abolition of Marriage: How We Destroy Lasting Love* (Washington, DC: Regnery Publishing, 1996); Charles Murray, *Losing Ground: American Social Policy, 1950–1980* (New York: Basic Books, 1984); and Lawrence Mead, *The New Politics of Poverty: The Nonworking Poor in America* (New York: Basic Books, 1993).

21. For recent data on the black–white marriage gap, see Bart Stykes, Krista K. Payne, and Larry Gibbs, "First Marriage Rate in the U.S., 2012," FP-14-08 (Bowling Green, OH: National Center for Family & Marriage Research, 2014).

22. Christina M. Gibson-Davis, "Expectations and the Economic Bar to Marriage among Low-Income Couples," in *Unmarried Couples with Children*, ed. Paula England and Kathryn Edin (New York: Russell Sage, 2007), 84–103.

23. Rebecca Mead, *One Perfect Day: The Selling of the American Wedding* (New York: Penguin, 2007), 24.

24. Kathryn Edin and Maria Kefalas, *Promises I Can Keep: Why Poor Women Put Motherhood before Marriage* (Berkeley: University of California Press, 2005).

25. On the skyrocketing growth in incarceration for black men, see Robert Perkinson, *Texas Tough: The Rise of America's Prison Empire* (New York: Picador, 2010). On the consequences of the criminal justice system for black men's employment, see Devah Pager, *Marked: Race, Crime, and Finding Work in an Era of Mass Incarceration* (Chicago: University of Chicago Press, 2007). On discrimination, see Joe R. Feagin and Melvin P. Sikes, *Living with Racism: The Black Middle-Class Experience* (Boston, MA: Beacon, 1995). On the deleterious consequences of discrimination for intimate relationships, see Velma McBride Murry et al., "Racial Discrimination as a Moderator of the Links among Stress, Maternal Psychological Functioning, and Family Relationships," *Journal of Marriage and Family* 63 (2001): 915–926.

26. US Census Bureau, *Current Population Survey*, March Demographic Supplement (2010). N = 10,671. These figures exclude multiracial individuals.

27. On the labor force argument, see Wilson, *The Truly Disadvantaged*. On the effects of racial disparities in imprisonment, see Bruce Western, *Punishment and Inequality in America* (New York: Russell Sage, 2006).

Note that black men generally marry black women. Vincent Kang Fu and Nicholas H. Wolfinger, "Broken Boundaries or Broken Marriages? Racial Intermarriage and Divorce," *Social Science Quarterly* 92 (2011): 1096–1117.

28. Robert D. Mare and Christopher Winship, "Socioeconomic Change and the Decline of Marriage for Blacks and Whites," in *The Urban Underclass*, ed. Christopher Jencks and Paul E. Peterson (Washington, DC: Brookings, 1991), 175–196.

29. Wilson, *The Truly Disadvantaged*. Another study shows that marriage rates decrease with the supply of marriageable men. Daniel T. Lichter et al., "Race and the Retreat from Marriage: A Shortage of Marriageable Men?" *American Sociological Review* 57 (1992): 781–799.

30. Wilson, *The Truly Disadvantaged*.

31. Mare and Winship, "Socioeconomic Change"; and Lichter et al., "Race and the Retreat from Marriage."

32. On racial/ethnic homogamy, see Fu and Wolfinger, "Broken Boundaries or Broken Marriages?"

33. This has long been the case. For marriage, see Neil G. Bennett, David E. Bloom, and Patricia H. Craig, "The Divergence of Black and White Marriage Patterns," *American Journal of Sociology* 95 (1989): 692–722. For divorce, see Steven Ruggles, "The Rise of Divorce and Separation in the United States, 1880–1990," *Demography* 34 (1997): 455–466.

34. NSRFL. N = 89 (white men), 125 (white women), 112 (black men), 291 (black women), 100 (Latino men), 171 (Latina women). The answers pertain to single men in general, and to boyfriends.

35. NSFG 2006–2010. N = 11,423 (white), 4,157 (black), 5,125 (Latino). Results are weighted.

36. Conservative observers have also made this point. See James Q. Wilson, "Why We Don't Marry," *City Journal* 12 (Winter 2002).

37. David E. Hayes-Bautista, *La Nueva California: Latinos in the Golden State* (Berkeley: University of California Press, 2004), 4.

38. R. S. Oropesa and Nancy S. Landale, "The Future of Marriage and Hispanics," *Journal of Marriage and Family* 66 (2004): 901–920.

39. Ibid. See also Nancy S. Landale and R. S. Oropesa, "Hispanic Families: Stability and Change," *Annual Review of Sociology* 33 (2007): 381–405. Moreover, foreign-born Latinos are disproportionately likely to marry their live-in partners and disproportionately less likely to dissolve their cohabiting relationships. Casey E. Copen, Kimberly Daniels, and William D. Mosher, "First Premarital Cohabitation in the United States: 2006–2010 National Survey of Family Growth," National Health Statistics Reports 64 (Hyattsville, MD: National Center for Health Statistics, 2013), table 3.

40. NSFG 2006–2010. N = 1,536 (white), 356 (black), 803 (Latino). Results are weighted.

41. Oropesa and Landale, "The Future of Marriage and Hispanics."

42. Pierette Hondagneu-Sotelo, *Domestica: Immigrant Workers Cleaning and Caring in the Shadows of Affluence* (Berkeley: University of California Press, 2001).

43. Roberto Suro, "The Hispanic Family in Flux" (Washington, DC: Center on Children & Families, Brookings Institution, 2007), 3.

44. Christopher G. Ellison, Nicholas H. Wolfinger, and Aida I. Ramos-Wada, "Attitudes toward Marriage, Divorce, Cohabitation, and Casual Sex among Working-Age Latinos: Does Religion Matter?" *Journal of Family Issues* 34 (2013): 295–322.

45. On the messages of contemporary religion, Nancy Ammerman, "Golden-Rule Christianity," in *Lived Religion in America: Toward a History of Practice*, ed. David D. Hall (Princeton, NJ: Princeton University Press, 1997), 196–216. On happy relationships, see Nicholas H. Wolfinger and W. Bradford Wilcox, "Happily Ever After? Religion, Marital Status, Gender, and Relationship Quality in Urban Families," *Social Forces* 86 (2008): 1311–1337.

46. Economic factors are income, education, employment, and employment history. Cultural variables are family structure of origin, sexual history, contraceptive use, cohabitation, and premarital fertility. The code of decency includes substance use (alcohol, marijuana, or hard drugs) and arrest history. More information about this analysis appears in the conclusion.

47. Wilcox and Wolfinger, "Then Comes Marriage?" None of the data sets analyzed for this book allow us to examine the religious participation of both romantic partners prior to marriage.

48. Most of the extant research on the paradox has been medical. See, for instance, Kyriakos S. Markides and Karl Eschbach, 2005. "Aging, Migration, and Mortality: Current Status of Research on the Hispanic Paradox," *Journals of Gerontology*, series 1, 60 (2005): S68–S75.

49. Nicholas H. Wolfinger, W. Bradford Wilcox, and Edwin I. Hernández, "Bendito Amor ('Blessed Love'): Religion and Relationships among Married and Unmarried Latinos in Urban America," *Journal of Latino-Latin American Studies* 3 (2010): 171–188.

Chapter 5

1. On African American religiosity, see our analysis of the 2000–2012 General Social Survey (GSS). Forty percent of African Americans

attend church several times a month or more (N = 2,716), compared
to 30 percent of whites (N = 13,729) and 31 percent of Latinos (N =
1,609). On union quality and stability, see Lorraine Blackman et al.,
*The Consequences of Marriage for African Americans: A Comprehensive
Literature Review* (New York: Institute for American Values, 2005). For
an overview of the paradox, see W. Bradford Wilcox and Nicholas H.
Wolfinger, "Then Comes Marriage? Religion and Marriage in Urban
America," *Social Science Research* 36 (2007): 569–589. On infidelity, see
the data presented later in this chapter.

2. Margaret L. Vaaler, Christopher G. Ellison, and Dan A. Powers,
"Religious Influences on the Risk of Marital Dissolution," *Journal
of Marriage and Family* 71 (2009): 917–934; W. Bradford Wilcox and
Nicholas H. Wolfinger, "Living and Loving 'Decent': Religion and
Relationship Quality among Urban Parents," *Social Science Research* 37
(2008): 828–843; and Nicholas H. Wolfinger and W. Bradford Wilcox,
"Happily Ever After? Religion, Marital Status, Gender, and Relationship
Quality in Urban Families," *Social Forces* 86 (2008): 1311–1337.

3. For recent data, see Casey E. Copen et al., "First Marriages in the
United States: Data from the 2006–2010 National Survey of Family
Growth," National Health Statistics Reports 49 (Hyattsville, MD:
National Center for Health Statistics, 2012).

4. Roberto Suro, "The Hispanic Family in Flux" (Washington, DC: Center
on Children & Families, Brookings Institution, 2007). This is also true
for Latino cohabiting relationships. Casey E. Copen, Kimberly Daniels,
and William D. Mosher, "First Premarital Cohabitation in the United
States: 2006–2010 National Survey of Family Growth," National
Health Statistics Reports 64 (Hyattsville, MD: National Center for
Health Statistics, 2013), table 3.

5. Maxine Baca Zinn and Angela Y. H. Pok, "Tradition and Transition
in Mexican-Origin Families," in *Minority Families in the United
States: A Multicultural Perspective*, ed. Ronald L. Taylor (Upper Saddle
River, NJ: Pearson, 2002), 79–100; R. S. Oropesa, "Normative Beliefs
about Marriage and Cohabitation: A Comparison of Non-Latino
Whites, Mexican Americans, and Puerto Ricans," *Journal of Marriage
and Family* 58 (1996): 49–62; R. S. Oropesa and Nancy S. Landale, "The
Future of Marriage and Hispanics," *Journal of Marriage and Family* 66
(2004): 901–920.

6. Zinn and Pok, "Tradition and Transition in Mexican-Origin Families";
A. Ginorio et al., "The Psychology of Latinas," in *Feminist Perspectives
on the Psychology of Women*, ed. C. Travis (Washington, DC: American
Psychological Association, 1995); and Vonnie C. McLoyd et al.,
"Marital Processes and Parental Socialization in Families of

Color: A Decade Review and Research," *Journal of Marriage and Family* 62 (2000):1070–1093. As discussed in chapter 2, an altogether different strain of machismo may produce benefits for marriages.

7. Wolfinger and Wilcox, "Happily Ever After?"

8. Amy M. Burdette, Stacy H. Haynes, and Christopher G. Ellison, "Religion, Race/Ethnicity, and Perceived Barriers to Marriage among Working-Age Adults," *Sociology of Religion* 73 (2012): 429–451.

9. Paul R. Amato and Alan Booth, *A Generation at Risk: Growing Up in an Era of Family Upheaval* (Cambridge, MA: Harvard University Press, 1997); Lorraine Blackman et al., *The Consequences of Marriage for African Americans: A Comprehensive Literature Review* (New York: Institute for American Values, 2005); Janice Kielcolt-Glaser and Tamara L. Newton, "Marriage and Health: His and Hers," *Psychological Bulletin* 127 (2001): 472–503; and W. Bradford Wilcox et al., *Why Marriage Matters, Third Edition: Thirty Conclusions from the Social Sciences* (New York: Institute for American Values, 2011).

10. Susan L. Brown and Alan Booth, "Cohabitation versus Marriage: A Comparison of Relationship Quality," *Journal of Marriage and Family* 58 (1995): 668–678; Steven L. Nock, "A Comparison of Marriages and Cohabiting Relationships," *Journal of Family Issues* 16 (1995): 53–76; and Linda J. Waite and Maggie Gallagher, *The Case for Marriage: Why Married People are Happier, Healthier, and Better off Financially* (New York: Doubleday, 2000).

11. Copen et al., "First Marriages in the United States"; R. Kelly Raley and Larry Bumpass, "The Topography of the Divorce Plateau: Levels and Trends in Union Stability in the United States after 1980," *Demographic Research* 8 (2003): 245–260; and Vincent Kang Fu and Nicholas H. Wolfinger, "Broken Boundaries or Broken Marriages? Racial Intermarriage and Divorce," *Social Science Quarterly* 92 (2011): 1096–1117. The story is different for cohabitation dissolution. Whites and blacks have similar dissolution rates, but Latino cohabiting unions dissolve at a far lower rate. Copen, Daniels, and Mosher, "First Premarital Cohabitation in the United States," table 3.

12. This finding may be an artifact of measurement error in marital quality. Nonmarital fertility and marriage are "hard" variables, while marital quality is subject to more variable interpretation by survey respondents.

13. These findings are based on a regression standardization of a logistic regression. Data are from the NSRFL (N = 1,385). Data are weighted. Standard errors are adjusted for survey design effects. Only respondents in married or cohabiting unions are included. Differences between whites and Latinos are not statistically significant.

All estimates control for region, age, sex, marital status, and the presence of children. Economic variables include income, education, and a measure of job stress. Cultural variables include belief that respondents will never leave their partner no matter how difficult the relationship becomes, the acceptability of divorce in a loveless marriage, the belief that marriage is an unbreakable vow before God, and a dichotomous item measuring whether a respondent has ever been divorced (family structure of origin is not available in the NSRFL). Relationship-related variables include a dichotomous variable measuring whether a respondent or his/her partner has ever been sexually unfaithful, and scales measuring the presence of affection, criticism, and generosity within the relationship.

14. Paul R. Amato and Stacey J. Rogers, "Do Attitudes toward Divorce Affect Relationship Quality?" *Journal of Family Issues* 20 (1999): 69–86; and W. Bradford Wilcox and Elizabeth Marquardt, *When Baby Makes Three* (Charlottesville, VA: National Marriage Project/Institute for American Values, 2011).

15. Joshua R. Goldstein, "The Leveling of Divorce in the United States," *Demography* 36 (1999): 409–414.

16. On the impact of racial segregation on African American social life, see Patrick Sharkey, *Stuck in Place: Urban Neighborhoods and the End of Progress toward Racial Equality* (Chicago: University of Chicago Press, 2013). On marriage markets and racial differences in marriage, see Daniel T. Lichter, Felicia B. Leclere, and Diane K. McLaughlin, "Local Marriage Markets and the Marital Behavior of Black and White Women," *American Journal of Sociology* 96 (1991): 843–867.

17. For a recent review, R. Kelly Raley and Megan M. Sweeney, "Explaining Race and Ethnic Variation in Marriage: Directions for Future Research," *Race and Social Problems* 1 (2009): 132–142.

18. Kathryn Edin and Maria Kefalas, *Promises I Can Keep: Why Poor Women Put Motherhood before Marriage* (Berkeley: University of California Press, 2005), 75.

19. On the timing of marriage and divorce for respondents of the National Longitudinal Survey of Youth 1979 cohort (NLSY79), Matthew McKeever and Nicholas H. Wolfinger, "Over the Long Haul: The Persistent Economic Consequences of Single Motherhood," in *Economic Stress and the Family*, ed. S. L. Blair (Bingley, UK: Emerald, 2012), 1–39. We use NLSY79 data for this analysis because neither NLSY97 nor the National Longitudinal Study of Adolescent to Adult Health (Add Health) follow respondents for long enough to provide adequate data on marital stability. As a cross-sectional survey, the National Survey of Family Growth (NSFG) has limited options for multivariate analysis of

divorce. Neither the GSS nor the NSRFL, both cross-sectional surveys, contain necessary data on marital history. For the NLSY79 analysis, socioeconomic variables include income, education, and employment. Family structure of origin, premarital fertility, and premarital cohabitation are our cultural variables. Additional measures of culture would be useful but are not available in NLSY79. All models include controls for fertility, region, and city size. Models are estimated using Cox proportional hazards with time-varying independent variables. We report robust standard errors to account for design effects. The overall NLSY sample size is about 9,400. See the appendix for more information about this analysis.

20. This is not uncommon. On the long-term effects of childhood sexual abuse on adult sexuality, see Christopher R. Browning and Edward O. Laumann, "Sexual Contact between Children and Adults: A Life Course Perspective," *American Sociological Review* 62 (1997): 540–560.

21. Elizabeth E. Brisco, *The Reformation of Machismo: Evangelical Conversion and Gender in Columbia* (Austin: University of Texas Press, 1995).

22. The relative importance of men's religious participation is consistent with our earlier research based on the Fragile Families and Child Wellbeing survey. Wolfinger and Wilcox, "Happily Ever After?"

23. Nicholas H. Wolfinger, W. Bradford Wilcox, and Edwin I. Hernández, "Bendito Amor ('Blessed Love'): Religion and Relationships among Married and Unmarried Latinos in Urban America," *Journal of Latino-Latin American Studies* 3 (2010): 171–188.

24. According to the NSRFL, there are twice as many couples in which just the woman attends (compared to couples in which only the man attends).

25. Wolfinger and Wilcox, "Happily Ever After?"

26. On men and relationships, see Eleanor E. Maccoby, *The Two Sexes: Growing Up Apart, Coming Together* (Boston: Harvard University Press, 1998); Thompson, Linda, and Alexis Walker. 1989. "Gender in Families: Women and Men in Marriage, Work, and Parenthood." *Journal of Marriage and the Family* 51:873–893.

27. For marriage, see Waite and Gallagher, *The Case for Marriage*; for religion, see Penny Edgell, *Religion and Family in a Changing Society* (Princeton: Princeton University Press, 2006); W. Bradford Wilcox and John P. Bartkowski, "Devoted Dads: Religion, Class, and Fatherhood," in *Situated Fathering: A Focus on Physical and Social Spaces*, ed. William Marsiglio and Greer Fox (Lanham, MD: Rowman & Littlefield, 2005), 299–320.

28. This runs contrary to our earlier work. Why the discrepancy? We raise two possibilities. First, our earlier finding is based only on

respondents in urban America. Second, the current finding is based on a cross-sectional survey while our earlier finding is based on longitudinal data. Therefore, we should acknowledge the reasonable possibility that relationship-related behaviors do indeed help explain the benefits of religious participation. W. Bradford Wilcox and Nicholas H. Wolfinger, "Living and Loving 'Decent': Religion and Relationship Quality among Urban Parents," *Social Science Research* 37 (2008): 828–843.

29. Secular social networks do not appear to provide the same benefit. See Chaeyoon Lim and Robert D. Putnam, "Religion, Social Networks, and Life Satisfaction," *American Sociological Review* 75 (2010): 914–933.

30. David C. Atkins and Deborah E. Kessel, "Religiousness and Infidelity: Attendance, but not Faith and Prayer, Predict Marital Fidelity," *Journal of Marriage and Family* 70 (2008): 407–418.

31. Michael E. McCullough and David B. Larson, "Prayer," in *Integrating Spirituality into Treatment: Resources for Practitioners*, ed. William R. Miller (Washington, DC: American Psychological Association, 1999), 85–110.

32. For further discussion of this finding, see Christopher Ellison, Amy Burdette, and W. Bradford Wilcox, "The Couple that Prays Together: Race and Ethnicity, Religion, and Relationship Quality," *Journal of Marriage and Family* 72 (2010): 963–975.

33. Émile Durkheim, *The Elementary Forms of Religious Life*, trans. by Karen E. Fields (New York: Free Press, 1995). See also Andrew L. Roth, "'Men Wearing Masks': Issues of Description in the Analysis of Ritual," *Sociological Theory* 3 (1995): 301–327.

34. This research is based on the Fragile Families and Child Wellbeing Study: http://www.fragilefamilies.princeton.edu. Wolfinger and Wilcox, "Happily Ever After?"

35. This finding should be interpreted with caution, as the data on spousal church attendance are limited.

36. Examples of these studies include Paul R. Amato and Stacy J. Rogers, "A Longitudinal Study of Marital Problems and Subsequent Divorce," *Journal of Marriage and Family* 59 (1997): 612–624; and Vaughn R. A. Call and Tim B. Heaton, "Religious Influence on Marital Stability," *Journal for the Scientific Study of Religion* 36 (1997): 382–392. We were able to reproduce this result in our analysis of NLSY79: frequent church attendance decreased divorce rates for all population groups when analyzed together, but only whites when analyzed separately.

37. This is undoubtedly a complex issue. Recall the findings presented in chapter 3, which indicate that Latinos and African Americans often have more traditional beliefs about the family than do whites.

38. W. Bradford Wilcox, Mark Chaves, and David Franz, "Focused on the Family? Religious Traditions, Family Discourse, and Pastoral Practice," *Journal for the Scientific Study of Religion* 43 (2004): 491–504.

39. Nicholas H. Wolfinger, *Understanding the Divorce Cycle: The Children of Divorce in Their Own Marriages* (New York: Cambridge University Press, 2005), chapter 2.

40. Christopher G. Ellison and Darren E. Sherkat, "The 'Semi-Involuntary Institution' Revisited: Regional Variations in Church Participation among Black Americans," *Social Forces* 4 (1995): 1415–1437.

Chapter 6

1. See, for instance, Heather Mac Donald, "Hispanic Family Values?" *City Journal* (Autumn 2006).

2. Paola Scommegna, "Exploring the Paradox of U.S. Hispanics' Longer Life Expectancy" (Washington, DC: Population Reference Bureau, 2013).

3. Institute for American Values and the National Marriage Project, "Social Indicators of Marital Health and Well-Being," in *The State of our Unions 2012* (Charlottesville, VA: National Marriage Project and Institute for American Values, 2012), under "Fragile Families with Children."

4. General Social Survey (GSS), 2000–2012. N = 4,751 (white), 855 (black), 667 (Latino). Results are unweighted.

5. Institute for American Values and the National Marriage Project, "Social Indicators of Marital Health and Well-Being," under "Fragile Families with Children."

6. GSS, 2000–2012. N = 3,963 (white), 958 (black), 773 (Latino). Percentage of respondents saying they are "moderate religious" or "very religious."

7. GSS, 2000–2012. N = 8,917 (white), 2,096 (black), 1,396 (Latino).

8. Elijah Anderson, *Code of the Street: Decency, Violence, and the Moral Life of the Inner City* (New York: Norton, 1999).

9. Kathryn Edin and Maria Kefalas, *Promises I Can Keep: Why Poor Women Put Motherhood before Marriage* (Berkeley: University of California Press, 2005), 75.

10. Daniel M. Hungerman, "Do Religious Proscriptions Matter? Evidence from a Theory-Based Test," *Journal of Human Resources* 49 (2014): 1053–1093.

11. This may not be true in all instances, however. See Chaeyoon Lim and Robert D. Putnam, "Religion, Social Networks, and Life Satisfaction," *American Sociological Review* 75 (2010): 914–933.

12. Alcoholics Anonymous, *Alcoholics Anonymous* (New York: Alcoholics Anonymous World Services, 2007).

13. T. M. Luhrmann, "Religion without God," *New York Times*, December 24, 2014.

14. Elizabeth Kneebone, "Economic Recovery and the EITC: Expanding the Earned Income Tax Credit to Benefit Families and Places," Research paper (Washington, DC: Brookings, 2009).

15. Robert Stein, "Taxes and the Family," *National Affairs* 2 (2010): 35–48.

16. Michael Jacobson, *Downsizing Prisons: How to Reduce Crime and End Mass Incarceration* (New York: New York University Press, 2005); and Steven Raphael and Michael Stoll, "A New Approach to Reducing Incarceration while Maintaining Low Rates of Crime," Discussion paper (Washington, DC: Hamilton Project, Brookings, 2014).

17. Bruce Western and Christopher Wildeman, "The Black Family and Mass Incarceration," *Annals of the American Academy of Political and Social Science* 621 (2009): 221–242; and Devah Pager, *Marked: Race, Crime, and Finding Work in an Era of Mass Incarceration* (Chicago: University of Chicago Press, 2007).

18. James J. Kemple, "Career Academies: Long-Term Impacts on Work, Education, and Transitions to Adulthood" (New York and Oakland, CA: MDRC, 2008).

19. Adam Carasso and C. Eugene Steuerle, "The Hefty Penalty on Marriage Facing Many Households with Children," *Future of Children* 15 (2005): 157–175.

20. For more information on the National Campaign, see http://www.the-nationalcampaign.org.

21. Ron Haskins and Isabel V. Sawhill, *Creating an Opportunity Society* (Washington, DC: Brookings, 2009).

22. For more information, see http://www.firstthings.org.

23. On the value of fidelity, see Denise Previti and Paul R. Amato, "Is Infidelity a Cause of a Consequence of Poor Marital Quality?" *Journal of Social and Personal Relationships* 21 (2004): 217–230. On the value of men's emotional engagement, see W. Bradford Wilcox and Steven L. Nock, "What's Love Got to Do with It? Equality, Equity, Commitment and Women's Marital Quality," *Social Forces* 84 (2006): 1321–1345. On the value of generosity in marriage, see Jeffrey Dew and W. Bradford Wilcox, "Generosity and the Maintenance of Marital Quality," *Journal of Marriage and Family* 75 (2013): 1218–1228.

24. See, for instance, Liana C. Sayer et al., "She Left, He Left: How Employment and Satisfaction Affect Men's and Women's Decisions to Leave Marriages," *American Journal of Sociology* 116 (2011): 1982–2018.

25. Galena K. Rhoades, Scott M. Stanley, and Emily Esfahani Smith, *Before "I Do": What Do Premarital Experiences Have to Do with Marital Quality among Today's Young Adults?* (Charlottesville, VA: National Marriage Project, 2014).
26. Annette Mahoney, "Religion in Families, 1999–2009: A Relational Spirituality Framework," *Journal of Marriage and Family* 72 (2010): 805–827.
27. Carolyn Pape Cowan and Philip A. Cowan, "Interventions to Ease the Transition to Parenthood: Why They Are Needed and What They Can Do," *Family Relations* 44 (1995): 412–423.
28. C. Eric Lincoln and Lawrence H. Mamiya, *The Black Church in the African American Experience* (Durham, NC: Duke University Press, 1990), 169.
29. Ibid., 3–5.
30. Orlando Patterson, *Rituals of Blood: Consequences of Slavery in Two American Centuries* (New York: Basic Books, 1998), 167.
31. Allan Figueroa Deck, *The Second Wave: Hispanic Ministry and the Evangelization of Cultures* (New York: Paulist Press, 1989).
32. GSS, 2000–2012. N = 259 (Protestant), 969 (Catholic). Results are unweighted.
33. This is presumably why Protestant Latinos hold more conservative attitudes about family-related issues than do their Catholic peers. Christopher G. Ellison, Nicholas H. Wolfinger, and Aida I. Ramos-Wada, "Attitudes toward Marriage, Divorce, Cohabitation, and Casual Sex among Working-Age Latinos: Does Religion Matter?" *Journal of Family Issues* 34 (2013): 295–322.
34. Arlene M. Sánchez Walsh, *Latino Pentecostal Identity: Evangelical Faith, Self, and Society* (New York: Columbia University Press, 2003).
35. On the relationship between marital status and interest in marriage, see Frank Newport and Joy Wilke, "Most in U.S. Want Marriage, but Its Importance Has Dropped," online article. Princeton, NJ: Gallup, 2013. http://www.gallup.com.

Appendix

1. Christopher Paul et al., "A Cautionary Case Study of Approaches to the Treatment of Missing Data," *Statistical Methods and Applications* 17 (2008): 351–372. This is a controversial finding, so we point out that Christopher Paul and his colleagues did what few proponents of sophisticated missing-data techniques have done: a head-to-head comparison of how the different techniques actually perform.

2. Our earlier research established the primacy of church attendance when studying how religion affects relationships. W. Bradford Wilcox, *Soft Patriarchs, New Men: How Christianity Shapes Fathers and Husbands* (Chicago: University of Chicago Press, 2004); see also Vaughn R. A. Call and Tim B. Heaton, "Religious Influence on Marital Stability," *Journal for the Scientific Study of Religion* 36 (1997): 382–392.

3. Brian Steensland et al., "The Measure of American Religion: Toward Improving the State of the Art," *Social Forces* 79 (2000): 291–318.

4. Paul D. Allison, *Survival Analysis Using the SAS System: A Practical Guide* (Cary, NC: SAS Institute, 1995), 216–219.

5. This is also the case for our previous research on relationship quality. W. Bradford Wilcox and Nicholas H. Wolfinger, "Living and Loving 'Decent': Religion and Relationship Quality among Urban Parents," *Social Science Research* 37 (2008): 828–843; and Nicholas H. Wolfinger and W. Bradford Wilcox, "Happily Ever After? Religion, Marital Status, Gender, and Relationship Quality in Urban Families," *Social Forces* 86 (2008): 1311–1337.

6. Joseph Altonji, Todd Elder, and Christopher Taber, "An Evaluation of Instrumental Variable Strategies for Estimating the Effects of Catholic Schooling," *Journal of Human Resources* 40 (2005): 791–821; and Daniel M. Hungerman, "Do Religious Proscriptions Matter? Evidence from a Theory-Based Test," *Journal of Human Resources* 49 (2014): 1053–1093.

7. Hungerman, "Do Religious Proscriptions Matter?"

BIBLIOGRAPHY

Akerlof, George A. 1998. "Men Without Children." *The Economic Journal* 108: 287–309.

Akerlof, George A., Janet L. Yellen, and Michael L. Katz. 1996. "An Analysis of Out-of-Wedlock Childbearing in the United States." *Quarterly Journal of Economics* 111: 277–317.

Alcoholics Anonymous. 2007. *Alcoholics Anonymous.* New York: Alcoholics Anonymous World Services.

Alexander, Michelle. 2012. *The New Jim Crow: Mass Incarceration in the Age of Colorblindness.* New York: New Press.

Allen, Elizabeth S., Galena Kline Rhoades, Scott M. Stanley, Howard J. Markman, Tamara Williams, Jessica Melton, and Mari L. Clements. 2008. "Premarital Precursors of Marital Infidelity." *Family Process* 47: 243–259.

Allison, Paul D. 1995. *Survival Analysis Using the SAS System: A Practical Guide.* Cary, NC: SAS Institute, 216–219.

Altonji, Joseph, Todd Elder, and Christopher Taber. 2005. "An Evaluation of Instrumental Variable Strategies for Estimating the Effects of Catholic Schooling." *Journal of Human Resources* 40: 791–821.

Amato, Paul R. 2005. "The Impact of Family Formation Change on the Cognitive, Social, and Emotional Well-Being of the Next Generation." *The Future of Children* 15: 75–96.

Amato, Paul R., and Alan Booth. 1997. *A Generation at Risk: Growing Up in an Era of Family Upheaval.* Cambridge, MA: Harvard University Press.

Amato, Paul R., Alan Booth, David R. Johnson, and Stacy J. Rogers. 2007. *Alone Together: How Marriage in America Is Changing.* Cambridge, MA: Harvard University Press.

Amato, Paul R., Laura Spencer Loomis, and Alan Booth. 1995. "Parental Divorce, Marital Conflict, and Offspring Well-Being during Early Adulthood." *Social Forces* 73: 895–915.

Amato, Paul R., and Stacy J. Rogers. 1997. "A Longitudinal Study of Marital Problems and Subsequent Divorce." *Journal of Marriage and Family* 59: 612–624.

Amato, Paul R., and Stacy J. Rogers. 1999. "Do Attitudes toward Divorce Affect Relationship Quality?" *Journal of Family Issues* 20: 69–86.

Ammerman, Nancy. 1997. "Golden-Rule Christianity." Pp. 196–216 in *Lived Religion in America: Toward a History of Practice*, edited by David D. Hall. Princeton, NJ: Princeton University Press.

Anderson, Elijah. 1999. *Code of the Street: Decency, Violence, and the Moral Life of the Inner City.* New York: Norton.

Arroyo, Julia, Krista K. Payne, Susan L. Brown, and Wendy D. Manning. 2013. "Crossover in Median Age at First Marriage and First Birth: Thirty Years of Change." FP-13-06. National Center for Family & Marriage Research.

Atkins, David C., and Deborah E. Kessel. 2008. "Religiousness and Infidelity: Attendance, but Not Faith and Prayer, Predict Marital Fidelity." *Journal of Marriage and Family* 70: 407–418.

Axinn, William G., and Arland Thornton. 1996. "The Influence of Parents' Marital Dissolutions on Children's Attitudes toward Family Formation." *Demography* 33: 66–81.

Bean, Frank D., Ruth R. Berg, and Jennifer V. W. Van Hook. 1996. "Socioeconomic and Cultural Incorporation and Marital Disruption among Mexican Americans." *Social Forces* 75: 593–617.

Bell, Daniel. 1978. *The Cultural Contradictions of Capitalism.* New York: Basic Books.

Bennett, Neil G., David E. Bloom, and Patricia H. Craig. 1989. "The Divergence of Black and White Marriage Patterns." *American Journal of Sociology* 95: 692–722.

Bernhardt, Annette, Martina Morris, and Mark S. Handcock. 1995. "Women's Gains or Men's Losses? A Closer Look at the Shrinking Gender Gap in Earnings." *American Journal of Sociology* 101: 302–328.

Bertrand, Marianne, Jessica Pan, and Emir Kamenica. 2013. "Gender Identity and Relative Income within Households." Working Paper 19023. Cambridge, MA: National Bureau of Economic Research.

Bianchi, Suzanne, John P. Robinson, and Melissa A. Milkie. 2006. *Changing Rhythms of American Family Life.* New York: Russell Sage.

Blackman, Lorraine, Obie Clayton, Norval Glenn, Linda Malone-Colon, and Alex Roberts. 2005. *The Consequences of Marriage for African Americans: A Comprehensive Literature Review*. New York: Institute for American Values.

Blau, Peter M., and Otis Dudley Duncan. 1967. *The American Occupational Structure*. New York: Wiley.

Blow, Charles M. 2013. "For Some Folks, Life Is a Hill." *New York Times*, November 29.

Bodenmann, Guy. 1997. "The Influence of Stress and Coping on Close Relationships: A Two-Year Longitudinal Study." *Swiss Journal of Psychology* 56: 156–164.

Brady, Kathleen T., and Susan C. Sonne. 1999. "The Role of Stress in Alcohol Use, Alcoholism Treatment, and Relapse." *Alcohol Research & Health* 23: 263–271.

Brooks, David. 2006. "Immigrants to Be Proud Of." *New York Times*, March 30.

Brown, Susan L., and Alan Booth. 1995. "Cohabitation versus Marriage: A Comparison of Relationship Quality." *Journal of Marriage and Family* 58: 668–678.

Brown, Tony N., David R. Williams, James S. Jackson, Harold W. Neighbors, Myriam Torres, Sherrill L. Sellers, and Kendrick T. Brown. 2000. "'Being Black and Feeling Blue': The Mental Health Consequences of Racial Discrimination." *Race and Society* 2: 117–131.

Browning, Christopher R., and Edward O. Laumann. 1997. "Sexual Contact between Children and Adults: A Life Course Perspective." *American Sociological Review* 62: 540–560.

Brusco, Elizabeth E. 1995. *The Reformation of Machismo: Evangelical Conversion and Gender in Colombia*. Austin: University of Texas Press.

Bumpass, Larry L., and Hsien-Hen Lu. 2000. "Trends in Cohabitation and Implications for Children's Family Contexts in the United States." *Population Studies* 54: 29–41.

Bumpass, Larry L., Teresa Castro Martin, and James A. Sweet. 1991. "The Impact of Family Background and Early Marital Factors on Marital Disruption." *Journal of Family Issues* 12: 22–42.

Burdette, Amy M., Christopher G. Ellison, Darren E. Sherkat, and Kurt A. Gore. 2007. "Are There Religious Variations in Marital Infidelity?" *Journal of Family Issues* 28: 1553–1581.

Burdette, Amy M., Stacy H. Haynes, and Christopher G. Ellison. 2012. "Religion, Race/Ethnicity, and Perceived Barriers to Marriage among Working-Age Adults." *Sociology of Religion* 73: 429–451.

Bureau of Labor Statistics. 2013. "Employment Projections." Washington, DC: US Department of Labor. http://www.bls.gov/emp/ep_chart_001.htm.

Bureau of Labor Statistics. 2015. "Labor Force Statistics from the Current Population Survey." Washington, DC: US Department of Labor. http://www.bls.gov/cps/tables.htm.

Caetano, Raul. 1987. "Alcohol Use and Depression among U.S. Hispanics." *British Journal of Addiction* 82: 1245–1251.

Call, Vaughn R. A., and Tim B. Heaton. 1997. "Religious Influence on Marital Stability." *Journal for the Scientific Study of Religion* 36: 382–392.

Carasso, Adam, and C. Eugene Steuerle. 2005. "The Hefty Marriage Penalty on Marriage Facing Many Households with Children." *The Future of Children* 15: 157–175.

Carlson, Marcia J., and Frank F. Furstenberg, Jr. 2006. "The Prevalence and Correlates of Multipartnered Fertility among Urban U.S. Parents." *Journal of Marriage and Family* 68: 718–732.

Chaves, Mark. 2004. *Congregations in America*. Cambridge, MA: Harvard University Press.

Cherlin, Andrew J. 1992. *Marriage, Divorce, Remarriage*. Rev. ed. Cambridge, MA: Harvard University Press.

Cherlin, Andrew J. 2004. "The Deinstitutionalization of American Marriage." *Journal of Marriage and Family* 66: 848–861.

Cherlin, Andrew J. 2009. *The Marriage-Go-Round: The State of Marriage and the Family in America Today*. New York: Vintage.

Chetty, Raj, Nathaniel Hendren, Patrick Kline, and Emmanuel Saez. 2013. "The Economic Impacts of Tax Expenditures: Evidence from Spatial Variation across the U.S." Cambridge, MA: Equality of Opportunity Project.

Clecak, Peter. 1983. *America's Quest for the Ideal Self: Dissent and Fulfillment in the 60s and 70s*. New York: Oxford University Press.

Cleck, Jessica N., and Julie A. Blendy. 2008. "Making a Bad Thing Worse: Adverse Effects of Stress on Drug Addiction." *Journal of Clinical Investigation* 118: 454–461.

Cohn, D'Vera, Jeffrey S. Passel, Wendy Wang, and Gretchen Livingston. 2011. "Barely Half of U.S. Adults Are Married—A Record Low." Washington, DC: Pew Research Center.

Coker, Ann L., Paige Hall Smith, Robert E. McKeown, and Melissa J. King. 2000. "Frequency and Correlates of Intimate Partner Violence by Type: Physical, Sexual, and Psychological Battering." *American Journal of Public Health* 90: 553–559.

Coontz, Stephanie. 2005. *Marriage, a History: From Obedience to Intimacy, or How Love Conquered Marriage*. New York: Viking.

Copen, Casey E., Kimberly Daniels, and William D. Mosher. 2013. "First Premarital Cohabitation in the United States: 2006–2010 National Survey of Family Growth." National Health Statistics Reports 64. Hyattsville, MD: National Center for Health Statistics.

Copen, Casey E., Kimberly Daniels, Jonathan Vespa, and William D. Mosher. 2012. "First Marriages in the United States: Data from the 2006–2010 National Survey of Family Growth." National Health Statistics Reports 49. Hyattsville, MD: National Center for Health Statistics.

Cowan, Carolyn Pape, and Philip A. Cowan. 1995. "Interventions to Ease the Transition to Parenthood: Why They Are Needed and What They Can Do." Family Relations 44: 412–423.

Crissey, Sarah. 2009. "Educational Attainment in the United States: 2007." Current Population Reports P20-560. Washington, DC: US Census Bureau.

Cunradi, Carol B., Michael Todd, Michael Duke, and Genevieve Ames. 2009. "Problem Drinking, Unemployment, and Intimate Partner Violence among a Sample of Construction Industry Workers and Their Partners." Journal of Family Violence 24: 63–74.

Davis, James A., Tom W. Smith, and Peter V. Marsden. 2006. GSS 1972–2006 Cumulative Codebook on CD-ROM. University of Connecticut: The Roper Center.

Deck, Allen Figueroa. 1989. The Second Wave: Hispanic Ministry and the Evangelization of Cultures. New York: Paulist Press.

DeMaris, Alfred, Michael L. Benson, Greer L. Fox, Terrence Hill, and Judy Van Wyk. 2003. "Distal and Proximal Factors in Domestic Violence: A Test of an Integrated Model." Journal of Marriage and Family 65: 652–667.

DeNavas-Walt, Carmen, Bernadette D. Proctor, and Jessica Smith. 2007. "Income, Poverty, and Health Insurance Coverage in the United States: 2006." Current Population Reports P60-233. Washington, DC: US Census Bureau.

DeNavas-Walt, Carmen, Bernadette D. Proctor, and Jessica Smith. 2013. "Income, Poverty, and Health Insurance Coverage in the United States: 2012." Current Population Reports P60-245. Washington, DC: US Census Bureau.

Dew, Jeffrey. 2009a. "The Gendered Meaning of Assets for Divorce." Journal of Family and Economic Issues 30: 20–31.

Dew, Jeffrey. 2009b. "Has the Marital Time Cost of Parenting Changed over Time?" Social Forces 88: 519–541.

Dew, Jeffrey, and W. Bradford Wilcox. 2013. "Generosity and the Maintenance of Marital Quality." Journal of Marriage and Family 75: 1218–1228.

Dixon, Travis L., and Daniel Linz. 2000. "Overrepresentation and Underrepresentation of African Americans and Latinos as Lawbreakers on Television News." Journal of Communication 50: 131–154.

Durkheim, Émile. 1995. The Elementary Forms of Religious Life. Translated by Karen E. Fields. New York: Free Press.

Edgell, Penny. 2006. *Religion and Family in a Changing Society.* Princeton, NJ: Princeton University Press.

Edin, Kathryn, and Maria Kefalas. 2005. *Promises I Can Keep: Why Poor Women Put Motherhood before Marriage.* Berkeley: University of California Press.

Ellingson, Stephen. 2004. "Constructing Causal Stories and Moral Boundaries: Institutional Approaches to Sexual Problems." Pp. 283–308 in *The Sexual Organization of the City,* edited by Edward O. Laumann, Stephen Ellingson, Jenna Mahay, Anthony Paik, and Yoosik Youm. Chicago: University of Chicago Press.

Elliott, Diana B., Kristy Krivickas, Matthew W. Brault, and Rose M. Kreider. 2012. "Historical Marriage Trends from 1890–2010: A Focus on Race Differences." Presented at the annual meeting of the Population Association of America. San Francisco, CA. SEHSD Working Paper 2012–12. http://www.Census.gov.

Ellison, Christopher G., Amy Burdette, and W. Bradford Wilcox. 2010. "The Couple that Prays Together: Race and Ethnicity, Religion, and Relationship Quality." *Journal of Marriage and Family* 72: 963–975.

Ellison, Christopher G., and Jeffrey S. Levin. 1998. "The Religion-Health Connection: Evidence, Theory, and Future Directions." *Heath Education and Behavior* 25: 700–720.

Ellison, Christopher G., and Darren E. Sherkat. 1995. "The 'Semi-Involuntary Institution' Revisited: Regional Variations in Church Participation among Black Americans." *Social Forces* 4: 1415–1437.

Ellison, Christopher G., and Robert Joseph Taylor. 1996. "Turning to Prayer: Social and Situational Antecedents of Religious Coping among African Americans." *Review of Religious Research* 38: 111–131.

Ellison, Christopher G., Nicholas H. Wolfinger, and Aida I. Ramos-Wada. 2013. "Attitudes toward Marriage, Divorce, Cohabitation, and Casual Sex among Working-Age Latinos: Does Religion Matter?" *Journal of Family Issues* 34: 295–322.

Ellwood, David T., and Christopher Jencks. 2004. "The Spread of Single-Parent Families in the United States since 1960." Pp. 25–65 in *The Future of the Family,* edited by Daniel P. Moynihan, Timothy M. Smeeding, and Lee Rainwater. New York: Russell Sage.

Espenshade, Thomas J. 1985. "Marriage Trends in America: Estimates, Implications, and Underlying Causes." *Population and Development Review* 11: 193–245.

Feagin, Joe R., and Melvin P. Sikes. 1995. *Living with Racism: The Black Middle-Class Experience.* Boston, MA: Beacon.

Finch, Brian Karl, et al. 2000. "Perceived Discrimination and Depression among Mexican-Origin Adults in California." *Journal of Health and Social Behavior* 41: 295–313.

Frazier, E. Franklin. 1974. *The Negro Church in America*. New York: Schocken Books.

Fry, Richard, and D'Vera Cohn. 2010. "Women, Men and the New Economics of Marriage." Washington, DC: Pew Research Center.

Fu, Vincent Kang, and Nicholas H. Wolfinger. 2011. "Broken Boundaries or Broken Marriages? Racial Intermarriage and Divorce." *Social Science Quarterly* 92: 1096–1117.

Gallagher, Maggie. 1996. *The Abolition of Marriage: How We Destroy Lasting Love*. Washington, DC: Regnery Publishing.

Geronimus, Arline T. 1991. "Teenage Childbearing and Social and Reproductive Disadvantage: The Evolution of Complex Questions and the Demise of Simple Answers." *Family Relations* 40: 463–471.

Gibson-Davis, Christina M. 2007. "Expectations and the Economic Bar to Marriage among Low-Income Couples." Pp. 84–103 in *Unmarried Couples with Children*, edited by Paula England and Kathryn Edin. New York: Russell Sage.

Ginorio, A., L. Gutierrez, A. M. Cauce, and M. Acosta. 1995. "The Psychology of Latinas." In *Feminist Perspectives on the Psychology of Women*, edited by C. Travis. Washington, DC: American Psychological Association.

Goldman, Noreen, and Anne Pebley. 1981. "Legalization of Consensual Unions in Latin America." *Biodemography and Social Biology* 28: 49–61.

Goldstein, Joshua R. 1999. "The Leveling of Divorce in the United States." *Demography* 36: 409–414.

Goldstein, Joshua R., and Catherine T. Kenney. 2001. "Marriage Delayed or Marriage Forgone? New Cohort Forecasts of First Marriage for U.S. Women." *American Sociological Review* 66: 506–519.

Gorman, Lisa, and Adrian Blow. 2008. "Concurrent Depression and Infidelity: Background, Strategies for Treatment, and Future Research." *Journal of Couple and Relationship Therapy* 7: 39–58.

Gross, Neil, and Solon Simmons. 2009. "The Religiosity of American College and University Professors." *Sociology of Religion* 70: 101–129.

Groves, Robert M., Grant Benson, William D. Mosher, Jennifer Rosenbaum, Peter Granda, William Axinn, James Lepkowski, and Anjani Chandra. 2005. "Plan and Operation of Cycle 6 of the National Survey of Family Growth." Vital and Health Statistics series 1, number 42. Hyattsville, MD: US Department of Health and Human Services.

Gruber, Jonathan. 2004. "Is Making Divorce Easier Bad for Children? The Long-Run Implications of Unilateral Divorce." *Journal of Labor Economics* 22: 799–833.

Hamilton, Brady E., Joyce A. Martin, and Stephanie J. Ventura. 2007. "Births: Preliminary Data for 2006." National Vital Statistics Reports 56(7). Hyattsville, MD: National Center for Health Statistics.

Hamilton, Brady E., Joyce A. Martin, and Stephanie J. Ventura. 2013. "Births: Preliminary Data for 2012." *National Vital Statistics Reports* 62(3). Hyattsville, MD: National Center for Health Statistics.

Haskins, Ron, and Isabel V. Sawhill. 2009. *Creating an Opportunity Society.* Washington, DC: Brookings.

Hayes-Bautista, David E. 2004. *La Nueva California: Latinos in the Golden State.* Berkeley: University of California Press.

Hernandez-Coss, Raul. 2005. *Lessons from the U.S.–Mexico Remittances Corridor on Shifting from Informal to Formal Transfer Systems.* New York: World Bank.

Hirschi, Travis, and Michael Gottfredson. 1983. "Age and the Explanation of Crime." *American Journal of Sociology* 89: 552–584.

Hochschild, Arlie, with Anne Machung. 1989. *The Second Shift.* New York: Avon Books.

Hondagneu-Sotelo, Pierette. 2001. *Domestica: Immigrant Workers Cleaning and Caring in the Shadows of Affluence.* Berkeley: University of California Press.

Hummer, Robert A., Richard G. Rogers, Charles B. Nam, and Christopher G. Ellison. 1999. "Religious Involvement and U.S. Adult Mortality." *Demography* 36: 273–285.

Hungerman, Daniel M. 2014. "Do Religious Proscriptions Matter? Evidence from a Theory-Based Test." *Journal of Human Resources* 49: 1053–1093.

Institute for American Values and the National Marriage Project. 2012. "Social Indicators of Marital Health and Well-being." Pp. 62–107 in *The State of our Unions 2012.* Charlottesville, VA: National Marriage Project and Institute for American Values.

Jacobson, Michael. 2005. *Downsizing Prisons: How to Reduce Crime and End Mass Incarceration.* New York: New York University Press.

Kantor, Glenda Kaufman. 1983. "Alcohol and Spouse Abuse: Ethnic Differences." Pp. 57–79 in *Alcohol and Violence,* vol. 13 of *Recent Developments in Alcoholism,* edited by Marc Galanter. New York: Plenum.

Kearney, Melissa S., and Phillip B. Levine. 2014. "Media Influences on Social Outcomes: The Impact of MTV's *16 and Pregnant* on Teen Childbearing." Working Paper 19795. Cambridge, MA: National Bureau of Economic Research.

Kemple, James J. 2008. "Career Academies: Long-Term Impacts on Work, Education, and Transitions to Adulthood." New York and Oakland, CA: MDRC.

Kennedy, Sheela, and Larry Bumpass. 2011. "Cohabitation and Trends in the Structure and Stability of Children's Family Lives." Paper presented at the annual meeting of the Population Association of America. Washington, DC.

Kessley, Ronald C., and Harold W. Neighbors. 1986. "A New Perspective on the Relationships among Race, Social Class, and Psychological Distress." *Journal of Health and Social* Behavior 27: 107–115.

Kielcolt-Glaser, Janice, and Tamara L. Newton. 2001. "Marriage and Health: His and Hers." *Psychological Bulletin* 127: 472–503.

Kneebone, Elizabeth. 2009. "Economic Recovery and the EITC: Expanding the Earned Income Tax Credit to Benefit Families and Places." Research paper. Washington, DC: Brookings.

Koball, Heather. 1998. "Have African American Men Become Less Committed to Marriage? Explaining the Twentieth Century Racial Cross-over in Men's Marriage Timing." *Demography* 35: 251–258.

Kreider, Ros, and Jason M. Fields. 2001. "Number, Timing, and Duration of Marriages and Divorces: Fall 1996." Current Population Reports P70–80. Washington, DC: US Census Bureau.

Krieger, Nancy, Kevin Smith, Deepa Naishadham, Cathy Hartman, and Elizabeth M. Barbeau. 2005. "Experiences of Discrimination: Validity and Reliability of a Self-report Measure for Population Health Research on Racism and Health." *Social Science & Medicine* 61: 1576–1596.

Kristof, Nicholas. 2014. "TV Lowers Birthrate (Seriously)." *New York Times*, March 19.

Krugman, Paul. 2007. *The Conscience of a Liberal*. New York: W. W. Norton and Company.

Lamidi, Esther. 2014. "Single, Cohabiting, and Married Households, 1995–2012" (FP-14-1). National Center for Family & Marriage Research. http://www.bgsu.edu.

Landale, Nancy S., and Nimfa B. Ogena. 1995. "Migration and Union Dissolution among Puerto Rican Women." *International Migration Review* 29: 671–692.

Landale, Nancy S., and R. S. Oropesa. 2007. "Hispanic Families: Stability and Change." *Annual Review of Sociology* 33: 381–405.

LeBlanc, Adrian Nicole. 2003. *Random Family: Love, Drugs, Trouble, and Coming of Age in the Bronx*. New York: Scribner.

Lemann, Nicholas. 1992. *The Promised Land: The Great Black Migration and How It Changed America*. New York: Vintage.

Lerman, Robert I., and W. Bradford Wilcox. 2014. *For Richer, for Poorer: How Family Structures Economic Success in America*. Washington, DC: AEI and Institute for Family Studies.

Lichter, Daniel T., and Deborah Roempke Graefe. 2001. "Finding a Mate? The Marital and Cohabitation Histories of Unwed Mothers." Pp. 317–343 in *Out of Wedlock: Causes and Consequences of Nonmarital Fertility*, edited by Lawrence L. Wu and Barbara Wolfe. New York: Russell Sage.

Lichter, Daniel T., Deborah Roempke Graefe, and J. Brian Brown. 2003. "Is Marriage a Panacea? Union Formation among Economically Disadvantaged Unwed Mothers." *Social Problems* 50: 60–86.

Lichter, Daniel T., Felicia B. Leclere, and Diane K. McLaughlin. 1991. "Local Marriage Markets and the Marital Behavior of Black and White Women." *American Journal of Sociology* 96: 843–867.

Lichter, Daniel T., Diane K. McLaughlin, George Kephart, and David J. Landry. 1992. "Race and the Retreat from Marriage: A Shortage of Marriageable Men?" *American Sociological Review* 57: 781–799.

Lichter, Daniel T., Zhenchao Qian, and Leanna M. Mellott. 2006. "Marriage or Dissolution? Union Transitions among Poor Cohabiting Women." *Demography* 43: 223–240.

Lim, Chaeyoon, and Robert D. Putnam. 2010. "Religion, Social Networks, and Life Satisfaction." *American Sociological Review* 75: 914–933.

Lincoln, C. Eric, and Lawrence H. Mamiya. 1990. *The Black Church in the African American Experience*. Durham, NC: Duke University Press.

Lippman, Laura, and W. Bradford Wilcox. 2014. *World Family Map*. Washington, DC: Child Trends.

Luhrmann, T. M. 2014. "Religion without God." *New York Times*, December 24.

Maccoby, Eleanor E. 1998. *The Two Sexes: Growing Up Apart, Coming Together*. Boston, MA: Harvard University Press.

MacDonald, Heather. 2006. "Hispanic Family Values?" *City Journal* (Autumn).

Mahay, Jenna, and Edward O. Laumann. 2004. "Neighborhoods as Sex Markets." Pp. 69–92 in *The Sexual Organization of the City*, edited by Edward O. Laumann, Stephen Ellingson, Jenna Mahay, Anthony Paik, and Yoosik Youm. Chicago: University of Chicago Press.

Mahoney, Annette. 2010. "Religion in Families, 1999–2009: A Relational Spirituality Framework." *Journal of Marriage and Family* 72: 805–827.

Major, Brenda, and Laurie T. O'Brien. 2005. "The Social Psychology of Stigma." *Annual Review of Psychology* 56: 393–421.

Mare, Robert D., and Christopher Winship. 1991. "Socioeconomic Change and the Decline of Marriage for Blacks and Whites." Pp. 175–196 in *The Urban Underclass*, edited by Christopher Jencks and Paul E. Peterson. Washington, DC: Brookings.

Markides, Kyriakos S., and Karl Eschbach. 2005. "Aging, Migration, and Mortality: Current Status of Research on the Hispanic Paradox." *Journals of Gerontology*, series 1, 60: S68–S75.

Marquardt, Elizabeth, David Blankenhorn, Robert I. Lerman, Linda Malone-Colón, and W. Bradford Wilcox. 2012. "The President's Marriage Agenda for the Forgotten Sixty Percent." Pp. 1–46 in *The State of Our Unions 2012*. Charlottesville, VA: National Marriage Project and Institute for American Values.

Martin, Joyce A., Brady E. Hamilton, Stephanie J. Ventura, Michelle J.K. Osterman, Sharon Kirmeyer, T. J. Mathews, and Elizabeth C. Wilson. 2011. "Births: Final Data for 2009." National Vital Statistics Reports 60(1). Hyattsville, MD: National Center for Health Statistics.

Mastro, Dana E., and Amanda L. Robinson. 2000. "Cops and Crooks: Images of Minorities on Primetime Television." Journal of Criminal Justice 28: 385–396.

Mays, Vickie M., Susan D. Cochran, and Namdi W. Barnes. 2007. "Race, Race-Based Discrimination, and Health Outcomes among African Americans." Annual Review of Psychology 58: 201–225.

Mazzaferro, Kathryn E., Pamela J. Murray, Roberta B. Ness, Debra C. Bass, Nadra Tyus, and Robert L. Cook. 2006. "Depression, Stress, and Social Support as Predictors of High-Risk Sexual Behaviors and STIs in Young Women." Journal of Adolescent Health 39: 601–603.

McCullough, Michael E., and David B. Larson. 1999. "Prayer." Pp. 85–110 in Integrating Spirituality into Treatment: Resources for Practitioners, edited by William R. Miller. Washington, DC: American Psychological Association.

McKeever, Matthew, and Nicholas H. Wolfinger. 2011. "Thanks for Nothing: Income and Labor Force Participation for Never-Married Mothers since 1982." Social Science Research 40: 63–76.

McKeever, Matthew, and Nicholas H. Wolfinger. 2012. "Over the Long Haul: The Persistent Economic Consequences of Single Motherhood." Pp. 1–39 in Economic Stress and the Family, edited by S. L. Blair. Bingley, UK: Emerald.

McLanahan, Sara. 2004. "Diverging Destinies: How Children Fare under the Second Demographic Transition." Demography 41: 607–627.

McLanahan, Sara, and Gary Sandefur. 1994. Growing Up with a Single Parent: What Helps, What Hurts. Cambridge, MA: Harvard University Press.

McLoyd, Vonnie C., Ana Mari Cauce, David Takeuchi, and Leon Wilson. 2000. "Marital Processes and Parental Socialization in Families of Color: A Decade Review and Research." Journal of Marriage and Family 62: 1070–1093.

McRoberts, Omar M. 2003. Streets of Glory: Church and Community in a Black Urban Neighborhood. Chicago: University of Chicago Press.

Mead, Lawrence. 1993. The New Politics of Poverty: The Nonworking Poor in America. New York: Basic Books.

Mead, Rebecca. 2007. One Perfect Day: The Selling of the American Wedding. New York: Penguin.

Mintz, Steven, and Susan Kellogg. 1988. Domestic Revolutions: A Social History of American Family Life. New York: Free Press.

Mishel, Lawrence, and Jared Bernstein. 1992. "Declining Wages for High School and College Graduates: Pay and Benefits Trends by Education, Gender, Occupation, and State, 1979–1991." Washington, DC: Economic Policy Institute.

Moffitt, Robert. 1998. "The Effect of Welfare on Marriage and Fertility." Pp. 50–97 in *Welfare, the Family, and Reproductive Behavior*, edited by Robert Moffitt. Washington, DC: National Academy Press.

Murray, Charles. 1984. *Losing Ground: American Social Policy, 1950–1980.* New York: Basic Books.

Murry, Velma McBride, P. Adama Brown, Gene H. Brody, Carolyn E. Cutrona, and Ronald L. Simons. 2001. "Racial Discrimination as a Moderator of the Links among Stress, Maternal Psychological Functioning, and Family Relationships." *Journal of Marriage and Family* 63: 915–926.

National Institute on Drug Abuse. 2008. "Epidemiologic Trends in Drug Abuse." Proceedings of the Community Epidemiology Work Group. Washington, DC: US Department of Health and Human Services, National Institutes of Health.

Neff, James Alan, and Sue Keir Hoppe. 1993. "Race/Ethnicity, Acculturation, and Psychological Distress: Fatalism and Religiosity as Cultural Resources." *Journal of Community Psychology* 21: 3–20.

Newport, Frank, and Joy Wilke. 2013. "Most in U.S. Want Marriage, but Its Importance Has Dropped." Online article. Princeton, NJ: Gallup. http://www.gallup.com.

Noah, Timothy. 2012. *The Great Divergence: America's Growing Inequality Crisis and What We Can Do about It.* New York: Bloomsbury.

Nock, Steven L. 1995. "A Comparison of Marriages and Cohabiting Relationships." *Journal of Family Issues* 16: 53–76.

Ono, Hiromi. 1998. "Husbands' and Wives' Resources and Marital Dissolution in the United States." *Journal of Marriage and Family* 60: 674–689.

Oropesa, R. S. 1996. "Normative Beliefs about Marriage and Cohabitation: A Comparison of Non-Latino Whites, Mexican Americans, and Puerto Ricans." *Journal of Marriage and Family* 58: 49–62.

Oropesa, R. S., and Nancy S. Landale. 2004. "The Future of Marriage and Hispanics." *Journal of Marriage and Family* 66: 901–920.

Osborn, Cynthia, and Sara McLanahan. 2010. "Partnership Instability and Child Well-Being." *Journal of Marriage and Family* 69: 1065–1083.

Pager, Devah. 2007. *Marked: Race, Crime, and Finding Work in an Era of Mass Incarceration.* Chicago: University of Chicago Press.

Pager, Devah, and Hana Shepherd. 2008. "The Sociology of Discrimination: Racial Discrimination in Employment, Housing, Credit, and Consumer Markets." *Annual Review of Sociology* 34: 181–209.

Paik, Anthony, Edward O. Laumann, and Martha Van Haitsma. 2004. "Commitment, Jealousy, and the Quality of Life." Pp. 194–225 in *The Sexual Organization of the City*, edited by Edward O. Laumann, Stephen Ellingson, Jenna Mahay, Anthony Paik, and Yoosik Youm. Chicago: University of Chicago Press.

Parker, Douglas A., Thomas C. Harford, and Irwin M. Rosenstock. 1994. "Alcohol, Other Drugs, and Sexual Risk-Taking among Young Adults." *Journal of Substance Abuse* 6: 87–93.

Passel, Jeffrey S., and D'Vera Cohn. 2008. "U.S. Population Projections: 2005–2050." Washington, DC: Pew Research Center.

Patterson, Orlando. 1998. *Rituals of Blood: Consequences of Slavery in Two American Centuries*. New York: Basic Books.

Pattillo-McCoy, Mary. 1999. *Black Picket Fences: Privilege and Peril among the Black Middle Class*. Chicago: University of Chicago Press.

Paul, Christopher, William M. Mason, Daniel McCaffrey, and Sarah A. Fox. 2008. "A Cautionary Case Study of Approaches to the Treatment of Missing Data." *Statistical Methods and Applications* 17: 351–372.

Perkinson, Robert. 2010. *Texas Tough: The Rise of America's Prison Empire*. New York: Picador.

Pew Research Center. 2010. "The Decline of Marriage and Rise of New Families." Washington, DC: Pew Research Center.

Phillips, Julie A., and Megan M. Sweeney. 2005. "Premarital Cohabitation and Marital Disruption among White, Black and Mexican American Women." *Journal of Marriage and Family* 67: 296–314.

Pinker, Steven. 2011. *The Better Angels of Our Nature: The Decline of Violence in History and Its Causes*. London: Allen Lane.

Popenoe, David, Jean Bethke Elshtain, and David Blankenhorn. 1996. *Promises to Keep: Decline and Renewal of Marriage in America*. Lanham, MD: Rowman & Littlefield.

Portes, Alejandro A., and Ruben G. Rumbaut. 2000. *Legacies: The Story of the Immigrant Second Generation*. Berkeley: University of California Press.

Press, Julie E., and Eleanor Townsley. 1998. "Wives' and Husbands' Housework Reporting: Gender, Class, and Social Desirability." *Gender and Society* 12: 188–218.

Previti, Denise, and Paul R. Amato. 2004. "Is Infidelity a Cause of a Consequence of Poor Marital Quality?" *Journal of Social and Personal Relationships* 21: 217–230.

Putnam, Robert. 2000. *Bowling Alone: The Collapse and Revival of American Community*. New York: Simon & Schuster.

Raley, R. Kelly, and Larry Bumpass. 2003. "The Topography of the Divorce Plateau: Levels and Trends in Union Stability in the United States after 1980." *Demographic Research* 8: 245–260.

Raley, R. Kelly, and Megan M. Sweeney. 2009. "Explaining Race and Ethnic Variation in Marriage: Directions for Future Research." *Race and Social Problems* 1: 132–142.

Raphael, Steven, and Michael Stoll. 2014. "A New Approach to Reducing Incarceration while Maintaining Low Rates of Crime." Discussion Paper. Washington DC: Hamilton Project, Brookings.

Rhoades, Galena K., Scott M. Stanley, and Emily Esfahani Smith. 2014. *Before "I Do": What Do Premarital Experiences Have to Do with Marital Quality among Today's Young Adults?* Charlottesville, VA: National Marriage Project.

Rhodes, Jean E., and Leonard A. Jason. 1990. "A Social Stress Model of Substance Abuse." *Journal of Consulting and Clinical Psychology* 58: 395–401.

Rideout, Victoria J., Ulla G. Foehr, and Donald F. Roberts. 2010. "Generation M^2: Media in the Lives of 8- to 18-Year-Olds." Menlo Park, CA: Kaiser Family Foundation.

Riolo, Stephanie A., Tuan Anh Nguyen, John F. Greden, and Cheryl A. King. 2005. "Prevalence of Depression by Race/Ethnicity: Findings from the National Health and Nutrition Examination Survey III." *American Journal of Public Health* 95: 998–1000.

Rivera, Jenny. 1994. "Domestic Violence against Latinas by Latino Males: An Analysis of Race, National Origin, and Gender Differentials." *Boston College Third World Law Journal* 14: 231–257.

Rivera-Batiz, Francisco L. 1999. "Undocumented Workers in the Labor Market: An Analysis of the Earnings of Legal and Illegal Mexican Immigrants in the United States." *Journal of Population Economics* 12: 91–116.

Roberts, Donald F., Ulla G. Foehr, Victoria J. Rideout, and Mollyann Brodie. 1999. "Kids and Media @ the New Millennium." Menlo Park, CA: Kaiser Family Foundation.

Roof, Wade Clark. 1993. *A Generation of Seekers: The Spiritual Journeys of the Baby Boom Generation.* New York: Harper Collins.

Roth, Andrew L. 1995. "'Men Wearing Masks': Issues of Description in the Analysis of Ritual." *Sociological Theory* 3: 301–327.

Ruggles, Steven. 1997. "The Rise of Divorce and Separation in the United States, 1880–1990." *Demography* 34: 455–466.

Sayer, Liana C., Paula England, Paul Allison, and Nicole Kangas. 2011. "She Left, He Left: How Employment and Satisfaction Affect Men's and Women's Decisions to Leave Marriages." *American Journal of Sociology* 116: 1982–2018.

Schneider, Daniel. 2011. "Wealth and the Marital Divide." *American Journal of Sociology* 117: 627–667.

Scommegna, Paola. 2013. "Exploring the Paradox of U.S. Hispanics' Longer Life Expectancy." Washington, DC: Population Reference Bureau.

Sharkey, Patrick. 2013. *Stuck in Place: Urban Neighborhoods and the End of Progress toward Racial Equality*. Chicago: University of Chicago Press.

Siennick, Sonja E. 2007. "The Timing and Mechanisms of the Offending-Depression Link." *Criminology* 45: 583–615.

Smiley, Tavis, and Cornel West. 2012. *The Rich and the Rest of Us: A Poverty Manifesto*. Carlsbad, CA: Hay House.

South, Scott J., and Glenna Spitze. 1994. "Housework in Marital and Nonmarital Households." *American Sociological Review* 59: 327–347.

Spain, Daphne, and Suzanne Bianchi. 1996. *Balancing Act: Motherhood, Marriage, and Employment among American Women*. New York: Russell Sage.

Stack, Carol B. 1974. *All Our Kin: Strategies for Survival in a Black Community*. New York: Harper & Row.

Steensland, Brian, Jerry Z. Park, Mark D. Regnerus, Lynn D. Robinson, W. Bradford Wilcox, and Robert D. Woodberry. 2000. "The Measure of American Religion: Toward Improving the State of the Art." *Social Forces* 79: 291–318.

Stein, Robert. 2010. "Taxes and the Family." *National Affairs* 2: 35–48.

Stevenson, Betsey, and Justin Wolfers. 2007. "Marriage and Divorce: Changes and Their Driving Forces." *Journal of Economic Perspectives* 21:27–52.

Story, Linda B., and Thomas N. Bradbury. 2004. "Understanding Marriage and Stress: Essential Questions and Challenges." *Clinical Psychology Review* 23: 1139–1162.

Stykes, Bart, Krista K. Payne, and Larry Gibbs. 2014. "First Marriage Rate in the U.S., 2012." FP-14-08. Bowling Green, OH: National Center for Family & Marriage Research.

Substance Abuse and Mental Health Services Administration. 2009. *Results from the 2008 National Survey on Drug Use and Health: National Findings*. NSDUH Series H-36, HHS Publication No. SMA 09-4434. Rockville, MD: Office of Applied Studies, US Department of Health and Human Services.

Suro, Roberto. 2007. "The Hispanic Family in Flux." Washington, DC: Center on Children & Families, Brookings Institution.

Sweeney, Megan M. 2002. "Two Decades of Family Change: The Shifting Economic Foundations of Marriage." *American Sociological Review* 67: 132–147.

Thornton, Arland, and Linda Young-DeMarco. 2001. "Four Decades of Trends in Attitudes toward Family Issues in the United States: The 1960s through the 1990s." *Journal of Marriage and Family* 63: 1009–1037.

Tucker, M. Belinda, and Claudia Mitchell-Kernan. 1995. *The Decline in Marriage among African Americans: Causes, Consequences, and Policy Implications*. New York: Russell Sage.

Upchurch, Dawn M., Lee A. Lillard, and Constantijn W.A. Panis. 2001. "The Impact of Nonmarital Childbearing on Subsequent Marital Formation and Dissolution." Pp. 344–380 in *Out of Wedlock: Causes and Consequences of Nonmarital Fertility*, edited by Lawrence L. Wu and Barbara Wolfe. New York: Russell Sage.

US Census Bureau. 1970. *Statistical Abstract of the United States: 1970* (90th edition).

US Census Bureau. 1970–2013. *Current Population Survey*. March Demographic Supplement.

US Census Bureau. 1995. *Statistical Abstract of the United States: 1995* (115th edition).

US Census Bureau. 2013. *Current Population Survey*. Annual Social and Economic Supplement.

Vaaler, Margaret L., Christopher G. Ellison, and Dan A. Powers. 2009. "Religious Influences on the Risk of Marital Dissolution." *Journal of Marriage and Family* 71: 917–934.

Vega, William A. 1990. "Hispanic Families in the 1980s: A Decade of Research." *Journal of Marriage and Family* 52: 1015–1024.

Waite, Linda, and Maggie Gallagher. 2000. *The Case for Marriage: Why Married People are Happier, Healthier, and Better off Financially*. New York: Doubleday.

Waldfogel, Jane, Terry-Ann Craigie, and Jeanne Brooks-Gunn. 2010. "Fragile Families and Child Wellbeing." *The Future of Children* 20: 87–112.

Walsh, Arlene M. Sánchez. 2003. *Latino Pentecostal Identity: Evangelical Faith, Self, and Society*. New York: Columbia University Press.

Western, Bruce. 2006. *Punishment and Inequality in America*. New York: Russell Sage.

Western, Bruce, Leonard M. Lopoo, and Sara McLanahan. 2004. "Incarceration and the Bonds between Parents in Fragile Families." Pp. 21–45 in *Imprisoning America*, edited by Mary Patillo, David Weiman, and Bruce Western. New York: Russell Sage.

Western, Bruce, and Christopher Wildeman. 2009. "The Black Family and Mass Incarceration." *Annals of the American Academy of Political and Social Science* 621: 221–242.

Whitehead, Barbara Dafoe, and David Popenoe. 2006. *The State of Our Unions 2006: The Social Health of Marriage in America*. New Brunswick, NJ: National Marriage Project.

Wilcox, W. Bradford. 2004. *Soft Patriarchs, New Men: How Christianity Shapes Fathers and Husbands*. Chicago: University of Chicago Press.

Wilcox, W. Bradford. 2006. "Suffer the Little Children: Marriage, the Poor, and the Commonweal." Pp. 242–253 in *The Meaning of Marriage: Family, State, Market, and Morals*, edited by Robert George and Jean Bethke Elshtain. Dallas, TX: Spence Publishing.

Wilcox, W. Bradford, Jared R. Andeson, William Doherty, David Eggebeen, Christopher G. Ellison, William Galston, Neil Gilbert, John Gottman, Ron Haskins, Robert I. Lerman, Linda Malone-Colón, Loren Marks, Rob Palkovitz, David Popenoe, Mark D. Regnerus, Scott Stanley, Linda Waite, and Judith Wallerstein. 2011. *Why Marriage Matters, Third Edition: Thirty Conclusions from the Social Sciences*. New York: Institute for American Values.

Wilcox, W. Bradford, and John P. Bartkowski. 2005. "Devoted Dads: Religion, Class, and Fatherhood." Pp. 299–320 in *Situated Fathering: A Focus on Physical and Social Spaces*, edited by William Marsiglio and Greer Fox. Lanham, MD: Rowman & Littlefield.

Wilcox, W. Bradford, Mark Chaves, and David Franz. 2004. "Focused on the Family? Religious Traditions, Family Discourse, and Pastoral Practice." *Journal for the Scientific Study of Religion* 43: 491–504.

Wilcox, W. Bradford, and Elizabeth Marquardt. 2011. *When Baby Makes Three*. Charlottesville, VA: National Marriage Project/Institute for American Values.

Wilcox, W. Bradford, Elizabeth Marquardt, David Popenoe, and Barbara Dafoe Whitehead. 2011. *The State of Our Unions 2011*. Charlottesville, VA: Institute for American Values and the National Marriage Project.

Wilcox, W. Bradford, and Steven L. Nock. 2006. "What's Love Got to Do with It? Equality, Equity, Commitment and Women's Marital Quality." *Social Forces* 84: 1321–1345.

Wilcox, W. Bradford, and Nicholas H. Wolfinger. 2007. "Then Comes Marriage? Religion and Marriage in Urban America." *Social Science Research* 36: 569–589.

Wilcox, W. Bradford, and Nicholas H. Wolfinger. 2008. "Living and Loving 'Decent': Religion and Relationship Quality among Urban Parents." *Social Science Research* 37: 828–843.

Williams, David R., and Selina A. Mohammed. 2008. "Discrimination and Racial Disparities in Health: Evidence and Needed Research." *Journal of Behavioral Medicine* 32: 20–47.

Williams, Norma. 1990. *The Mexican American Family: Tradition and Change*. New York: General Hall.

Wilson, James Q. 2002. "Why We Don't Marry." *City Journal* 12 (Winter).

Wilson, William Julius. 1987. *The Truly Disadvantaged: The Inner City, the Underclass, and Public Policy*. Chicago: University of Chicago Press.

Wilson, William Julius. 1997. *When Work Disappears: The World of the New Urban Poor*. New York: Knopf.

Wolfinger, Nicholas H. 2005. *Understanding the Divorce Cycle: The Children of Divorce in Their Own Marriages*. New York: Cambridge University Press.

Wolfinger, Nicholas H., and W. Bradford Wilcox. 2008. "Happily Ever After? Religion, Marital Status, Gender, and Relationship Quality in Urban Families." *Social Forces* 86: 1311–1337.

Wolfinger, Nicholas H., W. Bradford Wilcox, and Edwin I. Hernández. 2010. "Bendito Amor ('Blessed Love'): Religion and Relationships among Married and Unmarried Latinos in Urban America." *Journal of Latino-Latin American Studies* 3: 171–188.

Wu, Lawrence L. 1996. "Effects of Family Instability, Income, and Income Instability on the Risk of a Premarital Birth." *American Sociological Review* 61: 386–406.

Wu, Lawrence L., and Brian C. Martinson. 1993. "Family Structure and the Risk of a Premarital Birth." *American Sociological Review* 58: 210–232.

Yinger, John. 1998. "Evidence on Discrimination in Consumer Markets." *Journal of Economic Perspectives* 12: 23–40.

Youm, Yoosik, and Anthony Paik. 2004. "The Sex Market and Its Implications for Family Formation." Pp. 165–193 in *The Sexual Organization of the City*, edited by Edward O. Laumann, Stephen Ellingson, Jenna Mahay, Anthony Paik, and Yoosik Youm. Chicago: University of Chicago Press.

Zinn, Maxine Baca, and Angela Y. H. Pok. 2002. "Tradition and Transition in Mexican-Origin Families." Pp. 79–100 in *Minority Families in the United States: A Multicultural Perspective*, edited by Ronald L. Taylor. Upper Saddle River, NJ: Pearson.

INDEX

abortion, 11, 79–80, 82–83, 151
 and religion, 85, 88–91
abuse, 14, 40, 72, 114, 134
 molestation, 134, 136
 See also domestic violence
acculturation, 7, 16, 18, 24, 43, 112
Add Health, ix, 22, 83, 92, 111, 118–119,
 121, 165–167
African Methodist Episcopal, 116
Aid to Families with Dependent
 Children, 10
Akerlof, George, 11–12
Alcoholics Anonymous, 155
ambition, 148
Anderson, Elijah, 19, 28–29, 151–152
apprenticeship, 25, 157

Baptist, 51, 54, 60, 88, 98, 140, 159
Bell, Daniel, 11
Bible, 2, 54, 60, 99, 124, 136
birth control. *See* contraception
Blow, Charles, 9
Brisco, Elizabeth, 139
Brookings Institution, 158
Brooks, David, 15

Career Academies, 157
Catholic, 19, 50–51, 53, 56, 62, 70, 88,
 95–98, 112–116, 126, 138, 162–163

charismatic, 55, 138–139
child tax credit, 156
children
 attitudes about, ix–x, 1, 4, 10, 12,
  18, 25, 34, 53, 78–80, 82–85, 89,
  94–95, 100, 110–111, 124, 147,
  150–151, 154, 157, 159–160, 162
 living outside of two-parent, married
  family, 5, 7–8, 24, 41, 48, 80, 97,
  120, 134, 148
 outcomes of, when raised outside of
  happy, stable family, 21, 48, 70–76,
  91, 93, 100, 102, 126–127, 157
 See also nonmarital childbearing
churches (and religious services)
 activities of and attendance at, xi,
  53–55, 57, 60, 124, 134, 136, 138,
  143, 159
 black, 1–2, 4, 19, 23, 50–55, 57, 88,
  95, 116, 148, 151–152, 161–162
 and efforts to strengthen family life,
  24–25, 132–133, 159–163
 and family ministries, 97, 114, 124,
  134–135, 138, 143, 145, 159–160
 instill "code of decency," 19–20,
  24, 29, 51–56, 58–59, 60–62, 68,
  73, 75, 91–94, 112–114, 137–138
  (*see also* "code of decency," and
  religion)

churches (*Cont.*)
  Latino, 1, 53–59, 70, 73, 85–86,
    88–89, 91–94, 123, 151–152,
    162–163
  messages from, about sex and mar-
    riage, 11, 20, 24, 50–51, 88, 95,
    115–116, 122, 126, 142–143, 145,
    153–154, 163
  provide models of healthy relation-
    ships, 63–66, 97–98, 112–114, 142,
    153, 155
  provide social support, 18,
    20–21, 51, 54–55, 66, 97–98,
    115–121, 124–125, 134–142, 146,
    153–154, 156
  in qualitative data, 1–3, 53–54,
    56–59, 60, 62, 65, 67, 72, 86–87,
    89–92, 113–116, 124, 134–140
"code of decency," 92–93, 131
  instilled by secular
    organizations, 155
  prevalence of, 92, 147, 163
  and religion, 3, 19–20, 24, 29–30,
    49–56, 60, 62, 67–69, 95, 112–114,
    118–119, 122, 137–138, 151–154
    (*see also* churches (and reli-
    gious services), instill "code of
    decency")
"code of the street," 28–29, 47–49, 52,
  68, 83, 108, 141, 152
cohabitation
  attitudes about, 10, 73, 98–99,
    114–115, 126, 142–143 (*see also* sex,
    premarital)
  characteristics of persons in,
    103, 111
  as a factor, 80, 110, 119, 150
  fragility of, 5, 7, 17, 21, 24,
    71–72, 134
  prevalence of, 6, 15, 17, 24, 80–81,
    111, 115, 126, 147, 150
  in qualitative data, 26, 43, 56, 58–59,
    61–62, 71, 75–76, 98–99, 104,
    114–115, 120, 134, 137
  quality of relationship, 127–133, 142,
    144–145, 153–154

and religion, 63, 93, 95, 99,
  114–115, 122, 126–127, 139–143,
  145–146, 154
conservatives, x, 9, 12, 77, 81, 94,
  102, 116
contraception, 11, 81–82, 84, 94,
  110, 150
  and religion, 85, 88–89, 91
crime/criminal activity, 19, 21, 28, 30,
  34–37, 45, 47–50, 83, 119
  and religion, 19, 53, 58–60, 68,
    93, 152
  See also incarceration;
    substance abuse
culture
  and the family revolution, 4–5, 9,
    11–18, 102–103, 108–110
  and nonmarital childbearing, 77–84,
    86, 92–94, 150–151
  as part of solution, 23–25, 158, 164
  role of, in comparative Latino family
    stability, 110–112, 148
  role of, in fragility of black family,
    99, 110, 121, 129–130, 132–133,
    144, 148–150
  role of, in link between religion and
    marriage, 73, 119–120
  role of, in link between religious par-
    ticipation and relationship quality,
    51, 68, 141
  and street behavior, 45–49

dating, 2, 8, 27, 42, 70–71, 81, 85, 96,
  114–115, 117, 153, 158, 160
decency. *See* "code of decency"
depression. *See* health, mental
discrimination, racial and ethnic, x,
  4, 12, 16, 18, 23–24, 46–48, 54,
  66, 68, 72, 104, 108, 110, 125,
  149–151, 162
distrust, gender. *See* trust
divorce
  attitudes about, 12, 99, 130, 137, 141,
    145–146
  causes of, 29–34, 40, 42, 44–45, 75,
    132–133, 140, 144, 149

effects of, 21, 48, 97
employment reduces odds of, 57–58
as a factor to explain racial differences in relationship quality, 130
prevalence of, x, 3, 5–8, 15, 17, 75–76, 101, 111, 122, 125–126, 128–130, 144–145, 148
in qualitative data, 26–27, 32–33, 42, 44, 71, 75–76, 97–99, 104–105, 118, 124, 137, 140
racial and ethnic disparities in, 4, 12, 20–21, 29, 128–130, 132–133, 143–146, 148, 154–155
and religion, 4, 20–21, 24, 132, 137, 140, 143–146, 154–155
worries about, 75–76, 98–99, 104–105
domestic violence, 3, 17, 36–38, 40, 48–50, 53, 152, 161
See also abuse
drinking. *See* substance abuse
drugs. *See* substance abuse
Durkheim, Émile, ix, 29, 142

earned income tax credit, 156
economic shifts
as a factor in the family revolution, 5, 8–10, 12–16, 19, 21, 23–25, 68, 75, 92–94, 99, 102–105, 107, 110, 119, 122, 128–131, 133, 144, 147, 149, 151, 153, 160, 164
as a factor in street behavior, 45–46, 48–49
falling wages, 5, 9–10, 15, 46, 75, 110–112, 156–157
women's improved position, 9–10, 13, 32–33, 74–77, 104–105
Edin, Kathryn, xii, 13, 78, 131, 152
education, 16, 46–48, 56–57, 68, 128, 148, 156–158
See also socioeconomic condition
Ellison, Christopher, xii, 66
employment, 10, 27, 63, 67, 76, 86–87, 89–91, 147, 149
irregular hours, 34
among Latinos, 16, 33–34, 49, 111

long hours, 34
low-wage, 16, 28, 33–34, 45–47, 49, 99, 110–112, 133–136, 156
and marriage, 29, 57–58, 104–105, 107
and nonmarital childbearing, 76, 92
and relationship quality, 34, 57, 129, 135, 159
and religion, 19, 56–58, 68, 95, 112, 152, 159–160
role of churches, 25, 54, 57, 159
underemployment, 12, 25, 28, 30–32, 104
See also economic shifts; unemployment
Episcopal, 116, 155
ethic of marital generosity, 124–125, 130–131, 133, 159, 161
ethnography, xi, 23, 145
evangelical Protestant, 88, 163

familism, 5, 8–9, 11, 15–18, 70, 89, 110–112, 122, 126, 128, 130, 139, 148, 154, 162
family law, 10
family of origin, 48, 71, 80, 84, 97, 107, 109–110, 114–115, 132–134, 144
family revolution
causes of, 8–18, 102–110, 121
consequences of, 8, 21, 24, 50, 102, 150
description of, 4–8, 100–102, 120–121
feminism, second-wave, 11
fertility, multiple-partner, 4, 14, 25, 41, 43, 73, 108
fertility, nonmarital. *See* nonmarital childbearing
fidelity, 26, 30, 40, 45, 51, 63–68, 108, 112, 116–117, 152, 159, 161
See also infidelity
First Things First, 158
focus groups, xi, 23
food stamps (Supplemental Nutrition Assistance Program, SNAP), 10
forgiveness, 44, 114, 116–117, 122, 136, 161

General Social Survey (GSS), 22, 66–67, 160, 163, 165
Golden Rule, 20, 51, 53, 63, 116, 122, 126, 143, 145

Harvard, 162
Haskins, Ron, 158
Hayes-Bautista, David, 110–112
health, mental, 21, 28, 47, 49–50, 72, 100
    and religion, 55, 66–68
health, physical, 22, 100, 127
hedonism, 17, 46
Hispanic Paradox, 122, 147–148
Hungerman, Daniel, 154

immigrants/immigration, 4, 15–16, 18, 33–34, 43–44, 46, 70, 81, 111–114, 128, 137, 148, 157
incarceration
    causes of, 12, 35, 49
    more common among minority men, 12, 28, 35–36, 45, 147, 149
    as an obstacle to marriage, 104, 108, 149–150, 152
    reform of drug laws, 149, 156–157
    and religion, 58–60, 68
    undermines relationships, 12, 30, 34–35, 45, 152, 157
    See also crime/criminal activity; discrimination, racial and ethnic
income, 32, 34, 65, 67, 74, 93, 100, 103–105, 107, 111, 119, 121, 128–129, 132, 144, 148–149, 156–157, 164
    See also socioeconomic condition
individualism, 5, 11, 15, 17, 46
    and ambition, 148
    and prayer, 136
    and well-being, 168
infidelity
    causes of, 14, 45–50, 108
    concerns about, 108
    as a factor, 131, 133, 141
    more common among minorities, 17, 28, 41–45, 108, 125, 130–131, 149
    and multi-partner fertility, 41
    and nonmarital childbearing, 83
    in qualitative data, 26, 36–37, 40, 42, 65–66, 108, 117
    and religion, 3, 52, 117, 125, 141
    undermines relationships, 30, 42–44, 110, 131, 152

Jim Crow, 14–15, 110, 130, 144, 149, 162

Kefalas, Maria, 13, 78, 131, 152
King, Jr., Martin Luther, 161
King v. Smith, 10

liberals (also progressives), x, 8, 12, 94, 102
Lincoln, C. Eric, 161–162
Luhrmann, T. M., 155

MacDonald, Heather, 77
machismo, 16–17, 49, 68, 114, 126, 137, 139
Malcolm X, 161
Mamiya, Lawrence H., 161–162
Manhattan Institute, 77
manufacturing, 9, 16, 45–46, 104, 149
Mare, Robert, 107
marital quality, 21, 29–30, 124–142, 144–145, 160
    and children, 127
    and crime, 58
    and employment, 57
    and ethnic differences, 129–133, 150–153
    and happiness, 127
    and marital stability, 128
    and religion, 3–4, 20, 24, 29, 98, 122, 124–125, 133–142, 144–146, 154–155, 160
    See also marriage, challenges in; relationship quality
marriage
    attitudes about, 11–13, 16, 19, 43–44, 71, 74, 80, 97–100, 102, 105, 109, 112–114, 130, 141, 143, 145, 147, 153, 164

benefits of, 99–100, 102
challenges in, 4, 16, 26–45, 49–50,
  136–137, 139, 161
consequences of retreat from, x, 5,
  21, 100, 102–103, 111, 150 (*see also*
  family revolution)
deinstitutionalization of, 4–5
obstacles to, 12–13, 26–45, 72–76,
  83, 96–99, 101, 103–105, 107–110,
  120, 122–123, 150, 157, 162
penalties, 10, 156–157
prospects for, 29, 57–58, 60
racial divide in, x, 4, 6, 12, 14, 45, 47,
  72–77, 83–84, 91, 101, 103–106,
  108–110, 113, 118–121, 127–133,
  143–144, 149, 157, 160–161
rates, 6, 13, 19, 24, 30, 32, 48,
  100–102, 107, 110–111, 118–122,
  129–130, 149, 153, 157
and religion, 29, 85, 97–99, 112–123,
  137–138, 153, 163–164
same-sex, 155
timing of, 74, 100–101, 120–121,
  147–148, 153
media, 17, 46–47, 68, 81, 84, 109
  See also culture
Medicaid, 157
men, "marriageable," 9, 12–13, 32,
  104–105, 144, 150, 156
money, 1, 100, 140
  lack of, 32–34, 40, 74–76, 99,
  103–105, 129, 135–136
  See also marriage, obstacles to;
  socio-economic condition

National Campaign to Prevent Teenage
  and Unplanned Pregnancy, 158
National Center for Health
  Statistics, 22
National Longitudinal Survey of Youth
  (NLSY), 22, 57, 76, 83, 105, 107,
  109, 111, 118, 120–121, 132, 143
National Survey of Family Growth, 22
National Survey of Religion and Family
  Life (NSRFL), 22, 63–64, 129,
  139, 141

nomos, religious, 55
nonmarital childbearing
  attitudes about, 11–12, 14, 19, 77–80,
  82–86, 88, 93, 95, 149, 160, 163
  causes of, 8–18, 28–29, 48, 73–78,
  80–85, 88–89, 91, 94–95, 111, 115,
  149–151, 162
  as a challenge for couples, 25, 43,
  72–73, 101, 110, 121
  as a factor, 119, 121, 132
  prevalence of, 4, 7, 15, 71, 73–74,
  80–81, 88, 100–101, 111, 116, 122,
  148, 150, 154
  in qualitative data, 43, 70–71, 75, 80,
  96, 115, 120, 137
  racial and ethnic disparities in,
  3–4, 7, 12, 15–16, 19–20, 73–77,
  80–84, 91–92, 94–95, 101, 111,
  149–153
  and religion, 3, 19–20, 24, 70, 73,
  84–89, 91–95, 114–117, 122, 126,
  152–154, 163
  See also single parenthood
norms, 2, 5, 11, 14, 20, 47–49, 51, 66,
  80, 93, 95, 110, 126, 141, 145, 158

paradox, religion-family, 3–4, 24,
  20–21, 125, 147
  See also divorce, racial and ethnic
  disparities in; relationship quality,
  racial divide in
paradox, religion-nonmarital
  fertility, 73–95
  See also nonmarital childbearing
Patillo-McCoy, Mary, 28
Patterson, Orlando, 14, 46–47, 108,
  110, 162
Pentecostal, 1–2, 54–55, 85, 88, 95, 115,
  124, 163
policy, xi, 9–10, 12, 23–24, 68, 102–103,
  149–150, 156
popular culture. *See* media
poverty, 12–13, 16, 18, 21, 23–24,
  30–31, 48, 54, 66, 68, 72–73, 75,
  94, 100–101, 125, 150
  See also socioeconomic condition

prayer, 52, 55–57, 60, 117–118, 134–136, 140, 142, 146, 154, 163
Pre Cana, 97
promiscuity, 17, 19, 26, 49, 65, 126

racial uplift, 161–162
racism.
    See discrimination, racial and ethnic
relationship education, 158–160
relationship quality
    racial divide in, 121, 127–133, 144, 149
    and religion, 3–4, 20, 24, 29, 69, 124–126, 133–142, 144–146, 153–155
    and work, 30–34, 49, 51, 68–69, 110–111, 127, 132, 135–136, 160
religion
    limits of, 3–4, 20–21, 55, 58–59, 68, 93–94, 99, 125, 143–145, 155–156, 164
    prevalence of, 11, 23, 73, 125, 145–146, 148, 151, 159–160, 163
    See also churches (and religious services)
rituals, 51, 66, 125, 136, 138–139, 142, 154, 162

Sawhill, Isabell, 158
segregation, residential, 12, 110, 130, 144, 149
selection, 20, 145–146, 154–155
sermons, 51–55, 115–116, 142–143, 154, 160
sex
    and emotional health, 66
    multiple partnerships, 34, 41–43, 65, 70–71, 84, 92–93, 110
    quality of, 100
    sexual behavior as a factor, 3, 11, 42, 46, 48, 82–84, 92–93, 110, 119, 130–131, 133, 141, 149
    See also infidelity
sex, premarital, ix, 3
    attitudes about, 11, 13, 19, 24, 26, 34, 41–42, 47–48, 65, 73, 78–81, 83–86, 93, 95, 115, 126, 147, 152–153

prevalence of, 81–82, 86–88, 91–92, 94–95
and religion, 19, 84–88, 91–93, 95, 115, 126, 152–154
sexual revolution, 11–12, 50
single parenthood
    attitudes about, 78–80, 83–86, 149
    consequences of, 21, 24, 72, 102, 150
    as a legacy of slavery and Jim Crow, 14, 108
    policies affecting, 10
    prevalence of, 4, 8, 12, 15, 72, 80–81, 88, 95, 111, 116, 122, 148, 154, 160
    in qualitative data, 27, 88, 96, 133
    racial and ethnic disparities in, 15, 111
    and religion, 84–88, 95, 116–117, 122, 126, 154, 160
    See also nonmarital childbearing
slavery, 14–15, 108, 110, 149, 162
smoking, 100, 158
social marketing, 158
socioeconomic condition
    and divorce, 132–133, 144, 149
    and entry into marriage, 74–76, 99, 103–105, 110–112, 119, 121–122
    as a factor in the family revolution, 13–14, 16, 18–19, 102–107, 110, 121
    and nonmarital childbearing, 73, 75–77, 92–94, 149
    and relationship quality, 33–34, 128–129, 131, 144
    role of, in fragility of black family, 132–133, 144, 147–150
    role of, in link between marriage and religion, 119, 121
"soulmate," 74
Steuerle, Eugene, 10
street subculture. See "code of the street"
substance abuse
    and depression, 66–67
    and discrimination, 47–49
    drug business, 1, 19, 35–36, 60
    drunk driving, 158
    gender gap in, 37–38, 45, 123
    norms related to, 17, 46–49, 126

prevalence of, 28, 37, 40, 147
in qualitative data, 27, 36–37, 39–40,
  113, 119, 137–138
and religion, 19, 51–55, 60–62, 68,
  93, 98, 137–138, 161
undermines relationships, 30, 34,
  36–39, 126, 152
"success sequence", 158
Suro, Robert, 17, 112

teen pregnancy, 21, 80, 94, 158
temperance, 19, 29, 51, 67, 112, 138, 152
trust, 1, 27, 40, 42, 45, 97, 106, 108, 114,
  125, 134, 136

unemployment
among African Americans, 12, 26–28,
  31–33, 45, 49, 104–105, 129, 149

idleness, 50–52, 56–57, 68, 108, 152
levels, 31, 149–150
in qualitative data, 26–27, 104, 107,
  133–136
and religion, 66, 67, 135–136
as a threat to relationships, 30–33,
  104–105, 129, 132, 135–136
United Churches of Christ, 155

Washington, Booker T., 161
wedding, 13, 97, 99, 104
welfare, 10, 23
Wilson, William Julius, 9, 32, 105, 110
Winship, Christopher, 107
work. *See* employment
worship, 54–55, 124, 134
xenophobia, 16, 47, 68, 151
  See also discrimination, racial and
  ethnic